From Grey to Silver

Sven Kunisch · Stephan A. Boehm · Michael Boppel
Editors

From Grey to Silver

Managing the Demographic Change
Successfully

 Springer

Editors

Sven Kunisch
University of St. Gallen
Institute of Management
Dufourstr. 40a
9000 St. Gallen
Switzerland
sven.kunisch@unisg.ch

Stephan A. Boehm
University of St. Gallen
Center for Disability and Integration
Rosenbergstrasse 51
9000 St. Gallen
Switzerland
stephan.boehm@unisg.ch

Michael Boppel
University of St. Gallen
Institute of Management
Dufourstr. 40a
9000 St. Gallen
Switzerland
michael.boppel@unisg.ch

ISBN 978-3-642-15593-2   e-ISBN 978-3-642-15594-9
DOI 10.1007/978-3-642-15594-9
Springer Heidelberg Dordrecht London New York

Library of Congress Control Number: 2010936853

Cover design: WMXDesign GmbH, Heidelberg

Printed on acid-free paper

Springer is part of Springer Science+Business Media (www.springer.com)

In memory of
our colleague and true friend
Christian Welling

Foreword by the former President of the Federal Republic of Germany

Prof. Dr. Roman Herzog[*]

From Grey to Silver – with this memorable slogan this book addresses our future. The present demographic change will dramatically affect all areas of our society and future coexistence. Thus, continuous and well-founded discussions and examinations of this topic are not only particularly important, but also urgent.

In Germany, for example, the characteristics of the demographic change are easily summarised: The population is shrinking, there are fewer young people and there are more old people. These developments – especially the decreasing birthrate and the ageing of the over-represented middle-age group – lead to serious strains on the population's pyramidal age structure.

This 'distorted' age structure will drastically impact all areas of our society: family, labour, mobility, migration, welfare, social and health care, education and the economy. Admittedly, the present demographic change is not the sole cause of all challenges facing society, but it does exacerbate many of them dramatically. On examining this topic, the following becomes apparent: everything is interlinked, and it is very important to think holistically.

Owing to the topic's prime importance, the Federal Presidents have for some time been concerned with bringing it to the public's attention. An example of this is the Forum Demographischer Wandel (Demographic Change Forum) founded by the former President of the Federal Republic of Germany Dr. Horst Koehler and the Bertelsmann Foundation. This initiative aims at making the public aware of the significance of the topic, as well as developing concepts and suggestions for concrete actions. I have pointed to emerging problems related to the demographic change, such as the imminent danger of a 'pensioner's democracy' because political parties take the increasing number of ageing people disproportionally into consideration, which could lead to a permanent overburdening of younger people. This notion has certainly provoked controversies. An intense debate involving all of society, which will at times have to be controversial, is however necessary.

This book contributes to the debate – to the information and the discussion. The authors deal with the ominous challenges but also with the various opportunities for our economy arising from demographic change. Such a business perspective is significant for our future. Recognising the business consequences of the demo-

---

[*] translated version.

graphic developments and taking these into consideration are imperative for the competitiveness of not only companies, but also entire economies.

The book is notable for two features: Firstly, the topic is comprehensively examined by taking different company stakeholders into consideration. Demographic change eventually affects internal stakeholders, such as employees and management, as well as external ones, especially customers. There are enormous challenges. An acute shortage of professionals and university graduates has already become apparent in many industries. For companies, it is essential to preserve valuable know-how, to train and educate employees of all age groups, and to reconcile work and family life by means of childcare and flexible working hours. But there are also enormous opportunities! Especially with regard to the older customer segment. In Japan, the so-called 'silver market' is one of the fastest growing segments, but elsewhere it is still in its 'infancy'. Companies should promote meaningful innovations and address these new customer groups appropriately.

Secondly, the book is characterized by an interesting mix of contributions: it contains both academic and more practice-oriented chapters. The authors are of different nationalities and from varying age groups. Thus, this book – published to complement the DocNet Management Symposium 2010 at the University of St. Gallen – reflects the contents of the symposium as well as its special appeal. The variety and the bringing together of different generations always lead to lively debates and interesting solutions.

One aspect of this topic is beyond question: In principle, it is wonderful that we live longer and are also fit for a longer time. We should perceive this as an extraordinary opportunity. This book, published to complement the DocNet Management Symposium 2010, makes a contribution. – *Silver* light on the horizon.

Heilbronn, July 2010

Prof. Dr. Roman Herzog

Geleitwort von Bundespräsident a.D.

Prof. Dr. Roman Herzog[*]

From Grey to Silver – Unter diesem einprägsamen Motto geht es in dem vorliegenden Buch um unsere Zukunft. Der gegenwärtige demographische Wandel wird sämtliche Bereiche unserer Gesellschaft und unseres Zusammenlebens von morgen in dramatischer Weise beeinflussen. Fortwährende und fundierte Auseinandersetzungen mit dieser Thematik sind daher von besonderer Wichtigkeit und Dringlichkeit.

Für Deutschland lassen sich die Wesenszüge des demographischen Wandels auf eine einfache Formel bringen: Die Bevölkerung schrumpft, die Jungen werden weniger, und die Alten werden mehr. Diese Entwicklungen – vor allem die abnehmende Zahl der Geburten und das Altern der bevölkerungsstarken mittleren Jahrgänge – führen zu gravierenden Verzerrungen der Altersstruktur.

Diese „verkorkste" Altersstruktur wird einschneidende Folgen für alle Bereiche unserer Gesellschaft haben: Familie, Arbeit, Mobilität, Migration, Sozial-, Pflege- und Gesundheitswesen, Bildung und Wirtschaft. Zwar ist der demographische Wandel nicht die Ursache für alle gesellschaftlichen Herausforderungen der Gegenwart, aber er verschärft viele von ihnen auf dramatische Weise. Und bei der Auseinandersetzung mit dieser Thematik wird deutlich: Alles hängt mit allem zusammen, und es ist wichtig, ganzheitlich zu denken.

Aufgrund der enormen Bedeutung dieser Thematik ist es seit einiger Zeit auch ein Anliegen der deutschen Bundespräsidenten, diese in den Fokus einer breiten Öffentlichkeit zu rücken. Beispielsweise rief Bundespräsident a.D. Dr. Horst Köhler zusammen mit der Bertelsmann Stiftung das Forum Demographischer Wandel ins Leben. Diese Initiative zielt darauf ab, der Öffentlichkeit die enorme Bedeutung der Thematik bewusst zu machen sowie Konzepte und konkrete Handlungsvorschläge zu erarbeiten. Ich habe auf sich abzeichnende Probleme im Zuge des demographischen Wandels hingewiesen, etwa die drohende Gefahr einer „Rentnerdemokratie", weil die Parteien überproportional auf die immer mehr werdenden Älteren Rücksicht nehmen und dies zu einer anhaltenden Übervorteilung der Jüngeren führen könnte. Dieser gedankliche Anstoß hat sicher auch Meinungsverschiedenheiten ausgelöst. Eine intensive gesellschaftliche Debatte, die mitunter auch kontrovers geführt werden muss, ist jedoch notwendig.

Das vorliegende Buch trägt hierzu bei. Zur Information und zur Diskussion. Die Autoren setzen sich mit den bedrohlichen Herausforderungen, aber speziell auch mit den vielfältigen Chancen des demographischen Wandels für unsere Wirtschaft

---

[*] Original version in German language.

auseinander. Diese wirtschaftliche Perspektive ist bedeutsam für unsere Zukunft. Denn für die Wettbewerbsfähigkeit der Unternehmen, aber auch ganzer Volkswirtschaften ist es unerlässlich, die Konsequenzen der demographischen Entwicklungen für die Wirtschaft zu erkennen und das Handeln darauf auszurichten.

Das Buch setzt vor allem zwei Akzente: Erstens wird die Thematik möglichst umfassend betrachtet, indem verschiedene Anspruchsgruppen von Unternehmen berücksichtigt werden. Schließlich betrifft der demographische Wandel sowohl die internen Anspruchsgruppen wie die Mitarbeiter und die Führungskräfte, als auch die externen, vor allem die Kunden. Da gibt es enorme Herausforderungen. So zeichnet sich bereits heute ein akuter Mangel an Fachkräften und Akademikern in vielen Branchen ab. Für Unternehmen geht es beispielsweise darum, wertvolles Know-how zu erhalten, Mitarbeiter aller Altersgruppen aus- und weiterzubilden sowie die Vereinbarkeit von Beruf und Familie durch Kinderbetreuung und flexible Arbeitszeiten zu fördern. Aber es gibt auch enorme Potenziale! Insbesondere im Kundensegment der Älteren. In Japan zählt der sogenannte „Silver Market" zu den am schnellsten wachsenden Segmenten, bei uns steckt er jedoch noch in den „Kinderschuhen". Unternehmen müssen sinnvolle Innovationen vorantreiben und diese neuen Kundengruppen in geeigneter Art und Weise ansprechen.

Zweitens zeichnet sich das Buch durch einen interessanten Mix an Beiträgen aus: Es gibt Beiträge, die eher akademischer Natur sind, und solche, die sehr praxisnah gestaltet sind. Unter den Autoren sind verschiedene Nationalitäten sowie Jung und Alt. Damit reflektiert das vorliegende Buch, welches begleitend zum DocNet Management Symposium 2010 an der Universität St. Gallen erscheint, sowohl die Inhalte des Symposiums als auch dessen besonderen Reiz. Die Vielfalt und das Zusammentreffen von verschiedenen Generationen führen zu lebendigen Debatten und interessanten Lösungsansätzen.

Eines steht bei dieser Thematik außer Frage: Im Grunde ist es doch großartig, dass wir länger leben und auch länger fit sind. Wir müssen das als Chance begreifen. Das vorliegende Buch in Verbindung mit dem DocNet Management Symposium 2010 leistet einen Beitrag dazu. – Ein *Silberstreif* am Horizont.

Heilbronn, Juli 2010

Prof. Dr. Roman Herzog

Preface by the Editors

The demographic change – ageing and shrinking populations in some parts of the world and exploding populations in others – greatly affects all dimensions of societies. While economists, demographers, and policy makers have been debating the implications of demographic change for quite some time, the corporate world has reacted rather slowly. In recent years, however, companies have increasingly paid attention to the demographic change's challenges and opportunities.

This book sheds light on the challenges as well as the opportunities of the demographic change from a business perspective. Companies will be confronted with the difficult task of addressing the different needs of rather diverse age groups. For companies' future success it will be pivotal to keep employees of different age groups as motivated as possible and productive members of the workforce as long as possible. Besides these challenges, multiple opportunities arise from the demographic change. Among these are completely new fields of sales markets as older individuals develop into promising future customers. We strongly believe that those companies that can successfully adapt to the demographic change will develop a sustainable competitive advantage.

To fully capture the demographic change's far-reaching implications for companies, we pursue an interdisciplinary approach by bringing together practitioners and scholars from various fields and disciplines that include economics, organisational psychology, HR management, marketing, and consulting.

The insights are organised into five sections. Intended to set the stage, the first section fosters an understanding of the demographic change. The second section takes a macro-economic perspective in order to investigates the external environment in which companies operate. It describes the demographic change's impact on national labour markets, including potential changes in pension and vocational training systems. The third section centres on challenges related to the workforce and various aspects of diverse age groups in the workplace, focussing on HR and leadership systems. Finally, the fourth section addresses the distinct opportunities arising from the demographic change: emergent new markets, customer groups, sales prospects and innovations. We hope that the contents of the five sections provide a comprehensive picture of the topic from companies' perspective.

All the sections include two types of chapters: longer chapters present scientifically grounded insights into the challenges and opportunities of the demographic change, while shorter chapters – labelled viewpoints or insights from practice – highlight hands-on experiences as well as pioneering initiatives and actions. We believe that it is exactly this combination of research-driven and practice-oriented chapters which makes this book a profound and interesting read.

By presenting scientifically grounded, relevant insights, this book mainly addresses practitioners. It focuses on executives from various organisational fields, including HR and marketing managers, as well as on specialists in corporate strategy, change management and organisational development. Professional trainers, scholars and students of economy, strategy, marketing, organisational behaviour, and HR management may also gain valuable insights.

Many parties have been involved in our endeavour to foster the debate on how companies can seize the opportunities arising from the demographic change and tackle its challenges. We owe them a debt of gratitude. Firstly, we thank DocNet, the doctoral network at the University of St. Gallen, for providing us with the opportunity to organise the 8th DocNet Management Symposium titled *From grey to silver – How to successfully cope with the challenges and opportunities of demographic change* and to serve as the editors of this book, which complements the symposium.

   Secondly, we are grateful to the authors as well as the symposium speakers (many of whom also authored chapters of this book). All of them contributed their time and expertise generously. We are profoundly grateful for their efforts, their collegial spirit and ability 'to get the job done' under very strict time constraints.

   Thirdly, we are extremely thankful to those who supported this project in many other ways. We thank Alexandra Havrylyuk and Guido Mesmer, who helped organise the 8th DocNet Management Symposium. We also thank Ilse Evertse and her team for their willingness to support this project, but primarily for their enthusiasm that went far beyond the usual proofreading. It has been a great pleasure working with you! We are, of course, grateful to Christian Rauscher and his team from the publishing house Springer-Verlag who never wavered in their support of this book project.

   Finally, special thanks are due to the financial sponsors of this book project. They include this year's symposium lead sponsor KPMG, the World Demographic & Ageing Forum (WDA) and the Ecoscientia Foundation, the St. Gallen Research Centre for Ageing, Welfare and Labour Market Analysis (SCALA), and the alumni network of the University of St. Gallen (HSG Alumni). This project would not have been possible without their generosity.

St. Gallen, July 2010

Sven Kunisch, Stephan A. Boehm, Michael Boppel

Table of Contents

Part A   An introduction – Understanding demographic change

**Part B   An economic and social perspective – Taking the external
            environment into consideration**

List of Symbols

 Point of view
 Counterpoint
Practical insights

List of Abbreviations

BMW	Bayerische Motoren Werke AG (Bavarian Motor Works)
CEO	Chief Executive Officer
cf.	compare, consult (Latin: confer)
CUC	Customer Contact Centre
DFG	Deutsche Forschungsgemeinschaft (German Research Foundation)
DGFP	Deutsche Gesellschaft für Personalführung e.V. (German Association for Leadership)
DIJ	Deutsches Institut für Japanstudien (German Institute for Japanese Studies)
e.g.	for example (Latin: exempli gratia)
e.V.	Eingetragener Verein (Registered Association)
ESRC	British Economic and Social Research Council
EUR	Euro
FE	Fixed Effects
GBP	Pound Sterling
GCCIJ	German Chamber of Commerce and Industry in Japan
GDP	Gross Domestic Product
GPS	Global Positioning System
HRM	Human Resource Management
i.a.	among other things (Latin: inter alia)
i.e.	that is (Latin: id est)
IC	Innovation Contest
IFA	Internationale Funkausstellung Berlin (the International Radio Exhibition Berlin)
IIASA	International Institute for Applied Systems Analysis
IMMN	International Mature Marketing Network
ISP	International Study Program
IT	Information Technology
LA	Local Authority
LED	Light-emitting Diode
LTC	Long-term Care
MBA	Master of Business Administration

NL	Netherlands
NPD	New Product Development
NSD	New Service Development
OECD	Organisation for Economic Co-operation and Development
Ph.D.	Doctor of Philosophy (Latin: philosophiæ doctor)
R&D	Research & Development
SE	European Company (Latin: Societas Europaea)
SEK	Swedish Krona
SHARE	Survey of Health, Ageing and Retirement in Europe
SME	Small and medium-sized enterprise
SSW	Social Security Wealth
TFR	Total Fertility Rate
TTD	Time to Death
TUHH	Technische Universität Hamburg-Harburg (Hamburg University of Technology)
UK	United Kingdom
UN	United Nations
US	United States
USA	United States of America
USP	Unique Selling Proposition
VIP	Very Important Person

Part A

An introduction – Understanding demographic change

An integrated framework for investigating the challenges and opportunities of demographic change

Stephan A. Boehm, Sven Kunisch, Michael Boppel*

Demographic change is one of the most crucial issues of our time. Owing to its importance for companies, this topic has made it onto decision-makers' agendas in recent years. This chapter – which serves as the introductory chapter – sets out to first establish a common understanding of the term *demographic change*. The motivation is that one must first understand the specific developments of demographic change if one is to effectively consider its various implications. Secondly, by taking the company stakeholder perspective, this chapter introduces an integrated framework for examining demographic change's implications for companies. Thirdly, on the basis of the suggested framework, this chapter integrates and organises the individual book contributions.

---

* Dr. Stephan A. Boehm, Senior Lecturer and Director of the Center for Disability and Integration, University of St. Gallen.
Sven Kunisch, Ph.D. candidate and Chief Editor of the M&A REVIEW, Institute of Management, University of St. Gallen.
Michael Boppel, Ph.D. candidate, Institute of Management, University of St. Gallen.

S. Kunisch et al. (eds.), *From Grey to Silver*,
DOI 10.1007/978-3-642-15594-9_1, © Springer-Verlag Berlin Heidelberg 2011

Table of Contents

1   Understanding demographic change

The world is in the midst of a historically unprecedented demographic transition that is having – and will continue to have – profound effects on our population's size and age structure. While changes in populations' structure affect all dimensions of societies, companies, specifically, have started acknowledging that these changes come with enormous challenges as well as opportunities.

This introductory chapter serves three main purposes: Firstly, it seeks to establish a common understanding of the term *demographic change*. In order to deal effectively with its various implications for individual employees, the firm, and society as a whole, one must first understand the specific developments of the term *demographic change*.

Secondly, this chapter introduces an integrated framework based on the company stakeholder perspective and covering three major dimensions. Companies require an interdisciplinary approach to integrate knowledge from various fields and disciplines and thus fully capture demographic change's far-reaching implications.

Thirdly, this chapter seeks to integrate the individual contributions to this book. Within our integrated framework's three major perspectives, every chapter makes a distinct contribution to analysing the potential challenges and opportunities resulting from demographic change. Together, the chapters provide a comprehensive picture of the business challenges and opportunities of demographic change.

1.1   Triggers

Generally, there are three triggers of demographic change: *life expectancy*, *fertility rate*, and *migration rate*. Together, they explain how societies change in size as well as age composition.

Before 1900, the world population's age structure was more or less constant, with slow overall growth and relatively few people ageing beyond 65. During the first half of the 20th century, this began to change as *life expectancy* began to rise, especially in Western countries. In Switzerland, for example, life expectancy rose from 48 in 1900, to 62 in 1950, to more than 80 in 2008. While the age structure remained fairly constant, population size increased (Schweizer Bundesamt für Statistik[1] 2009). This trend towards a longer life-span continues.

In Germany, for example, demographic projections suggest that until the year 2060, men can expect a further increase of 7.8 years in their life expectancy, women 6.8 years (assumption 1). Anticipating extensive advancements in medical care, other forecasts predict an even higher additional life expectancy of 10.6 years for men and 8.8 years for women than that of the 2008 prediction (assumption 2). This would lead to an average life expectancy of 87.7 years for men and 91.2 for women. Figure 1 shows both projections as applied to Germany (Deutsches Statistisches Bundesamt[2] 2009a).

---

[1]   Swiss Statistics Office.
[2]   German Statistics Office.

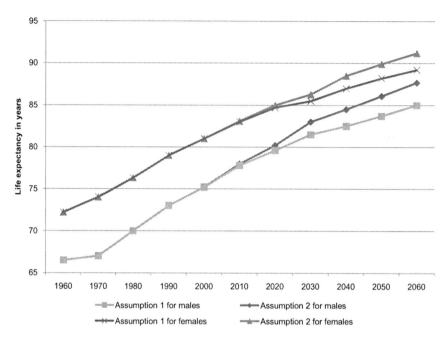

Figure 1: Life expectancy of those born between 1960 and 2060 in Germany (source: Deutsches Statistisches Bundesamt 2009a)

The second half of the 20th century saw the start of another phase in this transition as *fertility rates* declined dramatically by almost a half. The total fertility rate (TFR) represents the average number of children that would be born per woman if all women lived to the end of their childbearing years and bore children according to a given fertility rate at each age (CIA 2010). Internationally, TFR values differ significantly from around 5 in Africa to 1.5 in the European Union. In Switzerland, the fertility rate is 1.46 (in 2007), well below the *replacement rate* of 2.1 required for a stable population size (Schweizer Bundesamt für Statistik 2009).

Similar numbers apply to many European countries, for example, to Spain with a fertility rate of 1.40 and Hungary with a fertility rate of 1.32 (Eurostat 2010; Schweizer Bundesamt für Statistik 2009). Germany is a dramatic case. With its current reproduction rate of 1.37, Germany is in the bottom group of the EU 27 countries. In total, only 651,000 children were born in 2009 – 30,000 (3.6%) less than in 2008. If the 842,000 deaths in 2009 are taken into account, there was a population decrease of more than 190,000 inhabitants (Deutsches Statistisches Bundesamt 2010a). Countries like France (a fertility rate of 1.98), Ireland (2.03), and Turkey (2.10) face more positive situations, as their higher reproduction rates ensure stable population sizes (Eurostat 2010; Schweizer Bundesamt für Statistik 2009). Figure 2 summarizes the fertility rates of selected European countries.

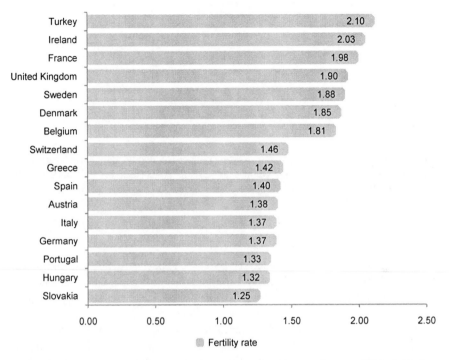

Figure 2: Fertility rates of selected European countries (source: Eurostat 2010; Schweizer Bundesamt für Statistik 2009)

The *migration rate* is considered the third important trigger affecting a society's demographic development. Specifically, the net migration rate reflects the difference between immigrants and emigrants in an area over time. A positive value means that more people enter the country than leave it and a negative value vice versa. Countries with a positive value profit from the inflow of foreign workers who contribute to their population growth, or at least to the stabilisation of their population size. Switzerland, for example, has mostly had a positive migration rate since 1890. In 2007 and 2008, the net migration reached new record highs of 75,500 (2007) and 98,200 persons (2008) (Schweizer Bundesamt für Statistik 2009). Since World War II, more than 2 million immigrants have entered Switzerland, accounting for 21% of the total population in 2009 (Schweizer Bundesamt für Migration 2009). Figure 3 compares the net migration rate of Switzerland and Germany with their population size.

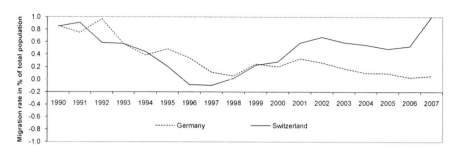

Figure 3: Migration rates in Germany and Switzerland 1990-2007 (source: own calculation based on Deutsches Statistisches Bundesamt 2010b, 2010c; Schweizer Bundesamt für Statistik 2010)

1.2 Direct effects

In short, the three above-mentioned triggers (life expectancy, fertility, and migration rate) determine a society's overall size and the age composition, and cause the effects summarised in the term *demographic change*. There are basically two main effects: *population decline* and *population ageing*.

One of the most obvious consequences of the demographic developments is the projected population decline in many industrialised countries. If the fertility rate and the migration rate are low, a population is likely to shrink. In Germany's case, demographers have calculated that from 2010, the population will shrink constantly. Until 2060, Germany is expected to lose 12 million inhabitants, which is equal to losing all the inhabitants of Bavaria! Furthermore, there will be large regional differences. While boom regions such as Munich or Frankfurt am Main are likely to grow, certain regions in East Germany (such as Mecklenburg-West Pomerania) are expected to undergo above-average inhabitant losses (Deutsches Statistisches Bundesamt 2009a, 2009b; Prognos AG 2007).

For companies the development of the *working population*, i.e. the number of persons between 20 and 65, is even more important than the development of the total population. Again, demographers project a decline of 10 million workers in Germany until 2050[3] (see Figure 4), which is 20% of the total workforce (Deutsches Statistisches Bundesamt 2009a, 2009b).

Interestingly, a completely different picture emerges for Switzerland. Owing to a higher net migration rate (see Figure 3), the total population is expected to stay stable or even increase slightly over the next 30 years (Schweizer Bundesamt für Statistik 2009). The same holds true for Switzerland's working population.

---

[3] These projections are based on a medium scenario, assuming a constant, low-fertility rate of 1.4, a further increase in life expectancy of about eight years (for males) and seven years (for females), as well as a comparably high net migration rate of 200,000 people per year. This medium scenario is applied throughout this chapter. Other, more pessimistic scenarios (e.g., implying a net migration rate of only 100,000 people) lead to even more dramatic results (e.g., a population size of only 65 million people in 2060).

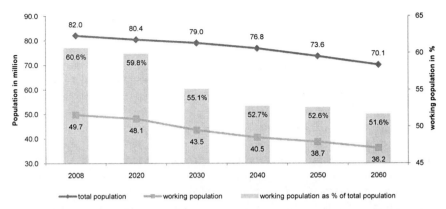

Figure 4: Projected population in Germany 2008-2060 (source: own calculation based on Deutsches Statistisches Bundesamt 2009a)

The change in population size is not the only direct effect of demographic change, which also has a strong impact on a society's age composition. In most European countries, the share of the young in the population has begun to decline, and the share of the elderly has started to increase. While there is currently a global trend, there is considerable variation between countries and regions, resulting from very different fertility, mortality, and migration trends.

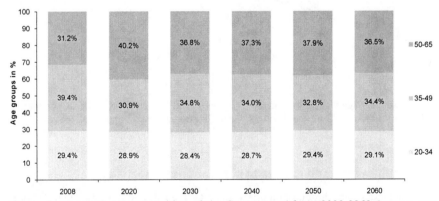

Figure 5: Projected age composition of the German workforce 2008-2060 (source: own calculation based on Deutsches Statistisches Bundesamt 2009c, 2010d)

Specifically Western Europe's and the United States' age structures are changing constantly due to the combined effect of low fertility rates, a rising average age, and the disproportionately large baby-boom generation born between 1946 and 1964 (Graig and Paganelli 2000). By 2010, nearly half of the US workforce will be composed of employees older than 45 (United Nations 2005). Similar numbers apply to Germany. From 2020, the group of older employees (50-65) will be the working population's largest subgroup (representing 40.2% of the total working population). Figure 5 shows the projected age composition of the German workforce from 2008 to 2060.

While the development of Switzerland's population size will differ from that of Germany (see above), it is in a similar situation as its neighbour when it comes to its population's age composition (see Figure 6 for the projected for Swiss and German age dependency ratios). As in Germany, the *age-dependency ratio* (the number of persons 65+ per 100 persons aged 20-64) is constantly increasing, i.e. the share of retired persons is growing compared to those who are economically active. In fact, the age dependency ratio for Switzerland is expected to increase from 0.26 in 2005 to 0.51 in 2050, i.e. for every senior person, there will only be two working age persons. Furthermore, from 2017, the group of inhabitants above 64 years will be larger than the group of children (0-19 years) (Schweizer Bundesamt für Statistik 2009). The figures for Germany are even more dramatic, with the age dependency ratio reaching a value of 60.5 in 2050.

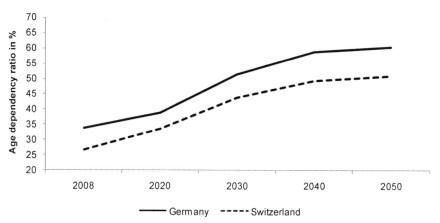

Figure 6: Age dependency ratio for Germany and Switzerland 2008-2050 (source: Schweizer Bundesamt für Statistik 2009, Deutsches Statistisches Bundesamt 2009a)

1.3 Medium-term and long-term implications for societies

Besides these rather direct, population-related effects of demographic change, there are various other implications for individuals, organisations, and society as a whole. While a detailed analysis is beyond the scope of this chapter (see Birg 2003 and Clark et al. 2004 for comprehensive reviews), the main implications for societies are described below.

From an economic perspective, social welfare systems will be strongly affected by demographic change. In Germany, for example, the main challenge will be reforming the pension system (Schröer and Straubhaar 2007). Retired people will soon outnumber the working population, leading to potential shortcomings in the financing of pensions. A higher effective retirement age and the prolonged, ongoing engagement of older people in the workforce seem unavoidable if this financial gap is to be at least partially closed (Beatty and Burroughs 1999; Bullinger 2001).

The financing of health and long-term care insurance is another challenge facing society. The expenditure on older people are expected to significantly exceed expenditure on younger people (Birg 2003). Thus, society's age distribution shift will put great pressure on social welfare systems. This also means that a higher share of individual employees' income will be deducted to pay for social insurances.

The nature of demographic change's impact on macroeconomic development is not yet known. Pessimistic forecasts for Germany expect economic growth to decline by 0.6-1.3% per year (Institut der deutschen Wirtschaft 2004). This would be a tremendous challenge for Western societies, which rely heavily on the expectation of continuous economic growth. However, the association between demographic change and a potential decline in a country's economic performance has not been proven (Wirsching 2005).

1.4 Challenges and opportunities for organisations

Demographic change confronts organisations with four primary challenges. Firstly, a large portion of the workforce will retire or have the choice to retire in the near future. Younger generations already working for companies or enrolled in educational institutions will most probably not fill the gap. Consequently, a labour supply shortage is expected, which is unlikely to be filled in terms of either quantity or quality (Dychtwald et al. 2004). Vivid terms such as 'the war for talent' (Michaels et al. 2001) call attention to this potential threat to companies in almost all developed economies. Although recent economic crises have attenuated this issue, the pressure on organisations to hire young, talented people will increase at the end of the current recession. This is especially true for companies that cut staff during the crisis. In Germany's case, calculations show that already in 2006, more than 73,000 engineering positions could not be filled, resulting in a potential loss of 18.5 billion EUR for Germany's economy (Institut der deutschen Wirtschaft 2007) – 0.8% of its gross domestic product (GDP).

Secondly, the average workforce age is increasing. It is not clear whether companies in Germany or Switzerland will still be able to compete against rising economies such as China or India, which can rely on a seemingly inexhaustible pool of young employees. This seems especially challenging, as the economy is increasingly driven by innovation (Davenport et al. 2006). Product life cycles are becoming shorter, pressurising companies to be more flexible and more effective. Therefore, innovative and age-specific human resource (HR) and leadership practices seem inevitable; only if such actions are undertaken will older employees stay on as productive workforce members.

Thirdly, not only will the average workforce age rise, the workforce will also become more age-diverse. Individuals from three or even four generations will work together in the same organisation. This overlap of different generations working together, which is sometimes referred to as the 'Prince Charles Effect' (Oertel 2007), might have positive or negative effects on overall company productivity (e.g., Jackson et al. 2003; Williams and O'Reilly 1998). On the one hand, people of different ages might have complementary skills and experiences, which they can use to enhance their joint productivity. On the other hand, certain forms of discrimination may occur in age-diverse organisations, which will have negative effects (see, for example, Kunze et al. 2010).

Finally, retiring age cohorts will increase over time. Soon, the first baby boomers – an especially large age cohort – will retire. In Germany, this generation is fundamental for today's workforce (Sinn 2005) and was chiefly responsible for the increases in productivity and innovation over the past decades (Voelpel et al. 2007). Owing to the more or less simultaneous drop-out of many of these qualified employees, organisations risk losing enormous amounts of knowledge, experience, and customer contacts (Dychtwald et al. 2004; The Concours Group 2003). There-fore, the retirement of the baby-boom generation will place significant pressure on organisations to ensure high-quality knowledge management to retain this critical knowledge.

The demographic change has been mainly discussed in terms of the various challenges emanating from it. Nevertheless, there are also multiple opportunities that arise from this change. An important factor is the consideration of a growing customer segment. This so-called *silver market* comprises people over 50 (Kohl-bacher and Herstatt 2009) who jointly hold almost half of Germany's purchasing power – approximately 610 billion EUR (GfK GeoMarketing GmbH 2008). Since companies in Europe – especially companies in German-speaking countries – can hardly compete with price offers from companies in Asia and other low-wage regions, they will have to be or need to swiftly become innovation leaders in their industry (Davenport et al. 2006). Therefore, if European companies can expand and meet the silver market's specific needs, they can achieve an important competitive advantage. One way to better understand older customers is to hire, employ, and retain older employees. Thus, companies that understand the silver market are very likely to prosper in the future.

2 An integrated framework for investigating business implications

While phenomena related to demographic change have attracted researchers and consultants from many different disciplines for some time now, they mostly focus on individual aspects and come from individual fields such as economics (e.g., Mason and Tapinos 2000; Hamm et al. 2009), HR management (e.g., Brandenburg and Domschke 2007; Prezewowsky 2007), or marketing (e.g., Reidl 2007; Kohl-bacher and Herstatt 2009). However, in order to fully capture the far-reaching implications of demographic change, it is crucial to pursue an interdisciplinary approach that brings together knowledge from various fields and disciplines.

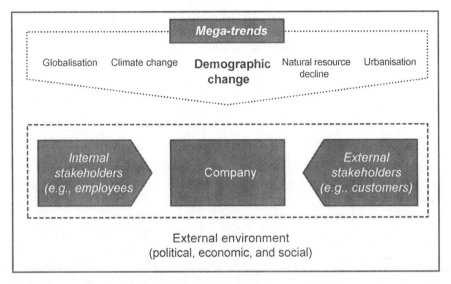

Figure 7: Framework for investigating the challenges and opportunities of demographic change from a business perspective (source: authors)

An integrated framework is a step in this direction, and serves to organise the contents of this book (see Figure 7). Two ideas are noteworthy in our suggested framework: Firstly, the framework highlights the strategic relevance of demographic change. From a company perspective, demographic change is one of the megatrends (others include globalisation, climate change, natural resources decline, and urbanisation) that has a profound impact and must be addressed. When developing strategy, it is imperative that companies consider mega-trends (e.g., Mueller-Stewens and Brauer 2009).[4]

Secondly, the framework adopts a stakeholder perspective of the firm, embracing internal stakeholders (employees, management, etc.) and external stakeholders (customers, state, society at large, etc.). Thereby, the framework integrates the underlying economic and social environment affecting companies and the successful management of both internal human resources and external customers.

---

[4] Siemens, for example, builds its strategy on four mega-trends. *"Urbanization and sustainable development, globalization and competitiveness, demographic change and healthcare, climate change and energy supply – the world is facing major challenges. [...] How can we provide efficient, patient-friendly and affordable healthcare systems in cities and rural areas alike? [...] These are far-reaching questions that demand comprehensive answers."* (Siemens Annual Report 2009, p. 6).

3   An integrated analysis of business implications

Based on the suggested framework, this book analyses potential challenges and
opportunities resulting from demographic change are from three major perspectives: (1) an economic and social perspective (the external environment), (2) a
human resource (HR) and leadership perspective (internal stakeholders), and (3) a
marketing and innovation perspective (external stakeholders).

3.1   An economic and social perspective

Firstly, demographic change is analysed and discussed from an economic and social
perspective. It appears pivotal to consider macro-economic implications as these
developments function as boundary conditions for the successful management of
demographic change.

Henseke (2011) sets the stage by highlighting that older workers could at least
partially compensate for the working population decline in most European countries
if certain institutional factors (e.g., employment protection laws or pension systems)
are configured in a specific way. Given that the working population is shrinking
tremendously and the ratio of economically active persons to dependent persons is
worsening constantly in many countries (e.g., Germany and Japan), these findings
are very important. Consequently, both governments and companies will have to
pave the way for more older workers becoming a normal part of a country's workforce.

Wilenius (2011) places demographic change in a larger societal context and
highlights many of its direct and indirect effects on Western economies. Among
others, social security arrangements will have to be redesigned and the state will
have to change its role from being a *full service provider* to becoming a *strategic
partner* for a prosperous retirement.

Karlsson and Klohn (2011) focus on one of the most relevant questions of demographic change: Does increased longevity also lead to an increase in care costs, or is
the remaining time-to-death the relevant predictor of morbidity and its related
effects? Using panel data from Sweden, the authors show that age as well as time-
to-death are indeed important determinants, although age has a much greater effect.
This finding has major implications for society, as it suggests that individuals and
social security systems will have to set aside larger financial reserves for old age.

Moerikofer-Zwez (2011) addresses a very similar topic. She points to societies
in general and especially nursing homes having to prepare for the changing needs of
future generations. Requirements (e.g., the living standards in nursing homes) may
vary tremendously between the generations now dependent on these services and
future generations, such as the baby boomers who have been used to higher levels of
prosperity throughout their lives.

Finally, Wolf (2011) closes the loop by describing how traditional notions of
work are changing and how demographic developments are complemented by additional triggers, such as the increasing number of women in the workforce or the shift
away from the Protestant work ethic.

As a whole, the book's first section helps organisations and decision-makers better understand the basic parameters of demographic change as well as its influences on the labour market.

3.2   A human resource and leadership perspective

Secondly, the book turns to employees as primary company stakeholders. In order to successfully manage demographic change, companies must develop a sound understanding of how demographic developments affect their workforce. As noted, companies must deal with multiple effects and challenges; these include a potential shortage of skilled employees, a higher average workforce age, the management of age-diverse workgroups, and the impending brain drain stemming from the retirement of experienced personnel (see DeLong 2004; Dychtwald et al. 2004; Smola and Sutton 2002; Tempest et al. 2002).

Kunze and colleagues (2011) address some of these issues and highlight the importance of age-specific leadership behaviour. In order to successfully deal with age-diverse employees, managers must know and respond to the specific leadership preferences, work values, and communication patterns within and between different generations – for example, the economic boom generation, the baby-boom generation, and the Internet generation. If leaders meet their subordinates' age-specific leadership expectations, they will build strong relationships with them.

Similarly, Schroder and colleagues (2011) call for innovative and age-related human resource (HR) practices in organisations. Building on case study data from the chemical, steel, and retail industries as well as from public schools in Germany and Britain, the authors urge organisations to consider the specific institutional and sectoral contexts in which they operate when designing HR systems.

Bilhuber Galli (2011) deliberately takes a very different view. While she acknowledges the need for companies to act in response to the challenges of demographic change, she warns decision-makers against implementing unidimensional age initiatives. In her opinion, age is neither a driver of (un)productivity nor do members of one age group necessarily share many commonalities. She advises companies to invest in a holistic organisational learning approach that appeals equally to all age groups.

Boehm and colleagues (2011) tackle the question of how companies can effectively deal with teams made up of age-diverse employees. The authors conduct an extensive literature review to show why age diversity may have positive and negative performance effects, and deduce practical recommendations to deal with age diversity in the workplace.

To some extent, Greve and Ruigrok (2011) leave organisational boundaries behind by investigating what career patterns executives follow after retiring. Using individual data from 104 top managers, they find that there are various post-executive career opportunities, including board memberships, consulting services, and teaching activities. Interestingly, the retiree's demographic characteristics (e.g., age, education level, and international experience) have a strong impact on post-executive activities. For companies and society as a whole, a vibrant post-executive labour market has many advantages as executives' human and social capital can be used effectively.

Hoerhager (2011) confirms this finding by sharing practical insights from the Consenec model. Consenec, a consulting firm employing former top managers of firms such as ABB and Alstom, implements some of Greve and Ruigrok's (2011) ideas and capitalises on post-executives' rich experience and know-how. This win-win situation enables managers over 60 to reduce their workload on a step-by-step basis and to enjoy more personal freedom, while sharing their knowledge for the sake of Consenec as well as the client.

In short, the second section highlights the importance of elaborate internal age management, including activities in the fields of generation-specific leadership, non-discriminatory HR management, and proactive retirement planning. By applying age management, companies can retain employees of different age groups as motivated and productive workforce members for as long as possible.

3.3 A marketing and innovation perspective

The third part adopts a marketing and innovation perspective. As noted, demographic change may also be a source of specific business opportunities for companies in developed economies. Among these are the completely new sales markets that arise as older individuals develop into promising future customers (see Reidl 2007; Kohlbacher and Herstatt 2009). For companies, however, this means recognising and adopting the preferences of such new customer groups, which were previously neglected. Nevertheless, a certain modification of the company's innovation process seems inevitable (Reichwald and Piller 2009).

Bullinger and colleagues (2011) follow this line of thought and analyse what companies can do to meet older customer groups' specific needs. They propose online innovation contests in which older people participate as an appropriate method to gain knowledge of older customers' preferences. By doing so, companies can successfully innovate for and with the ageing society and ultimately gain a sustainable competitive advantage.

Leyhausen and Vossen (2011) emphasise the growing importance of the silver market and describe different categories of older consumers as well as potential innovation and communication strategies to exploit these opportunities. They also call for the adoption of the open innovation paradigm and urge companies to make use of external seniors who are willing to share their ideas, preferences, and knowledge in special idea contests.

Pfeiffer (2011) provides practical insights and describes how Swisscom, Switzerland's largest telecommunication company, responds to business opportunities resulting from demographic developments. In seeking to address age-specific customer needs, Swisscom has initiated some highly visible pilot projects such as *silver shops*, in which highly experienced older employees serve senior customers, whose service expectations tend to differ from those of younger clients.

Finally, Kohlbacher and colleagues (2011) investigate whether European (and especially German companies) can profit from using Japan as a lead market for silver products. Given Japan's position as a forerunner with regard to the demographic shift, foreign companies can use the country as a test market for new age-specific technologies, products, and services. As the authors' empirical data show, German companies have not yet fully exploited the business potentials of Japan's silver market.

Overall, companies in developed economies are urged to analyse the potential business opportunities created by the demographic change and to adapt both their innovation and marketing activities accordingly. If a company manages to exploit the significant potentials offered by senior customers, it may achieve a sustainable competitive advantage.

4 Conclusion

Demographic change is one of the most crucial issues of our time. Owing to its primary importance for not only societies at large, but specifically for companies, this topic has been at the top of company decision-makers' agenda in recent years. This book sets out to contribute to a better understanding of demographic change's implications for companies – its tremendous challenges, but also its enormous opportunities – and to provide potential solutions for concrete actions. However, to identify further solutions, researchers as well as practitioners will need to do more work on this topic.

This is in line with the research agenda sketched by Walter (2011). He comments on the various effects that demographic change might have on developed economies and calls for further research on seven demographic mega-trends, which include the challenges for social security systems, the reasons for low fertility, the changes in family constructs and lifestyles, and issues of mobility and migration.

In short, fully capturing demographic change's far-reaching implications requires an interdisciplinary approach that integrates knowledge from various fields and disciplines. In order to address these diverse subjects, scholars and practitioners from economics, organisational psychology, HR management, marketing, and innovation management have contributed to this book. It provides companies with a more a holistic understanding of the demographic change's challenges and opportunities.

References*

Beatty, P. T., & Burroughs, L. (1999). *Preparing for an aging workforce: the role of higher education*. Educational Gerontology, 25, 585-611.
*Bilhuber Galli, E. (2011). From grey to silver – More than a question of age. In S. Kunisch, S. Boehm, M. Boppel (Ed.), *From Grey to Silver – Managing the Challenges and Opportunities of Demographic Change* (pp. 117-119). Heidelberg: Springer.

---

* Chapters in this book.

Birg, H. (2003). *Die demographische Zeitenwende: Der Bevölkerungsrückgang in Deutschland und Europa*. München: C.H. Beck.

*Boehm, S., Baumgaertner, M. K., Dwertmann, D. J. G., & Kunze, F. (2011). Age diversity and its performance implications – Analyzing a major future workforce trend. In S. Kunisch, S. Boehm, M. Boppel (Ed.), *From Grey to Silver – Managing the Challenges and Opportunities of Demographic Change* (pp. 121-141). Heidelberg: Springer.

Brandenburg, U. & Domschke, J-P. (2007). *Die Zukunft sieht alt aus: Herausforderungen des demografischen Wandels für das Personalmanagement*. Wiesbaden: Gabler.

*Bullinger, A. C., Rass, M., & Adamczyk, S. (2011). Using innovation contests to master challenges of demographic change – Insights from research and practice. In S. Kunisch, S. Boehm, M. Boppel (Ed.), *From Grey to Silver – Managing the Challenges and Opportunities of Demographic Change* (pp. 163-174). Heidelberg: Springer.

Bullinger, H.-J. (2001). *Zukunft der Arbeit in einer alternden Gesellschaft. Broschürenreihe Demographie und Erwerbsarbeit*. Stuttgart: IRB Verlag.

CIA (2009). *The CIA World Factbook 2010*. New York: Skyhorse Publishing.

Clark, R., Burkhauser, R., Moon, M., Quinn, J., & Smeeding, J. (2004). *The economics of an aging society*. Blackwell: London.

Davenport, T. D., Leibold, M., & Voelpel, S. C. (2006). *Strategic management and innovation in the company*. Erlangen: Publicis.

DeLong (2004). *Lost knowledge: confronting the threat of an aging workforce*. New York: Oxford University Press.

Deutsches Statistisches Bundesamt[5] (2009a). *Bevölkerung Deutschlands bis 2060 (report)*. http://www.destatis.de/jetspeed/portal/cms/Sites/destatis/Internet/DE/Presse/pk/2009/ Bevoelkerung/pressebroschuere__bevoelkerungsentwicklung2009,property=file.pdf. Accessed 20 July 2010.

Deutsches Statistisches Bundesamt[5] (2009b). *Demografischer Wandel in Deutschland: Auswirkungen auf die Entwicklung der Erwerbspersonenzahl*. http://www.statistik-portal.de/statistik-portal/demografischer_wandel_heft4.pdf. Accessed 20 July 2010.

Deutsches Statistisches Bundesamt[5] (2009c). *Bevölkerung Deutschlands bis 2060 (database)*. https://www-ec.destatis.de/csp/shop/sfg/bpm.html.cms.cBroker.cls?cmspath=struktur, Warenkorb.csp&action=basketadd&id=1024891. Accessed 21 July 2010.

Deutsches Statistisches Bundesamt[5] (2010a). Press release from May 17th, 2010. *2009: Weniger Geburten und Sterbefälle, Eheschliessungen nahezu konstant*. http://www. destatis.de/jetspeed/portal/cms/Sites/destatis/Internet/DE/Presse/pm/2010/05/ PD10__176__126,templateId=renderPrint.psml. Accessed 21 July 2010.

Deutsches Statistisches Bundesamt[5] (2010b). *Wanderungen von und nach Deutschland*. http://www.destatis.de/jetspeed/portal/cms/Sites/destatis/Internet/DE/Content/Statistiken/ Zeitreihen/LangeReihen/Bevoelkerung/Content75/lrbev07a,templateId=renderPrint.psml. Accessed 21 July 2010.

Deutsches Statistisches Bundesamt[5] (2010c). *Bevölkerung nach dem Gebietsstand*. http:// www.destatis.de/jetspeed/portal/cms/Sites/destatis/Internet/DE/Content/Statistiken/Zei-treihen/LangeReihen/Bevoelkerung/Content75/lrbev03a,templateId=renderPrint.psml. Accessed 21 July 2010.

Deutsches Statistisches Bundesamt[5] (2010d). *Bevölkerungsfortschreibung – Fachserie 1 Reihe 1.3 – 2008*. https://www-ec.destatis.de/csp/shop/sfg/bpm.html.cms.cBroker.cls? cmspath=struktur,vollanzeige.csp&ID=1025320. Accessed 21 July 2010.

---

[5] German Statistics Office.

Dychtwald, K., Erickson, T., & Morison, B. (2004). It's time to retire retirement. *Harvard Business Review, 82*, 48-57.

Eurostat (2010). *Population statistics for the European Union*. http://epp.eurostat.ec. europa.eu/portal/page/portal/population/data/main_tables. Accessed 20 July 2010.

GfK GeoMarketing GmbH (2008). *GfK purchasing power study*. http://www.gfk.com/ group/investor/key_figures_and_publications/investor_relations_news/news/002428/ index.de.html. Accessed 20 July 2010.

Graig. L. A., & Paganelli, V. (2000). Phased retirement. reshaping the end of work. *Compensation & Benefits Management, 16*, 1-9.

* Greve, P., & Ruigrok, W. (2011). Stepping down but not out – Characteristics of post-executive careers in Switzerland. In S. Kunisch, S. Boehm, M. Boppel (Ed.), *From Grey to Silver – Managing the Challenges and Opportunities of Demographic Change* (pp. 143-156). Heidelberg: Springer.

Hamm, I., Seitz, H., & Werding, M. (2009). *Demographic change in Germany: the economic and fiscal consequences*. Berlin, Heidelberg: Springer.

* Henseke, G. (2011). Demographic change and the economically active population in OECD countries – Could older workers compensate for the decline? In S. Kunisch, S. Boehm, M. Boppel (Ed.), *From Grey to Silver – Managing the Challenges and Opportunities of Demographic Change* (pp. 29-46). Heidelberg: Springer.

* Hoerhager, K. (2011). Insights from practice: Consenec – A well-proven model. In S. Kunisch, S. Boehm, M. Boppel (Ed.), *From Grey to Silver – Managing the Challenges and Opportunities of Demographic Change* (pp. 157-160). Heidelberg: Springer.

Institut der Deutschen Wirtschaft (2004). *Demographischer Wandel. Eine Grenze des Wachstums*. Köln.

Institut der Deutschen Wirtschaft (2007). *Mehr als 18 Milliarden Euro gehen verloren*. Pressemitteilung 49/2007.

Jackson, S.E., Joshi, A., & Erhardt, N.L. (2003). Recent research on team and organizational diversity: SWOT analysis and implications. *Journal of Management, 29*(6), 810-830.

* Karlsson, M., & Klohn, F. (2011). Ageing, health and disability – An economic perspective. In S. Kunisch, S. Boehm, M. Boppel (Ed.), *From Grey to Silver – Managing the Challenges and Opportunities of Demographic Change* (pp. 51-67). Heidelberg: Springer.

* Kohlbacher, F. Gudorf, P., & Herstatt C. (2011). Japan's growing silver market – An attractive business opportunity for foreign companies? In S. Kunisch, S. Boehm, M. Boppel (Ed.), *From Grey to Silver – Managing the Challenges and Opportunities of Demographic Change* (pp. 189-205). Heidelberg: Springer.

Kohlbacher, F. & Herstatt, C. (2009). *The silver market phenomenon: business opportunities in an era of demographic change*. Berlin, Heidelberg: Springer.

Kunze, F., Boehm, S., & Bruch, H. (2010). Age diversity, age discrimination climate, and performance consequences – A cross-organizational study. *Journal of Organizational Behavior, 31*(6), 1-30.

* Kunze, F., Boehm, S., & Bruch, H. (2011). Generational leadership – How to manage five different generations in the workforce. In S. Kunisch, S. Boehm, M. Boppel (Ed.), *From Grey to Silver – Managing the Challenges and Opportunities of Demographic Change* (pp. 87-100). Heidelberg: Springer.

* Leyhausen, F., & Vossen, A. (2011). We could have known better – Consumer-orientated marketing in Germany's ageing market. In S. Kunisch, S. Boehm, M. Boppel (Ed.), *From Grey to Silver – Managing the Challenges and Opportunities of Demographic Change* (pp. 175-184). Heidelberg: Springer.

Mason, A. & Tapinos, G. (2000). *Sharing the wealth: demographic change and economic transfer between generations.* New York: Oxford University Press.

Michaels, E., Handfield-Jones, H. & Axelrod, B. (2001). *The war for talent.* Boston: Harvard Business School Press.

* Moerikofer-Zwez, S. (2011). Demographic change – The role of the social context. In S. Kunisch, S. Boehm, M. Boppel (Ed.), *From Grey to Silver – Managing the Challenges and Opportunities of Demographic Change* (pp. 69-70). Heidelberg: Springer.

Mueller-Stewens, G., & Brauer, M. (2009): *Corporate Strategy & Governance: Wege zur nachhaltigen Wertsteigerung im diversifizierten Unternehmen.* Stuttgart: Schaeffer-Poeschel.

Oertel, J. (2007). *Generationenmanagement im Unternehmen.* Wiesbaden: Gabler.

* Pfeiffer, G. (2011). How Swisscom copes with the challenges of demographic change. In S. Kunisch, S. Boehm, M. Boppel (Ed.), *From Grey to Silver – Managing the Challenges and Opportunities of Demographic Change* (pp. 185-187). Heidelberg: Springer.

Prezewowsky, M. (2007). *Demografischer Wandel und Personalmanagement.* Wiesbaden: Gabler.

Prognos AG (2007). *Zukunftsatlas Deutschland 2007.* Basel: Prognos AG.

Reichwald, R., & Piller, F. (2009). *Interaktive Wertschöpfung: Open Innovation, Individualisierung und neue Formen der Arbeitsteilung* (2nd ed.). Wiesbaden: Gabler.

Reidl A. (2007). *Seniorenmarketing.* Landsberg am Lech: mi.

* Schroder, H., Flynn, M. & Muller-Camen, M. (2011). Rationale for and implementation of age-neutral HRM in divergent institutional contexts – Examples from Britain and Germany. In S. Kunisch, S. Boehm, M. Boppel (Ed.), *From Grey to Silver – Managing the Challenges and Opportunities of Demographic Change* (pp. 101-115). Heidelberg: Springer.

Schröer, S., & Straubhaar, T. (2007). Demographische Entwicklung: Problem oder Phantom. In E. Brölius & D. Schieck (Eds.), *Demographisierung des Gesellschaftlichen: Analysen und Debatten zur demographischen Zukunft Deutschlands* (pp. 165-183). Wiesbaden: VS Verlag.

Schweizer Bundesamt für Migration[6] (BFM) (2009). *Migrationsbericht 2009.* http://www.bfm.admin.ch/content/dam/data/migration/berichte/migration/migrationsbericht-2009-d.pdf. Accessed 20 July 2010.

Schweizer Bundesamt für Statistik[7] (2009). *Demografisches Porträt der Schweiz 2009.* http://www.bfs.admin.ch/bfs/portal/de/index/news/publikationen.Document.127584.pdf. Accessed 20 July 2010.

Schweizer Bundesamt für Statistik[7] (2010). *Bilanz der ständigen Wohnbevölkerung 1971-2008.* http://www.bfs.admin.ch/bfs/portal/de/index/themen/01/02/blank/dos/result.html. Accessed 20 July 2010.

Sinn, H. W. (2005). Das demographische Defizit: Die Fakten, die Folgen, die Ursachen und die Politikimplikationen. In H. Birg (Eds.), *Auswirkungen der demographischen Alterung und der Bevölkerungsschrumpfung auf Wirtschaft, Staat und Gesellschaft* (pp. 53-90). Münster: Lit Verlag.

Smola, K.W. & Sutton, C.D. (2002). Generational differences: revisiting generational work values for the new millennium. *Journal of Organizational Behavior*, 23(4), 363-382.

Tempest, S., Barnatt, C., & Coupland, C. (2002). Grey advantage – new strategies for the old. *Long Range Planning, 35*, 475-492.

---

[6] Swiss Migration Office.
[7] Swiss Statistics Office.

The Concours Group (2003). *Demography is destiny*. Research Report. Kingwood, Tx.

United Nations (2005). *Population challenges and development goals*. New York: United Nations.

Voelpel, S. C., Leibold, M., & Früchtenicht, J.-D. (2007). *Herausforderung 50 plus: Konzepte zum Management der Aging Workforce: Die Antwort auf das demographische Dilemma*. Erlangen: Publicis.

* Walter, N. (2011). Demographic change calls for change in the demographic research landscape – a German perspective. In S. Kunisch, S. Boehm, M. Boppel (Ed.), *From Grey to Silver – Managing the Challenges and Opportunities of Demographic Change* (pp. 23-25). Heidelberg: Springer.

* Wilenius, M. (2011). Demographic change as a challenge for societies at large. In S. Kunisch, S. Boehm, M. Boppel (Ed.), *From Grey to Silver – Managing the Challenges and Opportunities of Demographic Change* (pp. 47-49). Heidelberg: Springer.

Williams, K., & O'Reilly, C. (1998). Demography and diversity in organizations: A review of 40 years of research. *Research in Organizational Behavior, 20*, 77-140.

Wirsching, M. (2005). Der demographische Wandel und die Auswirkungen auf das Wirtschaftswachstum. *Mittelstands und Strukturpoliktik, 32*, 13-36.

* Wolf, C. (2011). Demographic change and the changing nature of the concept of work. In S. Kunisch, S. Boehm, M. Boppel (Ed.), *From Grey to Silver – Managing the Challenges and Opportunities of Demographic Change* (pp. 71-84). Heidelberg: Springer.

Demographic change calls for change in the demographic research landscape – a German perspective

Norbert Walter[*]

New challenges for demographic research

Demographic change has become one of the major social policy challenges confronting Germany. Its future will prove demanding for society, the state, politicians, academics, and every individual, as the population will age more rapidly over the next 20 years, while also shrinking in size. Furthermore, there is currently no appreciable resurgence in the birth rate, egalitarian gender roles will continue to become more common, a further increase in (healthy) life expectancy is probable, greater mobility will be required, more resources will be invested in integration, and demographic change will unfold in extremely diverse ways across Germany's regions.

These demographic trends will bring changes to the everyday lives of each of the country's inhabitants. While the state and society will need to develop appropriate strategies to manage these changes, new opportunities for shaping the future will open up, and these will need to be recognised and grasped. Changes must be implemented – especially in the education system, the labour market, the healthcare systems, infrastructure areas, the administrative and finance systems, and in security matters. There will be significant differences in the forms these changes take between one region and the next.

These challenges and changes also require a change in Germany's demographic research landscape, which has seen an increase in the number of institutions addressing these issues as well as a broadening of the spectrum of research topics. What are these changes? The hitherto classical principle of genealogy is becoming the focus of research activity. Theoretical research needs to be specified, the focus on research activity must intensify, and research must align more closely with the objective of advising on future policy. In particular, research into the consequences of demographic change is gaining prominence. Other new topics are the role of the family in the network of inter-generational relations, the impact of role models on reproductive behaviour, the impact of geographical mobility on family development and research into the potential benefits of demographic ageing.

One important objective is to inform and advise Germany's federal government and the federal ministries. This requires better coordination of contract research and

---

[*] Prof. Dr. Norbert Walter, Chief Economist emeritus of Deutsche Bank AG and Managing Director of Walter & Toechter Consult.

S. Kunisch et al. (eds.), *From Grey to Silver*,
DOI 10.1007/978-3-642-15594-9_2, © Springer-Verlag Berlin Heidelberg 2011

theoretical research. In order to achieve this goal, there must be comprehensive monitoring of demographic change as well as of current methodological developments and theories.

The goal is to achieve a better understanding of Germany's demographic situation by analysing the change in demographic structures and demographic behaviour patterns in a comparative international context. Demographic behaviour patterns must be explained more clearly, which is where differential analyses can be of help. Most of the differential analyses conducted to date suffer from their design as cross-sectional studies. The processes involved in migration or family development are thus largely ignored. Further research must therefore be conducted in the form of longitudinal studies, with a larger share of surveys designed to collect panel data. The objective of such research is to investigate demographic processes along their lines of development.

Furthermore, methodological pluralism is required. Analyses based predominantly on quantitative methods must be supplemented with qualitative research elements. Official statistical data should be strategically linked with surveys conducted by other institutions. The reappraisal of methodological approaches must include references to international comparisons and differential analyses.

Seven mega-trends for demographic research

1. Population ageing
Population ageing is producing new challenges for social security systems, especially pension, health, and long-term care insurance schemes. The elderly citizens of today and tomorrow constitute an impressive reservoir of potential that must be tapped if the ramifications of demographic change are to be dealt with. The opportunities presented by demographic ageing must be seized rapidly.

2. Low fertility situation
The causes of the low birth rate need to be investigated. Research should focus on the impact of changing values, the shift in notions of what constitutes an ideal family and ideal family upbringing, on the one hand, and differential analyses of fertility, on the other.

3. Changes in family constructs and lifestyles
Changes in family constructs and lifestyles, which refer to individualisation, pluralisation, and deinstitutionalisation, need to be addressed. Within the framework of differential analyses of fertility, more research needs to be conducted into the conditions and causes of the emergence of different lifestyles, their social situations and the consequences for the individuals and their reproductive decision-making.

4. Increasing life expectancy

Another issue to be addressed are the future opportunities that stem from the growing number of elderly people. Research should be focused on those age cohorts who have already retired or will soon leave the workforce. The imperatives are to identify the potentials of these cohorts and to determine the conditions – especially the influence of the labour market – under which the generations of retirees are prepared to translate their potential into active participation.

5. Inter-generational relationships under demographic change

The shared lifetimes of grandparents, parents, children, grandchildren, and great-grandchildren have increased significantly, thereby creating the opportunity for more diverse and differentiated inter-generational relations. The key areas will be the analyses of inter-generational relationships according to lifestyle, from the perspective of gender roles, of family constructs, socio-structural differentiation, and the formation of inter-generational relationships outside the traditional family. Another avenue of research is to investigate the potential assistance that elderly people without children of their own can offer, as well as what elderly people can do for one another.

6. Mobility and migration

Three primary issues related to mobility and migration must be addressed. First, internal migration and immigration can influence population numbers and structures (age structure, regional distribution, structure of lifestyles, proportions of the population with a migration background) as well as regional population distribution. However, emigration and inward immigration have a limited impact on demographic ageing. Second, the competition for skilled personnel has gained a new level of importance. In Germany, the debate focuses especially on the loss of highly qualified human resources (the brain drain). Third, the demands for job-related geographical mobility appear to be increasing.

7. Regional demographic trends

Regions in which the population is ageing and shrinking are expected to undergo a relative decline in their economic vibrancy and the range of public services they offer. Furthermore, these regions will become less attractive to new companies seeking business premises, while the regional ties of established companies will weaken as its workforce is ageing swiftly and highly skilled specialists leave the region. It is demographic change, not only in regions with shrinking populations, that generally results in new demands for the maintenance of public services. Regional planning, which has hitherto often been geared towards *expected growth*, must focus more closely on managing the processes of *population shrinkage*.

Part B

**An economic and social perspective –
Taking the external environment into
consideration**

Demographic change and the economically active populations of OECD countries – Could older workers compensate for the decline?

Golo Henseke[*]

Demographic change will reduce the proportion of people of working age in the total populations of all OECD countries, with potentially adverse effects on economic growth. However, this tendency could – at least partially – be countered by increasing employment rates. Employment is particularly low in the higher age groups.

Labour market institutions – for example, union involvement in wage setting or active labour market programmes – are major determinants of labour market performance and employment. Two particularly important institutions are the *level of employment protection* and the *generosity of the pension system*. On average, countries with relatively rigid employment protection laws and/or relatively generous pension systems experience lower employment rates among persons aged 55-64. Furthermore, more generous pension systems tend to lead to a more pronounced decline in employment after the ages 55-59. However, an isolated change in employment protection does not as such improve the employment of older workers.

---

[*] Golo Henseke, Ph.D. candidate and research assistant, Institute of Economics of the University of Rostock.

S. Kunisch et al. (eds.), *From Grey to Silver*,
DOI 10.1007/978-3-642-15594-9_3, © Springer-Verlag Berlin Heidelberg 2011

Table of Contents

1 Introduction

Demographic change is a global phenomenon. Populations in all developed and many developing countries have experienced a common demographic development: a (sudden) decline in birth rates has been followed by an increase in survival rates. As a result, a baby-boomer generation emerged that is larger than previous and subsequent generations (Lee 2003). This generation leaves a large footprint in a population's age structure. With the continued ageing of the baby boomers, the percentage older persons will inevitably rise.

Older and younger persons are typically economically dependent. Middle-aged persons, on the contrary, tend to be economically active and to participate in the production of goods and services. Dependent persons rely on transfers to sustain their consumption needs. The change in an entire population's age structure will therefore have an influence on the ratio of economically active persons to economically dependent persons, with potentially negative consequences for economic growth (Weil 1999).

Thus, the question arises whether an increase in labour usage can sufficiently counteract the working age population's expected growth rate decline, in order to stabilise the proportion of economically active persons in the population. This idea is also reflected in the EU Commission's suggestion that normal retirement age should be linked to gains in life expectancy (Ehrlich and Hoenighaus 2010).

A better understanding of the driving forces of employment in the age groups 55-59 and 60-64 can help answer the aforementioned question. Employment rates among older persons are generally below the levels of younger workers, but there is considerable time and cross-country variation that may facilitate a better understanding of the determinants of labour usage at higher ages.

A key factor in the functioning of economies is the underlying *institutional configuration*. The institutional configuration describes country-specific clusters of interdependent economic institutions that affect individual behaviour, economic and social outcomes, and even define the trajectories of economic development (C. Howell 2003). The role of *labour market institutions* in unemployment and economic performance has been discussed at length in the economic literature (Freeman 2005; D. R. Howell et al. 2007; Nickell et al. 2005). However, relatively little is known about the relationship between labour market institutions and the employment of older persons.

The *level of employment protection* and the *generosity of the pension system* might specifically shape the labour usage at higher ages. While the former influences the costs of firing and hiring workers and thus determines the employment dynamics (e.g., Heckman et al. 2000), the latter affects the retirement decision (e.g., Boersch-Supan 2000).

The objectives of this chapter are twofold: Firstly, it seeks to answer the question whether employment rate growth can feasibly counteract (at least partially) the population ageing's adverse effects on economic growth. Secondly, it seeks to shed some light on the relationship between labour market institutions and the employment of persons in the age groups 55-59 and 60-64.

Generally, the data indicate that growth is possible in the employment rate of older persons. Employment protection and pension system generosity are intuitively related to the employment of older persons: countries with high levels of employment protection and generous pension systems have lower levels of employment. Furthermore, a strong increase in the net replacement rate with additional work experience is associated with a sharp drop in the proportion of employed persons at higher ages. A change in employment protection appears to have no positive effect on employment rates, which is in line with the results of previous research (Lazear 1990; OECD 2004).

This chapter is structured as follows: the first part presents a simple model that links demographic change to economic growth. Thereafter, the second part reviews trends in demographic development and employment. Special attention is paid to the employment rate of persons aged 55-64. The third part addresses the role of employment protection and pension system generosity in explaining the differences between countries in the employment of older persons. The last section provides a conclusion.

2 Demographic change and economic growth

2.1 Demographic dividend

Populations basically fall into two groups: while the one group comprises economically active persons who produce and consume, the other group comprises economically dependent persons who only consume. Economically active persons participate in the labour market and produce an economy's aggregate income. Dependent persons receive transfers from the aggregate income to sustain their needs (Weil 1999).

Economic activity (henceforth *labour supply*) is limited by lower and upper age levels. The lower level is determined by legal restrictions (child labour) and is typically set at 15. The upper level is determined by the individual decision to retire, which is constrained by the statutory framework. Because labour supply beyond 65 is (still) negligible in most developed countries, the upper age limit can be set to 64, with almost no loss in generality. The population in the age interval 15-64 is called the *population of working age*. Not everyone in this interval actually supplies labour. Persons who supply labour for the production of goods and services are part of the *labour force*. A certain percentage of the labour force is unemployed but looking for work. Only the *employed* form the actual labour input, which is involved in the production of goods and services and the generation of aggregate income. The proportion of employment in the total population can be interpreted as the gross approximation of the percentage of net producers in the total population.

An economy's income per capita equals the product of average labour productivity and the proportion of employed persons in the total population. In other words, the proportion of employed persons translates average labour productivity into income per capita. This multiplicative relationship can easily be transformed into growth rates. Then, growth of the income per capita is the sum of labour productivity growth and the changes in the proportion of employed persons in the total population. Changes in the proportion of employed persons mirror the effect of demographic change and variations in the demand and supply of labour[1] (Kelley and Schmidt 2005).

For example, in the US, output per worker (average labour productivity) has grown by around 1.4%, while the proportion of employed persons remained approximately stable between 2003 and 2008. The growth of income per capita is the sum of both growth rates – thus, about 1.4%.

These considerations suggest a straightforward connection between economic growth and a certain aspect of demographic change, namely the varying growth rate of the proportion of working age persons in the total population (see Figure 1). As baby boomers entered working age, this lead to an increase in the proportion, while their exit will lower it. These shifts affect the growth rate of income per capita with approximately the same magnitude. However, since demographic change is only one determinant of economic growth, intensified labour usage and faster productivity growth could compensate for adverse demographic developments.

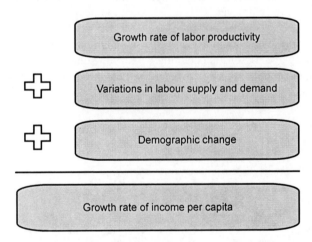

Figure 1: Model of income growth (Source: Kelley and Schmidt 2005; own representation)

---

[1] In algebraic terms: The relationship between income, productivity, the employment rate, and the proportion of working age persons can be expressed as (GDP/N) = (GDP/EMP) · (EMP/WA) · (WA/N), with GDP/N as the gross domestic product per capita, GDP/EMP denotes the average labour productivity, EMP/WA describes the employment rate, and WA/N the proportion of working age persons in the total population. Taking logs and differentiating the equation with respect to time yields an additive relationship between the growth rates of the components, gr(GDP/N) = gr(GDP/EMP) + gr(EMP/WA) + gr(WA/N), where gr(•) denotes the respective growth rate (Kelley and Schmidt 2005).

2.2 Demographic trends

Demographic change today is the result of past demographic developments. Currently observed and projected developments result from past changes in fertility, life expectancy, and migration. The most significant – and, in the medium term, most challenging – development is the ageing of the baby-boomer generation. The baby boomers' entrance into the labour market generated a *demographic dividend* that could turn into a *demographic burden* once this generation begins to retire.

All OECD countries have experienced (and some still experience) periods with a growing proportion of working age persons, but this proportion will start declining in the OECD in the near future (see Figure 2). The peak in the average growth rate was reached around 1985, when the baby boomers in most countries reached the age of 15. In future, however, the proportion will decline – according to recent UN figures. From around 2010 onward, the average growth rate of the proportion of working age persons turns negative in the OECD. Some countries (e.g., Germany, Italy, Japan, and South Korea) will experience negative growth of -1% per year over the course of this demographic development. The decline is less severe in other countries (e.g., France, the US, and the UK), but there are only a few positive growth rates beyond 2010. In Mexico, the demographic transition began later and, as a result, the period with a declining proportion of persons of working age will start later. Poland will experience a small temporary break, but the proportion of working age persons is declining overall. In some countries (e.g., Sweden and the US), the population's age structure will have stabilised by 2040.

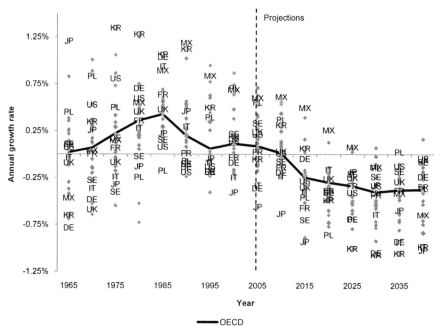

Figure 2: Changes in the proportion of persons of working age in the OECD between 1965 and 2040 (Source: UN world population prospects 2008)

Assuming constant employment and labour force participation rates as well as a stable growth rate in labour productivity, this development will directly affect the income per capita's growth rate. As the growth rate of the GDP per capita has been approximately 1.5% in the OECD, even modest declines in the proportion of persons of working age could have a significant impact on economic development. Most OECD countries will at least temporarily have experienced a decline in the proportion of the population of working age by 0.5% or below per year after 2005. When this development is considered, the question arises regarding the extent to which improvements in the employment rate could counteract the consequences of demographic change.

2.3 Trends in employment and unused productive capacity

Employment is the joint outcome of labour supply and demand decisions. The supply of labour is fairly stable over time, depending on individual decisions, and is influenced by the institutional configuration. Labour demand can be disaggregated into a volatile *business cycle* component and a *structural* component that relates to the underlying institutional configuration (Blanchard 2006).

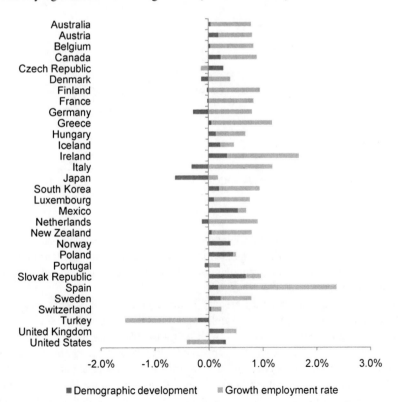

Figure 3: The annual employment growth in OECD countries, 1998-2008 (Source: OECD labour force statistics)

The proportion of employed persons in the total population approximates the percentage of net producers. On the one hand, it depends on the ratio of persons who can work (working age population) to the total population and, on the other hand, on the percentage of persons of working age who actually work, i.e. the employment rate. A demographically induced reduction in the proportion of persons of working age could thus be counteracted by an employment rate increase.

If the employment growth in the OECD is analysed, this reveals several interesting aspects (see Figure 3): Firstly, employment rates change over time. The assumption of stability is misleading. Secondly, employment rate changes dominate the demographic development in almost all countries during the period under investigation. Thirdly, a reduction in the proportion of persons of working age in the total population can be counteracted by an increase in the employment rate – as shown by the development in Denmark, Germany, Italy, the Netherlands, and Portugal. Finally, the demographic development is not always counteracted by employment shifts, as can be seen in the case of Japan and Turkey.

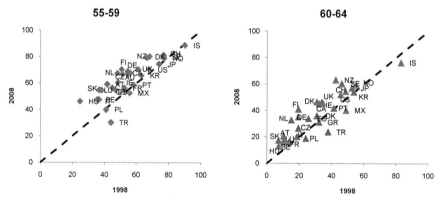

Figure 4: Employment rates in the OECD, 1998 and 2008 (Source: OECD labour force statistics)

Employment rate growth can only take place if there is room for improvement, i.e. if not every person of working age is employed. Generally, employment rates differ across age and gender. In particular, older persons are characterized by below-average employment.

However, there are large differences in the degrees to which older persons are still in employment – between as well as within OECD countries (see Figure 4). Generally, figures are below (often, well below) 100%; only the Icelandic figures are rather close to the maximum. There is therefore room for improvements in employment rates in most countries and hence a way to (at least partially) counteract the consequences of demographic change. Past trends show that improvements in employment rates are feasible; most data points are located above the angle bisectors. The figures rose in 87% (55-59) and 83% (60-64) of the countries between 1998 and 2008. Another common finding is the difference between employment rates in the age group 55-59 and 60-64: the former is generally higher than the latter, but the figures are not independent from each other. On average, countries with a high employment rate among persons aged 55-59 exhibit higher rates in the age group 60-64, and vice versa.

Unemployment due to job loss or exiting the labour force can be interpreted as lost productive capacity. Gruber and Wise (1998; 1997) use labour force participation figures to develop a rough measure of *unused productive capacity*. Their approach naturally extends to employment rates. The idea is to first calculate the age-specific proportion of unemployed persons (one minus the employment rate). In a second step, the figures are averaged over a certain age range (e.g., 55-64). The result is a measure of the unused productive capacity, as a proportion of the total labour capacity in the age range. As Gruber and Wise (1997) note, the figures provide an idea of the broad differences in labour usage at higher ages between countries, but they do not imply that everyone in the age range *"should, or could, work"* (p. 5).

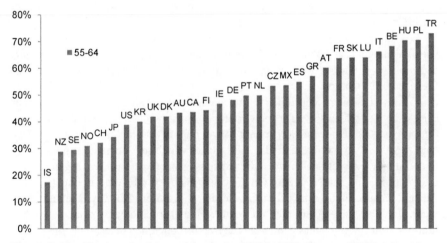

Figure 5: Unutilised productive capacity in the OECD, 2008 (Source: OECD labour force statistics)

Hungary, Poland, and Turkey have the highest levels of unused productive capacity in 2008 (see Figure 5). Belgium is the country with the highest level of unused capacity in Western Europe. By far the highest degree of labour usage can be observed in Iceland, followed by New Zealand, Sweden, and Norway. The difference in labour usage between the latter group and the group consisting of Turkey, Poland, and Hungary is approximately 40 percentage points.

In short, employment rates differ strongly between and within countries. Furthermore, employment rate changes can counteract demographic effects. Most importantly, employment rates, particularly at higher ages, could increase; current labour usage is low in most countries, and past trends indicate that improvement is feasible.

3 Labour market institutions

3.1 Overview

It is widely believed that *labour market institutions* affect employment, unemployment, and participation through various channels. Firstly, labour market institutions can influence labour supply and demand decisions by changing the wage-formation mechanism, by affecting the elasticity of product demand, and by stimulating technical change (Arpaia and Mourre 2005). Secondly, the institutional configuration affects the bargaining power of companies and workers as well as the efficiency of the matching process by modifying the costs of hiring and firing workers (Blanchard 2006).

Labour market institutions refer to the degree of employment protection, the extent of unionisation, the level of wage bargaining centralisation, taxes on labour (including social security contributions), and active labour market policies, for example. Furthermore, they describe the generosity of the unemployment and pension systems, the provision of early retirement programmes, and the availability of disability benefits (Eichhorst et al. 2008).

Institutions do not work in isolation, but interact with one another in complex ways, within and across markets. The optimal configuration depends on the primary coordination pattern between economic agents (Hall and Gingerich 2009; Hall and Soskice 2001). Companies are seen as the crucial actors (C. Howell 2003). Based on companies' dominant coordination mechanisms, two ideal types of capitalism evolve, both of which solve the coordination problem with distinct institutional configurations. On the one hand, there are liberal market economies such as New Zealand, USA, UK, Australia, Canada, and Ireland, which rely on market mechanisms to coordinate interactions between the various agents (e.g., workers, organisations, trade unions, and shareholders). On the other hand, coordination in countries like Austria, Japan, South Korea, France, Germany, Sweden, Norway, Finland, Denmark, Belgium, the Netherlands, and Switzerland is dominated by strategic interaction between the relevant agents. The degree of coherence determines the overall economic performance (Hoepner 2005).

Evidence of institutional influences on age-specific employment patterns is scarce. Differences are plausible, since older and younger workers have better alternatives to labour market participation than prime-aged workers; while younger workers can participate in education, older workers have the option to retire. Unions could therefore benefit from focusing their efforts on prime-aged workers with potentially adverse effects on employment outside the prime-age range; indeed, data show that union involvement in wage-setting reduces the employment propensity of older and younger persons (Bertola et al. 2007). There is another direct link between the decision to retire, i.e. labour force exit, and pension system features. Pension systems characterized by strong early retirement incentives are typically accompanied by a relatively low retirement age and thus low levels of labour supply at higher ages (e.g., Duval 2003; Gruber and Wise 2004).

Unionisation and the pension system describe important features of the institutional configuration. An institution that has to date been largely ignored in the context of older workers' employment is *employment protection laws*. In contrast, the role of the *pension system* in the retirement decision is well understood. However, scholars have concentrated on *labour force participation* (Boersch-Supan and Schnabel 1998; Coile and Gruber 2007; Gruber and Wise 2004), but early retirement incentives could also mirror the low employment chances of older workers, i.e. be a response to weak labour demand. A closer look at both institutions can contribute to a better understanding of the mechanisms that stimulate the employment of older persons.

3.2 Employment protection

Employment protection is believed to be the primary source of labour market inflexibility (Nickell et al. 2005). Employment protection may have ambiguous effects on the employment of older workers. On the one hand, it makes lay-offs more costly and should thus reduce the flow of older workers into retirement or unemployment. On the other hand, it could increase the costs of job mobility and job creation, thereby hampering gradual retirement and decreasing the re-employment chances of older unemployed persons, which in turn leads to earlier labour market exits. Employment protection might also influence the employment of older persons indirectly through the overall employment level. It is not clear which effects dominate a priori.

The degree of employment protection is most likely related to the shape of other labour market institutions. For example, early retirement programmes could help *open up* jobs for younger workers in regimes with rigid employment protection laws that increase worker lay-off costs, especially of workers with long tenure. Consequently, cross-sectional differences, which reflect the direct effect of employment protection, also reflect the influence of related institutions. A change in employment protection is more likely to occur in isolation, but its effect could of course still be confounded by other covariates that exhibit a similar time trend.

On average, countries with fairly rigid employment protection laws reveal lower older worker employment rates. However, reductions in employment protection within a country do not improve employment per se (see Figure 6).

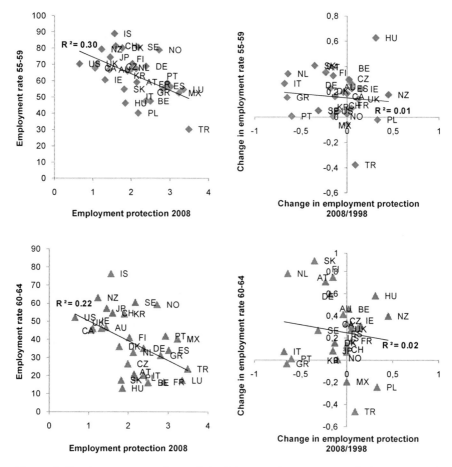

Figure 6: Employment protection and the labour market outcomes of older persons in OECD countries (Source: OECD labour force statistics, OECD index of employment protection)

A closer look also reveals three additional aspects: Firstly, employment protection appears to be more relevant at ages that are usually associated with labour force participation. Other determinants of employment might become more important at higher ages.

Secondly, the observed patterns indicate that not only the degree of employment protection, but the whole institutional configuration influences the result. Both panels on the left of Figure 6 reveal clusters of countries with similar configurations and similar levels of employment, particularly regarding the employment rate of persons aged 55-59. For example, there are the liberal market economies such as New Zealand, USA, UK, Australia, Canada, and Ireland, which have relatively low employment protection and comparably high employment rates of persons aged 55-59. Some coordinated market economies (e.g., Finland, Sweden, Norway,

Denmark, and Japan) reach equally high or even higher employment rates with more rigid employment protection laws. Other coordinated market economies (e.g., Portugal, Spain, France, Italy, and Greece) have rigid employment protection in conjunction with low employment rates. An explanation for the differing level of employment across coordinated market economies is the degree of institutional coherence. The Nordic countries and Japan are characterized by high levels of strategic coordination in the labour market, whereas the southern European countries only reach moderate degrees of coordination: the institutional configuration appears to be less coherent in this case, with negative consequences for the employment rate at higher ages (Hall and Gingerich 2009). Central European countries such as Germany, the Netherlands, Austria, and the Czech Republic, which are also coordinated marker economies, have an average degree of employment protection and reach average employment rates.

The differences between national employment rates are escalated for the age group 60-64. Liberal market economies, some Scandinavian countries, Japan, and South Korea have comparably high employment rates with very different degrees of employment protection. On average, other countries (e.g., France, Belgium, Italy, Austria, Hungary, and Poland) have strict employment protection (to varying degrees), but all reach equally low employment rates. In other words, while employment protection is one important feature of the institutional configuration that influences the employment propensities of older persons, it is not the only one.

Thirdly, a change in employment protection between 1998 and 2008 did not lead to a corresponding shift in the employment rates over this period. In both cases, the explained variation is quasi nil. This lack of evidence must be interpreted with caution. As this is a univariate analysis of the differences between two years, there might be confounding effects and trends that cover the real influence. A thorough multivariate analysis might give a more precise answer (e.g., Heckman et al. 2000). However, it becomes clear that a simple change (reduction) in employment protection will not as such lead to a different labour market outcome for older persons.

In summary, the results show that, on average, countries with higher employment protection levels tend to be characterised by lower older person employment rates. However, relatively rigid employment protection can coexist with high older worker employment rates. A simple reduction in a country's employment protection does not automatically lead to better subsequent labour market outcomes for older persons.

3.3 Generosity of pension systems

The individual decision to exit the labour force is dependent on the characteristics of the social security system, particularly the generosity of the pension system and early retirement incentives (Boersch-Supan 2000; Gruber and Wise 1998). Most OECD countries have a normal retirement age of around 65, but offer possibilities to retire earlier at the cost of an actuarial adjustment of pension benefits. On average, old age pensions are available from around age 62 onwards (Turner 2007).

Retirement incentives depend on the design and resulting generosity of pension schemes. A common measure of this generosity is the *old-age pension replacement rate*, which is the ratio of pension benefits to the last or average wage prior to retirement.

Actual replacement rates depend on several factors other than the pension system, for example, the age at labour market entrance, the career patterns, and the retirement age (Duval 2003). The OECD calculates prospective replacement rates based on several simplifying assumptions to facilitate cross-national comparisons. These prospective replacement rates are estimated for a representative private sector worker who entered the labour force in 2006 at the age of 20, will work until normal retirement age while earning the country-specific mean wage, and will then receive pension according to currently legislated rules. Pension benefits include income from all mandatory and quasi-mandatory pension schemes (OECD 2009 for more information). To take cross-national differences in personnel income taxes and contributions to social security into account, the following analysis is based on *prospective net replacement rates*. Unfortunately, there is no time series data available. If the figures for men and women differ, the replacement rates for men are taken.

Higher net replacement rates should encourage early retirement and thus lead to lower employment rates. The effect should be stronger in the age group 60-64 than in persons aged 55-59, as old age pensions are usually available after the age of 60. Furthermore, more generous retirement systems might lead to faster transition into retirement and hence to a larger difference in employment rates between the age group 55-59 and persons aged 60-64.

The data show that countries with more *generous retirement systems* are on average characterized by lower older person employment (see Figure 7). Surprisingly, the strength of the relationship is independent of age. Prospective net replacement rates predict cross-national differences in employment rates in both age groups equally well.

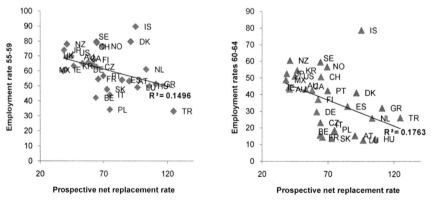

Figure 7: The prospective net pension replacement rates and employment as at 2006 (Source: OECD labour force statistics; OECD pensions at a glance 2009)

Iceland appears to be a special case, as it is characterised by very high employment rates despite a high net replacement rate. If Iceland is treated as an outlier[2] and excluded from the sample, the observed relationship becomes clearer and behaves as expected. Countries with a higher *net replacement rate* tend to exhibit lower employment rates, and the relationship is stronger at higher ages.

Countries are not as clearly clustered as before. The majority of the liberal market economies are still found in the upper left part of the graphs; net replacement rates are low and employment rates are high. But the remaining picture is more mixed. Pension systems appear to be diverse, even across countries with similar institutional configurations (OECD 2009).

If net replacement rates measure retirement incentives, they will help explain the difference in employment rates between persons aged 55-59 and persons aged 60-64. To approximate the change in retirement incentives over both age groups, the difference in prospective net replacement rates between labour market entry at age 20 and at age 25 is taken as the explanatory variable.

In fact, on average, countries with larger replacement rate increases after five years of additional work experience have a larger decline in employment rates at higher ages (see Figure 8). This finding indicates that at least some pension systems provide strong (early) retirement incentives. France, the Slovak Republic, and Hungary experience a strong decline in employment in conjunction with large increases in net replacement rates after five years of additional work, while in New Zealand, Ireland, and the US, the employment decline is less severe and the net replacement rates remain constant.

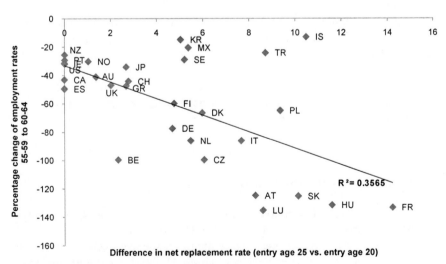

Figure 8: Retirement incentives and employment patterns, OECD 2006 (Source: OECD labour force statistics, OECD pensions at a glance 2009)

---

[2] An outlier is a data point that deviates markedly from other observations.

It is, of course, possible and even likely that governments could set retirement incentives and thus the generosity of pension systems in accordance with the structural labour market situation. Especially in times of restructuring, high levels of youth unemployment and rigid labour markets, governments could consider implementing early retirement strategies to ease this situation.

Similarly, the degree of generosity could be linked to the rigidity of employment protection laws. Stricter laws increase the costs of laying off older workers and hamper younger persons' labour market entrance. In this case, generous pension systems could provide the necessary incentives to *open up* jobs for younger workers. The data confirm this consideration. On average, countries with stronger employment protection are characterised by more generous pension systems. There is a positive (linear) relationship between these two indicators. Turkey, Greece, and Spain, for example, have relatively rigid employment protection laws as well as generous pension systems, with prospective net replacement rates exceeding 100% in Turkey and Greece. At the other end of the scale are the usual suspects: the USA, UK, and New Zealand, with low replacement rates and low employment protection. This supports the idea that labour market institutions do not work in isolation, but are structurally linked to one another.

The observed patterns should be interpreted as tentative evidence. The indicator of retirement incentives is imperfect. Voluntary pension schemes should gain importance in countries with low replacement rates, which will have consequences for the role that mandatory schemes' retirement incentives play. Furthermore, the institutional configuration's related features will confound the observed univariate correlation.

Despite these limitations, the data reveal the following: Firstly, across countries, high net replacement rates are associated with older persons' low employment rates. Secondly, strong increases in replacement rates over career length are associated with sharper drops in employment rates at higher ages. Thus, the design of the pension system is related to national differences in older persons' employment. Thirdly, the generosity of the pension system and the degree of employment protection are positively related, which supports the idea of certain stable institutional configurations.

4   Summary and conclusion

Demographic change will lead to a shrinking proportion of working age persons in all OECD countries. This will have an adverse effect on the ratio of net producers to net consumers and could ultimately reduce future economic growth.

However, many countries are characterised by large unutilised productive capacity. Particular at higher ages, labour usage is low and could improve to counteract this demographic tendency. Past experiences confirm that rising employment rates are possible.

Labour demand and supply strongly depend on a country's labour market institutions. Two major institutions are the rigidity of employment protection laws and the generosity of the pension system. Both are predictive of country differences in employment rates at higher ages. On average, countries with more rigid employment protection and/or more generous pension systems have lower employment propensities in the age groups 55-59 and 60-64. Furthermore, more generous pension systems also lead to larger drops in employment between the age groups 55-59 and 60-64. However, a change in employment protection within countries does not appear to influence the employment rates of older workers.

Institutions do not work in isolation, but form rather stable institutional configurations. The degree of employment protection and the generosity of the pension system are related; countries tend to be characterised by either high or low levels of both.

Thus, a more coherent institutional configuration design might help improve employment at higher ages. This would also help ease the financial pressure of population ageing on pension systems, especially in continental Europe. Suggestions by the EU Commission to link the normal retirement age and gains in life expectancy require employees to have the opportunity as well as the incentive to continue working to higher ages. Currently, just less than 40% of persons aged 60-64 are employed in the EU 19 (EU 15 and the Czech Republic, Hungary, Poland, and the Slovak Republic), compared to roughly 60% in North America.

A promising approach to increase labour usage at older ages could be to further reduce early retirement incentives in mandatory pension schemes. However, this will simultaneously require an improvement in older persons' employability, for example, through active labour market programmes as well as increased workforce training and development efforts in companies, as also suggested by Blossfeld et al. (2010). A simple change in one indicator might not automatically improve the labour market outcome, as can be seen by changes in employment protection's lack of effects. To improve the effectiveness of reforms, changes in one institution should be accompanied by reforms in complementary institutions. This could bring countries closer to counteracting the results that demographic change has on the economically active population.

References

Arpaia, A., Mourre, G. (2005). Labour market institutions and labour market performance: A survey of the literature. *European Commission – Economic Papers*, 238.

Bertola, G., Blau, F., Kahn, L. (2007). Labor market institutions and demographic employment patterns. *Journal of Population Economics*, 20(4), 833-867.

Blanchard, O. (2006). European unemployment: The evolution of facts and ideas. *Economic Policy*, 21(45), 5-59.

Blossfeld, H. P., Hofaecker, D., Buchholz, S., Pollnerová, S. (2010). Late careers and retirement under globalization: Becoming retired in times of accelerating social change. Paper presented at the annual meeting of the American Sociological Association Annual Meeting, Boston.

Boersch-Supan, A. (2000). Incentive effects of social security on labor force participation: Evidence in Germany and across Europe. *Journal of Public Economics*, 78(1-2), 25-49.

Boersch-Supan, A., Schnabel, R. (1998). Social security and declining labor-force participation in Germany. *The American Economic Review*, 88(2), 173-178.

Coile, C., Gruber, J. (2007). Future social security entitlements and the retirement decision. *Review of Economics and Statistics*, 89(2), 234-246.

Duval, R. (2003). Retirement behaviour in OECD countries: Impact of old-age pension schemes and other social transfer programmes. *OECD Economic Studies*, 37.

Ehrlich, P., Hoenighaus, R. (2010). EU-Bürger sollen später in Rente gehen. *Financial Times Deutschland*, p. 9.

Eichhorst, W., Feil, M.T., Braun, C. (2008). What have we learned? Assessing labor market institutions and indicators. *IZA discussion paper*, no. 3470.

Freeman, R. B. (2005). Labour market institutions without blinders: The debate over flexibility and labour market performance. *International Economic Journal*, 19(2), 129-145.

Gruber, J., Wise, D. (1998). Social security and retirement: An international comparison. *The American Economic Review*, 88(2), 158-163.

Gruber, J., & Wise, D.A. (eds.) (2004). *Social security programs and retirement around the world: Micro-estimation* 1st ed., Chicago: University Of Chicago Press.

Hall, P. A., Gingerich, D. W. (2009). Varieties of capitalism and institutional complementarities in the political economy: An empirical analysis. *British Journal of Political Science*, 39(03), 449-482.

Hall, P. A., & Soskice, D. (2001). An introduction to varieties of capitalism. In P. A. Hall, & D. Soskice (eds.). *Varieties of capitalism: the institutional foundations of comparative advantage* (pp. 1-69). Oxford: Oxford University Press.

Heckman, J., Pagés-Serra, C., Edwards, A. C., Guidotti, P. (2000). The cost of job security regulation: Evidence from Latin American labor markets [with comments]. *Economía*, 1(1), 109-154.

Hoepner, M. (2005). What connects industrial relations and corporate governance? Explaining institutional complementarity. *Socio-Economic Review*, 3(2), 331-358.

Howell, C. (2003). Review: Varieties of capitalism: And then there was one? *Comparative Politics*, 36(1), 103-124.

Howell, D. R., Baker, D., Glyn, A., Schmitt, J. (2007). Are protective labor market institutions at the root of unemployment? A critical review of the evidence. *Capitalism and Society*, 2(1).

Kelley, A., Schmidt, R. (2005). Evolution of recent economic-demographic modeling: A synthesis. *Journal of Population Economics*, 18(2), 275-300.

Lazear, E. P. (1990). Job security provisions and employment. *The Quarterly Journal of Economics*, 105(3), 699-726.

Lee, R. (2003). The demographic transition: Three centuries of fundamental change. *The Journal of Economic Perspectives*, 17(4), 167-190.

Nickell, S., Nunziata, L., Ochel, W. (2005). Unemployment in the OECD since the 1960s. What do we know? *The Economic Journal*, 115(500), 1-27.

OECD (2004). *OECD employment outlook*, Paris: OECD Publishing.

OECD (2009). *Pensions at a glance 2009 – Retirement-income systems in OECD countries*, Paris: OECD Publishing.

Turner, J. (2007). Social security pensionable ages in OECD countries: 1949-2035. *International Social Security Review*, 60(1), 81-99.

Weil, D. N. (1999). Population growth, dependency, and consumption. *The American Economic Review*, 89(2), 251-255.

Demographic change as a challenge for societies at large

Markku Wilenius[*][1]

Demographic change has a devious, but predictable impact on the economy. In industrialised countries, ageing will exacerbate the decline in the human capital base while increased longevity will place an enormous burden on public welfare systems. The two most populous countries, China and India, are set to become global heavyweights in education and qualification: China within the next decade and India some time later. As the demographic change penetrates societies over time, the massive impact will unfold in various ways. Occasionally, this is reflected in a country's performance, as in Japan.

The world will experience great demographic changes: The baby-boomer generation will be retired by 2020. Consequently, a large age group will cease contributing to the economy, while not being fully substituted by a younger generation. This means the workforce is shrinking. Consequently, nations are challenged with finding a way to deal with a declining workforce with the age group that is the basis for economic development.

Moreover, ageing populations in Western countries also imply that the elderly will be healthier. Interest in this topic will therefore not only be generated by improved medical care, but will also be primarily based on senior citizens playing a far more proactive role in societies. Consequently, the influence of the elderly will increased in all areas of society. How can societies and pension providers support elderly people to maintain their economic activity? This demand will probably materialize as new sets of products and services.

Scholars[2] from the International Institute for Applied Systems Analysis (IIASA) have intensively investigated the relationship between wealth creation and education. Their findings suggest that a population's level of education is key for maintaining or increasing the level of economic welfare. The research takes into account that education generally leads to a lower fertility rate and later child bearing. Moreover, the higher a population's education level the more productive the workforce, i.e. the quality of the workforce improves. Therefore, when discussing the state of the workforce, one has also to take the population's education level into account.

---

[*] Prof. Markku Wilenius, Finland Futures Research Centre, University of Turku; Senior Advisor, Allianz SE.
[1] Sources: Allianz SE (2009a). *Shape Your Future: Structuring the Future in an Aging Society.* Munich: Allianz SE. Allianz SE (2009b). *Digitalized Globe 2019.* Munich: Conference Report, Allianz SE.

[2] Professor Wolfgang Lutz.

S. Kunisch et al. (eds.), *From Grey to Silver*,
DOI 10.1007/978-3-642-15594-9_4, © Springer-Verlag Berlin Heidelberg 2011

For instance, as a developing country, China has a relatively well-developed education system. Therefore, one can assume the Chinese population has a good chance of overcoming its ageing-related economic problems with an increased education level. In contrast, India's situation seems more gloomy, since the country's education level is not well-developed. One reason for this is the impact that the ancient caste system still partially has, thus depriving a massive number of people of vocational education.

As a consequence of ageing, social security systems in the Western Countries require fundamental redesigns. In the private sector, there is a clear lack of awareness of private savings, and one needs to increase the general awareness of the need to channel additional private money into retirement assets. Like many other mature societies, Germany is exemplary of a familiar phenomenon. Instead of discarding the current circumstances and looking for the best long-term scenarios related to social security systems, the prevailing tendency is to be locked into initiatives designed to create short-term solutions. Whatever these solutions entail, the state will have to shift its role from being a full service provider towards that of a strategic partner for its citizens and the business community. German citizens need to become more aware of the costs of their behaviour and lifestyle, while companies will have to support their customers by explaining this issue.

The fundamental problem could lie in determining an appropriate retirement age now that people are enjoying increasing longevity. One solution might be to fix the retirement period to a certain number of years instead of having a fixed retirement age. If one defines the start of the retirement period 10 years prior to the statistical life expectancy, many of today's financing problems for pensions and health care would be solved. For example, some health-related costs could then be transferred to the working/earning phase. The importance of education and flexibility in engaging the elderly in economic activities needs to be emphasised. If the elderly are productive for longer, their contribution to the economy can help tackle the demographic challenges that lie ahead.

The future, including the demographic future, is ultimately very hard to predict. This is best illustrated from past attempts to estimate life expectancy. The chart below depicts women's life expectancy, and clearly demonstrates that whatever age one estimates, it will be confounded by reality. However, it is certain that there is an ageing trend. Consequently, longevity is one of the key issues societies need to tackle.

HOW OLD CAN YOU GROW?

Expert predictions on the limits of human life have been continually confounded by reality, as this chart on women's life expectancy shows. For example, in 1936, Dublin and Lotka projected a hypothetical expectation of life at birth of 69.93 years for women. This was surpassed in Iceland in 1941.

▦ *Recorded life expectancy in years*

95 *1994 United Nations – 92.5 → ?*

90

1990 Olchansky et al. – 85 → 1995 (Japan)
85
1955 Coale – 84.2 → 2000 (Japan)

80 *1981 Frejka – 77.5 → 1972 (Sweden)*

75

70 *1936 Dublin & Lotka – 69.9 → 1941 (Iceland)*

65

60

55

50

45

| 1840 | 1860 | 1880 | 1900 | 1920 | 1940 | 1960 | 1980 | 2000 | 2020 | 2040 |

Source: J. Oeppen and J. W. Vaupel, "Broken Limits to Life Expectancy," *Science 296*, no. 5570 (2002): 1029–1031.

Ageing, health and disability –
An economic perspective

Martin Karlsson, Florian Klohn[*]

It has been established that morbidity increases with age, which leads to a reduction in labour productivity and an increase in care costs. However, in the health economic literature, it is sometimes argued that an individual's age is not a good predictor of morbidity and care costs once 'time to death' is taken into account. In other words, age itself is not significant because the period in which older people need help is simply postponed when life expectancy increases.

This chapter reviews the economic literature on ageing's impact on health and labour market productivity. In particular, this chapter focuses on how future morbidity and care needs can be projected given current demographic trends. A simple empirical study, provided at the end of the chapter, suggests that observed positive trends in the morbidity of older people may not be enough to offset the impact of population ageing. Subsequently, care costs are expected to increase considerably as populations age. As far as labour markets are concerned, the analysis presented suggests that the possibilities to offset demographic changes by increasing the state retirement age might be limited. Even though morbidity only starts increasing rapidly from the age of 80 onwards, this period of increased dependency hardly shifts when life expectancy increases.

---

[*] Dr. Martin Karlsson, Assistant Professor for Applied Econometrics, Technische Universität Darmstadt.
Florian Klohn, Research and Teaching Assistant at the chair for Applied Econometrics, Technische Universität Darmstadt.

S. Kunisch et al. (eds.), *From Grey to Silver*,
DOI 10.1007/978-3-642-15594-9_5, © Springer-Verlag Berlin Heidelberg 2011

Table of Contents

1   Introduction

Most developed countries' populations are ageing rapidly with consequent implications for labour markets and public spending on long-term care (LTC), pensions and
health care. The Swedish dependency ratio (the number of retired people per
100 people of working age) is projected to increase from the current 28 to 40 in
2050. Although substantial, the increase is lower than in many other countries. In
Germany, for instance, the ratio is projected to increase from the current 31 to 59 in
2050 (United Nations 2008). An overview of projected trends in dependency ratios
for some OECD countries is given in Figure 1.

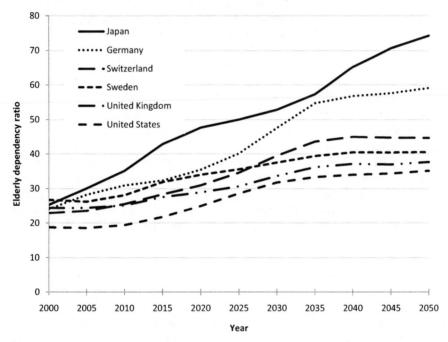

Figure 1: Projected elderly dependency ratio in some countries (Source: United Nations
2008)

Such demographic changes are expected to have a significant impact on the demand
for care services. Most consumers of LTC are 80+; for example, in Sweden, almost
80% of care home inhabitants belong to this age group (SALAR 2009). Since
increasing life expectancy implies that this group is growing faster than the general
retired population, there is concern that the demographic burden could make the
current system of financing LTC unsustainable. Indeed, in many countries, there has
been a trend towards concentrating resources on individuals with severe disability
(Karlsson et al. 2004).

However, the impacts of an ageing population do not stop there. Several countries are planning to increase their state retirement age. In the US and in Germany, the normal retirement age will increase gradually over the next few decades: the German state retirement age will be 67 in 2029. In the UK, female state pension age will gradually increase to 65 by 2020, at which point it will be equal to male state pension age. Thereafter, the state pension age will rise to 66 between 2024 and 2026 and then eventually to 68. In contrast, Sweden has no set retirement age: working individuals may retire from the age of 61 onwards, and they have a right to stay in employment – at least until they are 67.

Although life expectancy is undoubtedly increasing, the question arises as to whether older workers will be healthy enough to work or whether they will become an increasing burden on the economy by swelling the ranks of people on long-term sickness and disability benefits. Furthermore, if they continue to work, will they be as productive as younger workers? The UK's direct and indirect benefit costs have been estimated at 30 billion GBP per year and the annual loss of output at three times that figure. This is before taking possible changes in age-related productivity into account for those who continue working (Blake and Mayhew 2006; Backes-Gellner and Veen 2009).

To prepare for all possible eventualities, policy makers need to be able to calibrate social policy over the next few decades. However, this requires a much greater understanding of healthy life trajectories and disablement processes. There is currently no mechanism for quantifying the percentages of people who will be unable to work at higher retirement ages, whether healthy life expectancy as well as life expectancy is increasing, which sub-groups are the most vulnerable to sickness and disability, the extent to which risk is socially rather than biologically determined, and whether risk in these cases can be manipulated by the policy process.

This chapter has two main aims: Firstly, to provide an overview of recent research on the interplay between population ageing, health and labour market outcomes. The emphasis is on economic research, but contributions from epidemiology and health services research are considered as well. Secondly, to conduct an empirical analysis of the relationship between ageing and social care expenditure, using data from Swedish municipalities. The main objective of this analysis is to estimate whether age is still a good predictor of care costs if time-to-death (TTD) and its related costs are taken into account.

The chapter is organised as follows: The following section reviews the implications of current demographic trends for labour market policies. The third section discusses the epidemiological and economic literature on the relationship between ageing, morbidity and care expenditure. Then, a simple empirical analysis is conducted. The final section summarises the findings and their implications for policy.

2 Health, ageing and labour market outcomes

Health and ageing have important implications for labour supply and labour market participation, but also for the workforce's productivity. In this section, the literature on these issues is reviewed, starting with the relationship between health and labour market participation. A more comprehensive overview is provided by Karlsson et al. (2009).

2.1 Morbidity and labour market participation

Concerning the relationship between health and work, there is an emerging trend within economics literature to take people's health into account when modelling their labour market participation. As Disney et al. (2006) pointed out, health can influence the decision to work in many ways:

- People in poorer health might experience higher disutility from work.
- Poor health might reduce the income from work, if reduced productivity is reflected in wages.
- Poor health might entitle the individual to non-wage income, which is conditional on not working.

All these factors suggest that health has a positive influence on the decision to work. However, an individual in poor health might need a higher income to cover medical expenses – which implies a higher propensity to work.

French (2005) carried out a rigorous analysis of health and retirement. Taking health into account, he estimated a life cycle model of consumption and labour supply. Health, mortality and wages are assumed to be exogenous: an individual's lifetime utility is maximised according to a given stochastic process for health and mortality. The author finds that throughout the life cycle, health affects how many hours an individual works. Nevertheless, it only accounts for a small amount of the total variation in work hours over the life cycle. Furthermore, health seems to affect the decision of whether or not to work more than it influences the number of hours actually worked. Nevertheless, the explanatory power of health is also limited also in this case. Hence, declining health only accounts for about 10% of the reduction in participation between 55 and 70.

However, French's analysis is limited (and this applies to Heyma 2004, and Domeij and Johannesson 2006, as well) in that he assumes an individual's health trajectory is given: the analysis presupposes that health is unaffected by labour market decisions. There are several reasons to believe that this assumption is problematic. As Disney et al. (2006) point out, reported health statuses may be untenable because:

- Inactive individuals have an incentive to over-report poor health, to justify their inactiveness.
- Individual heterogeneity is of great importance.
- Individuals with permanent and very poor health may never have worked – and can hence not be observed 'retiring'.

- Ill health may impact the worker's other labour market attributes (productivity, etc.).
- Individual health may be affected by the individual's labour market state.

To remedy this problem, it has been suggested that a time-dependent 'health stock' should be estimated based on self-assessed health and a number of 'objective' health criteria. This approach is believed to overcome some of the problems mentioned above. Using this approach, Disney et al. (2006) find that current health changes and previous health have the expected effects on labour market participation. Furthermore, they find no evidence that health shocks are 'asymmetric' in the sense that a deterioration in health has a different effect on labour supply than an improvement in health. The authors also find that cohabiting individuals have significantly higher probabilities of both being in paid employment.

2.2 Ageing and productivity

There are different reasons why labour productivity can be affected by population ageing. Firstly, there are direct effects due to changes in individuals' physical and intellectual abilities. Secondly, looking at the organisational level, there is some evidence that the relation is not as clear for aggregate productivity.

Moreover, economic research has addressed the connection between ageing and productivity on an individual level. In many microeconomic models, productivity is assumed to follow a specific age profile so that productivity increases at younger ages but reaches a peak when people reach middle age. Empirical research also indicates that individual-level productivity decreases with older workers' age. Nevertheless, the actual shape of individual productivity profiles remains an open issue (Martins et al. 2005).

There is a prolific literature dealing with age-related factors and cognitive functioning. Small and Bäckman (1999) investigate the question of how cognitive abilities and ageing are related for older people. They suggest that the relationship between TTD and cognitive decline is influenced by the incidence of specific diseases and a decrease in physical vitality. Another important issue is whether retirement itself has an influence on cognitive functioning. Bonsang et al. (2010) suggest that retirement has a considerable negative causal effect on cognitive abilities.

Backes-Gellner and Veen (2009) measure productivity on the organisational level and evaluate age diversity's effect on company performance. They suggest that individual ageing is less important at the firm level. They hypothesise that firm productivity is not just the aggregate of individual measures, but also depends on the effects of age diversity. The authors use an individual-level German panel dataset, and their results suggest that a diverse workforce has an economically and statistically significant positive impact on productivity in companies with a strong focus on innovation.

Boersch-Supan et al. (2001) assess the extent to which the demography influences productivity in the US using aggregate data. Their findings indicate that age-induced productivity losses have a much smaller impact on total production than the size of the economically active population. Hence, they conclude that the ageing workforces' productivity is not a major challenge for the future.

After this discussion on the direct impact of ageing on the labour market, the next section gives a detailed overview of the literature on morbidity and demand for health care.

3   Health and population ageing

3.1 Three hypotheses

Relatively little is known about long-term trends and the disablement process's determinants. One important issue that has not yet been resolved is the long-term trends in healthy life expectancy and disabled life expectancy. Three competing hypotheses have been proposed.

The most optimistic one, suggesting a *compression* of morbidity, was proposed by Fries (1980). According to this perspective, adult life expectancy is approaching its biological limit so that if disability spells can be postponed to higher ages, the result will be an overall reduction in the time spent disabled. In contrast, Gruenberg (1977) suggested an *expansion* of morbidity based on the argument that the observed decline in mortality was mainly due to declining accident rates. The third hypothesis was proposed by Manton (1987) according to whom the development in mortality and morbidity is a combination of the two, which could lead to an expansion of the time spent in good health as well as the time spent in disability.

Official statistics as to which of these three hypotheses prevails in reality are, however, surprisingly inconclusive (Bone et al. 1995; Bebbington and Darton 1996; Bebbington and Comas-Herrera 2000). In general, results seem to be sensitive to the definition of disability (activities of daily living or limiting long-standing illness) as well as to the severity of disability taken into account.

Despite this ambiguity in the statistics, the long-term trends have very strong implications for the future funding of LTC. In a long-term projection model for the UK, Karlsson et al. (2006) find that a pessimistic scenario ('expansion of morbidity') implies some 2 million disabled older people greater than the most optimistic scenario ('compression of morbidity'). The implications for public finances are similar: in the pessimistic scenario, public expenditure on formal LTC would have to increase by around 80% of its present level, whereas virtually no increase would be necessary in the optimistic scenario.

3.2 Perspectives from health economics

There is related literature in economics, which analyses how health care costs are affected by population ageing. Much attention has been devoted to the so-called *red herring hypothesis*, according to which care costs are unrelated to age once remaining lifetime has been controlled for. The implications of this hypothesis – for public spending and labour market policies as well as for individual welfare – are obviously positive, since they imply that healthy years are added to life when longevity increases.

In a seminal paper, Zweifel et al. (1999) use individual-level Swiss data to investigate this issue. They show that age's impact on health care costs decreases once 'time to death' (TTD) is taken into account. During the last two years of life, an individual's actual age seems to be completely irrelevant. This leads to their conclusion that age is not necessarily an important determinant of health care expenditures.

Subsequent studies by Salas and Raftery (2001) as well as Seshamani and Gray (2004) criticise Zweifel et al.'s approach on several grounds. Firstly, they claim that there might be a problem concerning the explanatory variables' collinearity, which makes it impossible to disentangle different explanatory factors' contributions. Secondly, there is possibly reverse causation running from care expenditures to TTD, which could lead to a biased estimate. Using a similar dataset and a similar approach to Zweifel et al. (1999) but including additional variables, Seshamani and Gray (2004) conclude that while morbidity is highly relevant for health care costs, age also remains important.

Zweifel et al. (2004) address these issues. They use past health care expenditures as instrumental variables for current expenditures and estimate their model in two steps, analysing the decision to seek care and the amount of care provided separately. Nevertheless, they conclude that, in most age groups, TTD is more important than age. In a related study, Stearns and Norton (2004) use an American panel data set. They find that while both age and TTD are statistically significant, TTD has a much greater impact. Werbelow et al. (2007) focus on LTC and use panel data from Switzerland. They decompose the effect for different categories of care and show that most components of health care expenditure are driven by TTD instead of age. An exception is expenditures on acute care for long-term patients for which TTD appears to be irrelevant.

In a related study from the US, Shang and Goldman (2008) find that age has limited predictive power once remaining individual life expectancy is introduced into the model. Similarly, Weaver et al. (2009) use panel data from the US and focus mainly on LTC costs since they account for the bulk of care costs for older people. They implement a sophisticated statistical model to address decisions of demand for LTC and cohabitation with an adult child jointly. Their findings suggest that TTD is the main cost driver, but being married reduces its importance.

Using a Dutch data set on home care utilisation, de Meijer et al. (2009) differentiate between different causes of death and analyse the impact of morbidity. Once morbidity and disability are controlled for, the age effect remains relevant whereas TTD becomes insignificant. They conclude that TTD cannot causally affect care expenditures and might also be considered a red herring: it is simply a proxy for morbidity and disability. In a recent study, Zweifel et al. (2009) address the reverse causality problem by using instrumental variables for TTD. Their findings suggest that the increase in health care expenditures is much more likely due to a shift in medical technology than the population's ageing – therefore, TTD seems significant.

The argument that TTD is a proxy for morbidity (see de Meijer et al. 2009) can be challenged with reference to Gerstorf et al. (2010). In their study, the decline in well-being prior to death is being investigated. Using individual-level data from Germany, the UK and the US, they estimate separate well-being curves for each country. Their findings suggest that there is a significant kink in the well-being curve in the last few years of life. The use of different data sources allows comparing this phase of decline in different populations, and it appears to vary between three and five years.

This study presented in this chapter is among the first to analyse the red herring hypothesis using Swedish data. The authors are only aware of one previous study that investigates this hypothesis: Larsson, Kareholt and Thorslund (2008) evaluate the effect of age and TTD on care for older people in Sweden. Their emphasis is on utilisation of home help services, institutional care and hospital care. They conclude that TTD has twice the impact of actual age – thus supporting the red herring hypothesis. Other studies that address the age profile of care costs in Sweden have been conducted by Gerdtham (1993), Thorslund and Parker (1995), as well as Gerdtham et al. (2005).

In conclusion, the jury is still out on the red herring hypothesis, and there is clearly a need for more studies which corroborate previous findings with more sophisticated methods.

4   Ageing, morbidity and social care in Sweden

This section presents an empirical analysis to illustrate some of the ideas expressed in the previous sections. It focuses on population ageing's impact on the provision of and expenditure on social care services in Sweden. Using high-quality Swedish data, a simple demographic model for explaining social care expenditure can be contrasted with models that allow for compression of morbidity by assuming that old-age disability is a function of TTD as well as age.

Evidently, this analysis is of great importance to public finances and labour market policies. If the period of physical deterioration is not expanded but delayed when longevity increases, it means that public spending on care will increase less rapidly in the future – but also that policies aimed at increasing the normal retirement age will not be obliterated by the onset of old-age disability.

In Sweden, social care policies are the responsibility of municipalities, of which there are 290 in total. Directly elected politicians decide on the supply of services and also raise the revenues necessary to cover operating costs. Local income taxes are the main source of funding, and out-of-pocket payments are of limited importance (3.7% of total costs, as of 2007; SALAR 2009). The national government lays down general principles and responsibilities for social care in law, and monitors the quality in care homes. Furthermore, the government redistributes funds to create equal opportunities for the provision of LTC in all parts of the country, despite immense differences in need as well as in the local tax bases.

Even though private providers' market share has tripled over the last two decades (e.g., from 5.4% to 13.7% for nursing home slots; see Socialstyrelsen 2002, 2008), virtually all formal social care provided in Sweden is still funded and monitored by local authorities, which keep meticulous records of the amounts, types and costs of care services provided. These data are collected by the National Board for Health and Welfare which ensures that data are comparable between municipalities and over time. Thus, due to the availability of high-quality data that cover the entire population, there are excellent possibilities to conduct analyses of demographic changes' impact on demand for social care.

4.1 Dataset

The main variable of interest captures the average local costs of social care, defined as the sum of institutional and home care expenditures for older people, plus the total costs per inhabitant of disabled care. Standardised information is available for the time range 1998-2008. For demographic data, official records provided by Statistics Sweden are used. These datasets include the number of residents in each age cohort and for each municipality. Moreover, mortality rates are available for each local authority.

Table 1: Descriptive statistics (source: Statistics Sweden and own calculations)

Variable	Description	Mean	Std. Dev.	Min.	Max.
costolddis08	Care costs per inhabitant in 2008 prices	14.982	3.639	3.278	27.484
cmr	mortality rate period t	0.011	0.003	0.004	0.026
cmrL1	mortality rate period t+1	0.011	0.003	0.004	0.023
cmrL2	mortality rate period t+2	0.011	0.003	0.004	0.023
pop064	share of population of age 0-64	0.810	0.037	0.700	0.926
pop6569	share of population of age 65-69	0.049	0.008	0.028	0.085
pop7074	share of population of age 70-74	0.044	0.009	0.019	0.078
pop7579	share of population of age 75-79	0.040	0.009	0.015	0.068
pop8084	share of population of age 80-84	0.031	0.008	0.008	0.057
pop8589	share of population of age 85-89	0.017	0.005	0.004	0.035
pop9094	share of population of age 90-94	0.007	0.002	0.001	0.014
pop9599	share of population of age 95-99	0.001	0.001	0.000	0.005
pop100	share of population of age 100+	0.000	0.000	0.000	0.001

The 290 municipalities are the main unit of observation. Their population sizes range between 2,500 and 830,000. The main explanatory variables are those capturing each municipality's age structure. Measured in intervals of five years, this dataset includes older people's population shares. To avoid the possibility of reverse causation, these variables are measured at the beginning of each year.

Since the purpose of this study is to formally test the red herring hypothesis, the contemporary and future mortality rates are also considered (to capture aggregate

TTD). These are calculated as the number of inhabitants deceased within a year divided by the number of inhabitants alive at the beginning of each period. All variables are expressed in terms of averages per inhabitant, which makes the interpretation of results particularly easy.

To account for inflation, all costs were standardised according to the Swedish producer price index: they are expressed in 2008 crowns. As can be seen in Table 1, the average cost of care is around 15,000 SEK (1,500 EUR) per person, but they range between 3,300 and 27,500 SEK. Crude mortality rates range between 0.004 and 0.03. The variables representing the age structure follow the expected pattern: the shares decrease rapidly at advanced ages.

4.2 Econometric method

The econometric model allows for a flexible relationship between the explanatory variables (age groups and mortality rates) and the dependent variable (care costs per capita). An underlying assumption is that other determinants of care costs, which are not included in this model, are unrelated to the explanatory variables of interest. If this assumption holds, the estimation results are unbiased. If there are region-specific factors (so-called *confounders*) which correlate with both demographics and the dependent variable, estimates will be biased.

However, it should be noted that the dataset's panel structure is very useful in this regard. If possible confounders are assumed to be constant over time, the fixed effects estimator can be used, by including municipality dummies, to identify the parameters of interest with reference to deviations from municipality-specific means. This problem of unobserved heterogeneity can also be present at the individual level, but if these underlying factors are assumed to remain constant within the 10 years of the analysis, they are not a problem.

4.3 Results

In Table 2, the Fixed Effects regression results are displayed. The first column shows the coefficients of a regression of care costs per capita on older people's population shares. In the following columns, contemporary and future mortality rates are introduced successively to see whether the age group coefficients are affected – which would indicates a red herring problem. As expected, the coefficients for all age groups are positive, although they only start becoming statistically significant at the 5%-level from the 80+ age groups. In these age groups, coefficients are significant even at the 1%-level.

In the column excluding the mortality rate, the coefficient for 80 to 84-year-old people indicates that an individual in this age group incurs care costs of 69,250 SEK (7,000 EUR) per year (in addition to the average of a working age individual). The coefficients increase successively with rising age up to the estimate of 683,000 SEK (69,000 EUR) for the oldest age group.

Table 2: Regression output (Source: Statistics Sweden and own calculations)

Variable	Care cost for older and disabled per inhabitant (kSEK)			
	FE (1)	FE (2)	FE (3)	FE (4)
Pop6569	19.21*	19.02	18.77	18.31
	(1.66)	(1.65)	(1.62)	(1.57)
Pop7074	3.562	2.474	1.507	1.113
	(0.3)	(0.21)	(0.13)	(0.09)
Pop7579	10.82	8.992	7.394	6.305
	(0.82)	(0.68)	(0.55)	(0.47)
Pop8084	69.25***	66.31***	63.45***	61.75***
	(4.02)	(3.87)	(3.62)	(3.41)
Pop8589	141.7***	136.4***	132.7***	130.5***
	(5.54)	(5.29)	(5.05)	(4.93)
Pop9094	237.5***	230.4***	223.7***	221.1***
	(6.47)	(6.37)	(6.07)	(5.94)
Pop9599	294.0***	283.6***	278.0***	274.4***
	(3.53)	(3.42)	(3.35)	(3.24)
Pop100	683.0**	655.7**	652.1**	653.4**
	(2.2)	(2.14)	(2.13)	(2.13)
CMR		29.24*	32.41*	34.68*
		(1.73)	(1.78)	(1.82)
CMRL1			23.69	25.39
			(1.26)	(1.26)
CMRL2				14.52
				(0.66)
_cons	5.781***	5.807***	5.812***	5.791***
	(5.62)	(5.65)	(5.65)	(5.63)
N	2,334	2,334	2,334	2,334

t statistics under corresponding intra group correlation and homoscedasticity robust standard errors, year dummies included, * $p<0.10$, ** $p<0.05$, *** $p<0.01$

In accordance with the red herring hypothesis, the coefficients for the age groups decrease once the mortality rate and its future values are included. However, the effect of including these variables seems to be rather modest. Thus, the results give some evidence of a red herring, but age itself seems to have a strong impact on care costs even after controlling for TTD. Figure 2 visualises this relationship.

The mortality rate is significant at the 10%-level in all specifications. In economic terms, mortality rates are highly significant: Each additional death is associated with cost increases of 29,000 to 75,000 SEK, depending on the specification. The higher estimate is derived from the specification where two leads (i.e. future values) of the mortality rate are included alongside the current mortality rate. However, these effects are dwarfed by the increase in expected costs at higher ages.

Thus, our conclusion differs significantly from that of Larsson et al. (2008), who find that TTD is twice as important as age.

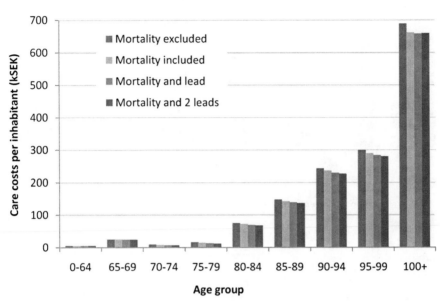

Figure 2: Estimated impact of age on care costs (Source: Statistics Sweden and own calculations)

To further illustrate these results' implications, the costs arising due to a one-year increase in life expectancy were calculated. This was done on the basis of the estimators for the different age groups, the Swedish age structure and age-specific mortality rates of 2008. Results are presented in Figure 3: The top panel shows the implied change in lifetime care costs (from the current level of 1,213 kSEK) and the bottom panel shows the corresponding increase in average costs per person per year (assuming a stationary population). These results are contrasted with a 'no red herring' scenario (i.e. a 'naive' demographic extrapolation) and a 'complete red herring' scenario (i.e. all age-related costs are costs of dying). Although all three specifications imply somewhat lower cost increases than a simple demographic extrapolation, it is obvious that they are much closer to this scenario than to the 'pure red herring' scenario.

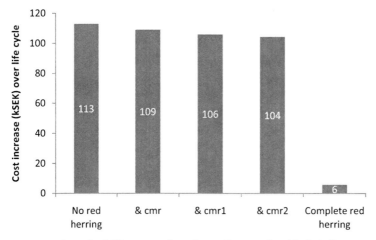

Scenarios [different number of mortality rates (cmr) included]

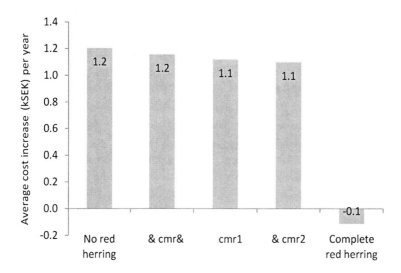

Scenarios[different number of mortality rates (cmr) included]

Figure 3: Cost increases associated with a one-year increase in life expectancy for various scenarios (Source: Statistics Sweden and own calculations)

Some issues have not been considered in this analysis. Firstly, there might be a bias arising due to reverse causality running from LTC costs to mortality rates. If high care expenditures reduce subsequent mortality rates, TTD's impact could have been underestimated. However, dealing with this problem requires going beyond the scope of this study. Secondly, local mortality rates are used for all ages and causes of death. These mortality rates could be an imprecise proxy for the variable: an individual entering the final period of life. This could in turn explain the insignificance of the coefficients related to mortality.

5   Conclusion

In this chapter, a broad view of population ageing's economic implications is given, paying particular attention to the effects of ageing and increases in longevity on physical limitations and care costs. These relationships are of immense importance to policy makers since they determine future care costs and also the possibility of extending working life in step with increases in life expectancy.

There are many missing pieces in this puzzle. The epidemiological literature on increased longevity's implications for morbidity and population health remains inconclusive. Moreover, the related economic literature on the relationship between ageing and health care costs has failed to deliver unambiguous results. Furthermore, very little is known about the relationship between age and labour productivity.

In an attempt to increase our knowledge on these issues, Swedish data were used to estimate an econometric model of the determinants of LTC costs in Swedish municipalities. By controlling for the local mortality rate, it was possible to address the issue of whether TTD is a better predictor of care costs than age. Since the dataset covers the entire Swedish population, parameter estimates represent Sweden as a whole. Moreover, since a panel dataset is used, the econometric model allows for unobserved regional differences which are constant over time. These two advantages clearly imply that the results might be more robust than those of some previous studies.

The general message emerging from this analysis regarding future care costs is pessimistic. Even though local mortality rates are strongly associated with care costs – the estimates for this variable are not very precise, but the economic significance is considerable – a municipality's age structure remains a strong predictor of LTC costs even after mortality is considered. Hence, it appears that, as far as LTC in Sweden is concerned, an 'expansion of morbidity' can be expected, meaning that unhealthy years are added to life when life expectancy increases. Although it is not possible to derive detailed implications regarding older people's labour market outcomes from this analysis, it is obvious that ageing's largest impact on care costs arises from the 80+ age cohorts. Since morbidity and care needs are strongly related to factors that influence productivity, one might interpret this as an indicator that age-related changes in productivity are not as high in the age groups younger than 80. One preliminary conclusion that could be drawn from this result is that physical functioning does not represent a serious obstacle to increasing retirement age well beyond the current levels. However, since the analysis presented here covers only a single aspect of ageing and disability, such a strong conclusion seems premature.

Of course, several caveats apply, and this study's findings should be corroborated with more sophisticated methods and data from other countries. For example, even though the used panel data estimator can be expected to reduce possible reverse causality considerably, there is still a possibility that current LTC costs influence future mortality rates. If this is the case, the estimates of the mortality effect are downwards biased. However, even if addressing this problem would further reduce the estimated impact of age on LTC costs, it is unlikely that this study's general conclusion will change.

References

Backes-Gellner, U., Veen, S. (2009). The impact of aging and age diversity on company performance. University of Zurich, Institute for Strategy and Business Economics. http://ssrn.com/abstract/=1346895. Accessed 02 July 2010.

Bebbington, A. C., Darton, R. A. (1996). Healthy life expectancy in England and Wales: Recent evidence. *PSSRU discussion paper*, No. 1205.

Bebbington, A., Comas-Herrera, A. (2000). Healthy life expectancy: Trends to 1998, and the implications for long-term care costs. *PSSRU Discussion Paper*, No. 1695.

Blake, D. P., Mayhew, L. D. (2006). On the Sustainability of the UK State Pension System in the Light of Population Ageing and declining fertility. *Economic Journal*, 116(512), 286-305.

Boersch-Supan, A. (2001). Labor market effects of population aging. *NBER working paper*, No. 8640.

Bone, M., Bebbington, A. C., Jagger, C., Morgan, K., Nicolaas, G. (1995). *Health expectancy and its uses*. London: HMSO.

Bonsang, E., Adam, S., Perelman, S. (2010). Does retirement affect cognitive functioning? Maastricht University, RM/10/005.

Disney, R, Emmerson, C., Wakefield, M. (2006). Ill health and retirement in Britain: A panel data-based analysis. *Journal of Health Economics*, 25(4), 621-649.

Domeij, D., Johannesson, M. (2006). Consumption and health. *Contributions to Macroeconomics*, 6(1), 1314-1314.

French, E. (2005). The effects of health, wealth, and wages on labour supply and retirement behaviour. *Review of Economic Studies*, 72(2), 397-427.

Fries, J. (1980). Aging, natural death and the compression of morbidity. *New England Journal of Medicine*, 303(3),130-135.

Gerdtham, U.-G. (1993). The impact of ageing on health care expenditure in Sweden. *Health Policy*, 24(1), 1-8.

Gerdtham, U.-G., Lundin, D., Sáez-Martí, M. (2005). The ageing of society, health services provision and taxes. *Journal of Population Economics*, 18(3), 519-537.

Gerstorf, F., Ram, N., Mayraz, G., Hidajat, M., Lindenberger, U., Wagner, G., Schupp, J. (2010). Late-life decline in well-being across adulthood in Germany, the UK, and the US: Something is seriously wrong at the end of life. *SOEP papers*, No. 286.

Gruenberg, E. M. (1977). The failures of success. *Milbank Memorial Foundation Quarterly/ Health and Society*, 55(1), 3-24.

Heyma, A. (2004). A structural dynamic analysis of retirement behavior in the Netherlands. *Journal of Applied Econometrics*, 19(6), 739-759.

Karlsson, M., Mayhew, L., Plumb, R., Rickayzen, B. (2004). An international comparison of long-term care arrangements. *Actuarial Research Centre Report*, No. 156.

Karlsson, M., Mayhew, L., Rickayzen, B. (2009), Individualised life tables. Investigating dynamics of health, work and retirement in the UK, *Journal of Population Ageing*, 1(2-4), 153-191.

Larsson, K., Kareholt, I., Thorslund, M. (2008). Care utilisation in the last years of life in relation to age and time to death: Results from a Swedish urban population of the oldest old. *European Journal of Ageing*, 5(4), 349-357.

Manton, K. G. (1987). Response to an introduction to the compression of morbidity. *Gerontologica Perspecta*, 1, 23-30.

Martins, J. O., Gonand, F., Antolin, P., Maisonneuve, C. de la, Yoo, K.-Y. (2005). The impact of ageing on demand, factor markets and growth. *Economic Working Papers*, No. 420.

Meijer, C. de, Koopmanschap, M., d'Uva, T. B., Doorslaer, E. van (2009). Time to drop time-to-death? Unraveling the determinants of LTC spending in the Netherlands, *Netspar discussion paper*, 11/2009-045.

SALAR (2009). *Developments in elderly policies in Sweden*. Stockholm: SALAR.

Salas, C., Raftery, J. P. (2001). Econometric issues in testing the age neutrality of health care expenditure. *Health Economics*, 10(7), 669-671.

Seshamani, M., Gray, A. (2004). Ageing and health-care expenditure: The red herring argument revisited. *Health Economics*, 13(4), 303-314.

Shang, B., Goldman, D. (2008). Does age or life expectancy better predict health care expenditures? *Health Economics*, 17(4), 487-501.

Small, B. J., Bäckman, L. (1999). Time to death and cognitive performance. *Current Directions in Psychological Science*, 8(6), 168-172.

Socialstyrelsen (2008). *Äldre – vård och omsorg 2007*. Stockholm: Socialstyrelsen. Stearns, S. C., Norton, E. C. (2004). Time to include time to death? The future of health care expenditure predictions. *Health Economics*, 13(4), 315-327.

Thorslund, M., Parker, M. G. (1995). Strategies for an ageing population: Expanding the priorities discussion. *Ageing and Society*, 15, 199-217.

United Nations (2008). *World population prospects: The 2008 revision*. Population Division of the Department of Economic and Social Affairs.

Weaver, F., Stearns, S. C., Norton, E. C., Spector, W. (2009). Proximity to death and participation in the long-term care market. *Health Economics*, 18(8), 867-883.

Werbelow, A., Felder, S., Zweifel, P. (2007). Population ageing and health care expenditure: A school of 'red herrings'? *Health Economics*, 16(10), 1109-1126.

Zweifel, P., Felder, S., Meiers, M. (1999). Ageing of population and health care expenditure: a red herring, *Health Economics*, 8(6), 485-496.

Zweifel, P., Felder, S., Werblow, A. (2004). Population ageing and health care expenditure: New evidence on the 'red herring', *Geneva papers on pisk and insurance: Issues and practice*, Special Issue on Health Insurance 29, 653-667.

Zweifel, P., Felder, S., Werblow, A. (2009). Do red herrings swim in circles? Controlling for the endogeneity of time to death. *Journal of Health Economics*, 29(2), 205-212.

Demographic change –
The role of the social context

Stéphanie Moerikofer-Zwez[*]

In 2025, which is rather close, the baby-boomer generation will start reaching old age (80+). In Switzerland, this latter age group will then have increased by almost 50% since 2008.[1] What physical and personal needs will they have? What place will this group of more than half a million people have in society?

Looking into the future and trying to make predictions, we tend to use linear extrapolations of the actual situation. For predictions on the growth of the elderly population, this is a valid method if the time covered is not too long and factors such as life expectancy and immigration can be estimated quite accurately. However, predictions of the 80+ age group's health and their need for care, for example, are much more difficult, and linear extrapolations are most likely to be wrong. Health in old age is influenced by social conditions during youth and adult life, as well as by lifestyle factors before and after the age of 65. Research[2] indicates that the increase in healthy old age years is more pronounced than the increase in life expectancy itself – thus reducing the years of required external help and care. Therefore, it is obvious that the linear extrapolation of actual data will overestimate the future need for care in old age. This effect may be even more pronounced if public support for health promotion after retirement is increased and/or if, for example, a drug is developed that prevents or delays the onset of dementia. Consequently, for predictions on the 80+ age group's future health, we have to consider the influence of external factors, especially social and medical ones, that determine the health of a certain age cohort.

The difference between age cohorts is even more pronounced when we look at elderly people's personal and social needs. Nursing homes in Switzerland and elsewhere still have rooms with two, and sometimes even four, beds. The men and women of the age cohort that now – in need of institutional care – lives in nursing homes were born before 1930 and were used to sharing rooms with other persons from an early age. Moreover, this age group has also experienced sharing hospital rooms with four or more beds. Therefore, even if they are not entirely happy with the situation, they mostly accept sharing a room with other people. For the baby-

---

[*] Dr Stéphanie Moerikofer-Zwez is president of the Swiss Home Care Association (Spitex).
[1] Swiss Federal Statistical Office.
[2] Hoepflinger F. (2003). Gesunde und autonome Lebensjahre – Zur Entwicklung der behinderungsfreien Lebenserwartung. In: Perrig-Chiello and Hoepflinger (Ed.), *Gesundheitsbiographien. Variationen und Hintergründe* (pp. 59-74). Huber Verlag: Bern.

S. Kunisch et al. (eds.), *From Grey to Silver*,
DOI 10.1007/978-3-642-15594-9_6, © Springer-Verlag Berlin Heidelberg 2011

boomer cohort, such a situation will be unacceptable. The need for privacy and the possibility to be alone is fundamental for people who grew up after World War II. When we plan future nursing homes or renovate existing ones, this will have to be taken into account. However, we also have to extend the possibilities for home care, thus allowing people to remain in their customary surroundings.

From an economic viewpoint, we should also take into account that the baby-boomer cohort will be healthier and more mobile than the actual 80+ cohort. Furthermore, the period in which the baby boomers were professionally active was economically prosperous and they had more possibilities to save money for their retirement than earlier generations. Moreover, a substantial proportion of this cohort is capable of using the Internet. Thus, on the basis of their social background, they are an economically interesting group of well-informed consumers who, even in later years, will want to live a self-determined and – within certain limits – active life.

Demographic change and the changing nature of the concept of work

Carola Wolf[*]

The changing nature of the *concept of work* is one example of demographically associated social change. The definition of the concept of work, as referred to in this chapter, relates to the nature of activities that qualify as working activities in our perceptions and our thoughts about work – the meaning we attribute to our professional work. This includes aspects such as: Is our professional work a central life interest? Do we regard work as a financially motivated necessity or as a means of personal self-fulfilment? Which social values shape our understanding of what qualifies as 'hard work'?

The perception of work has consequences for the design of workplaces, leadership styles and the shaping of our professional careers; it is, among others, heavily influenced by changes in Western industrialised countries' demographic workforce patterns. Ageing, with its resultant higher percentage of older workers and longer individual professional biographies, is only one demographic trend. Ageing must be considered within a complex set of demographic patterns and economic influences, including aspects such as male-female workplace participation, increases in service and knowledge workers, and more complex skill sets required by today's workforce.

[*] Carola Wolf, research assistant, Institute of Management, University of St. Gallen.

S. Kunisch et al. (eds.), *From Grey to Silver*,
DOI 10.1007/978-3-642-15594-9_7, © Springer-Verlag Berlin Heidelberg 2011

Table of Contents

1   Introduction

Demographic change – such as the ageing of the population in many industrialised countries – goes hand in hand with social changes in Western societies. Such social changes include, for example, the changing status of women and their integration into workplaces, or changing family structures with more single-parent families. Another social phenomenon linked to demographic changes is a shift in the *concept of work*[1].

When discussing the effects of demographic change on organisations, it must be kept in mind that a demographically changing workforce not only includes aspects of ageing, but also other demographic characteristics. Furthermore, the effects of demographic changes in industrialised countries cannot be studied in isolation; other *economic developments* and job developments have to be considered as well. The changing concept of work might simultaneously be a consequence and an antecedent of *changing workforce demographics*. It is therefore important to understand the modern work concept and become aware of the taken-for-granted assumptions of a traditional work concept, which still influence individual and organisational thinking on how to deal with demographic change.

The following discussion is based on a holistic view on the interplay between demographic changes in the workforce and economic developments related to job structures in Western societies. An organisational perspective is applied to summarise general observations on changes in the work concept[2]. The overall goal is sensitisation to the need for integrated approaches to study and respond to demographic change in the context of other related economic trends. The problem of an ageing workforce is therefore not discussed as a stand-alone and dominant demographic change issue. Instead, related aspects are considered that are closely interlinked with ageing but are sometimes neglected when, for example, focusing only on an increase in older workers.

To illustrate the complex set of interrelated developments with regard to the nature of work and demographic change, some dominant trends are explored in this chapter. Examples include a value shift from a *Protestant work ethic* and changes in work activities, to an increase in *emotional work* as a major component of professional work in modern societies. Furthermore, an analysis is provided of the consequences for the work concept as a result of women's increasing participation in professional life. Finally, addressing the increase in generational conflicts in

---

[1]   The notion of work in this context refers primarily to employment in organisations, rather than to a broader notion of work that includes work activities outside employment (such as family work, etc.).

[2]   While the author is aware that similar discussions on the work concept in organisational psychology make a more detailed distinction that is far more grounded in psychological discussion, she acknowledges that this chapter is based on insights from organisational studies and personal experiences. Readers interested in the scientific origins and developments of concepts touched on in this chapter are referred to the specialist literature (e.g., in the field of organisational psychology).

workplaces highlights the tension created by the shifting work values in generations confronted with one another in the workplace.

2   Conceptual background: Major demographic trends and the work concept

2.1 Changing workforce demographics

Discussions on demographic changes in the workforce often centre around ageing. While ageing is certainly one of the most important changes in demographic patterns, workforce demographics are characterised by more than an increase in the average workforce age (e.g., Johnston and Packer 1987; Morris and Venkatesh 2000; Miles 1999; Milliken et al. 1990). Demographic workforce patterns based on individual attributes fall into three categories: "*attributes that describe immutable characteristics such as age, gender, and ethnicity; attributes that describe individuals' relationships with organizations, such as organizational tenure or functional area; and attributes that identify individuals' positions within society, such as marital status*" (Lawrence 1997, p. 5). Relevant demographic variables include "*age, race, gender, tenure (company or group), education (specialization or level), and functional background diversity*" (Hope Pelled 1996, p. 619).

Therefore, aspects other than age, such as changes in the male-female employee ratio in an organisation as well as an increase in workforce cultural diversity, are equally important and must be addressed along with ageing. Furthermore, by including economic developments, a broader view of shifting demographic patterns should also consider the increase in service workers and a decline in blue-collar worker positions, which are closely interlinked with other demographic patterns such as an increase in the female workforce participation (e.g., Cascio 1995; Loden and Rosener 1991; Geissler 2002; Milliken et al. 1990; Oppenheimer 1973). Especially in Western societies and industrialised countries, industrialisation has led to an upgrading of work profiles with workers requiring more complex skill sets (Spenner 1983).

2.2 The work concept

The developments summarised above change our personal perceptions of work and the role of work in our lives. Work (or the modern term 'occupation') is defined as the work activities which "*people do to 'earn a living' [...] Thus, work includes both making things and performing services which are of value to one-self, as well as others*" (Applebaum 1992b, p. X). From an anthropological point of view, work represents much more than the mere creation of material and immaterial things to secure one's living. "*Work is like the spine which structures the way people live, how they make contact with material and social reality, and how they achieve status and self-esteem*" (Applebaum 1992b, p. IX). Therefore, an extended definition of the concept of work is applied in this chapter, not only including the nature of activities that qualify as work activities in our perceptions, but also our thoughts about work – the meanings we attribute to our professional work.[3] This includes aspects such as: Is our professional work a central life interest? Do we see work as a financially motivated necessity or as a means of personal self-fulfilment? Which social values shape our understanding of what qualifies as 'hard work' (e.g., Harpaz and Fu 2002; Mirchandani 1998; Morse and Weiss 1955)?

The meanings and ideas we relate to the notion of work are institutionalised, historically developed conceptions that we absorb during socialisation (e.g., von Rosenstiel 2000). Owing to institutionalised work notions, for example, we associate specific attributes and symbols with work. However, economic and demographic developments might necessitate changes in an established idealised idea of work (e.g., Cascio 1995). The following descriptions are tailored to a Western workforce in (post)industrialised countries characterised by an increasing demand for service and *white-collar workers* (e.g., Spenner 1983; Woelfl 2005).

3   Aspects of a shifting work concept: Expanding traditional work notions

As noted, demographic changes are best considered in combination with other changes in the workplace, such as globalisation, industrialisation, technological developments and their effects on workforce structures (e.g., Cascio 1994; Smola and Sutton 2002). Technological developments in industrialised societies, for example, demand new skill sets of employees. *"Automation eliminates routinized work; workers experience less close supervision and have more responsibility; work is more complex and interrelated, particularly in high technology fields"* (Spenner 1983, p. 824). This skill sets shift is intensified by an increasing proportion of service and knowledge worker positions comprising a large percentage of the currently available jobs (e.g., Cascio 1995; Johnston and Packer 1987; Woelfl 2005).

3.1 From physical to emotional work components

For employees, work has more than a solely materialistic function. However, in the past, the notion of work was often primarily associated with hard physical work to produce specific things and to satisfy material needs (e.g., Applebaum 1992b; von Rosenstiel 2000). However, there are a number of occupations, such as researchers, salespersons, health-care workers, administrative assistants etc. with no physical output (Applebaum 1992b).

Furthermore, our traditional perception of work is still influenced by specific ideas of gender and family roles. Hard physical work is associated with a male workforce. Male/Female stereotypes still influence gender segregation in workplaces. Women in the workplace are often associated with characteristics such as

---

[3] The extended definition includes aspects of the concept of 'meaning of work' in the specialist literature (e.g., Harpaz and Fu 2002; Mirchandani 1998; Morse and Weiss 1955).

emotionality, empathy, care for others, etc. The stereotype of the hard-working, per-formance-oriented, powerful, and highly productive male has endured (e.g., Neu-bauer 1990; von Rosenstiel 2000). Although, in the past century, emancipation and the women's movement had successfully begun breaking down these taken-for-granted perceptions of gender roles, most generations in today's workforce have been socialised in environments influenced by traditional role models.

However, these traditional patterns have changed with the increase in female integration into the workforce during the past century. This is not only due to the success of the women's movement, but also an economic necessity (e.g., Cox 1993; Johnston and Packer 1987). On the one hand, in Western economies, current demo-graphic developments urge employers to exploit all available workforce potential, including the female workforce, to satisfy the demand for a workforce. On the other hand, the increase in service and knowledge jobs as well as in white-collar workers also benefit from skill sets traditionally associated with female characteristics (e.g., Neubauer 1990; von Rosenstiel 2000). Therefore, demographic developments prompt us to go beyond the traditional gender segregation in work environments.

An example[4] is the increasing role of *emotion work* which is associated with many service jobs in the post-industrial era in Western economies (Johnston and Packer 1987; Mirchandani 1998; Pleck 1977). *Emotion work* or *emotional labour* relates to the need to manage our emotions at work and to produce specific desired emotions when facing customers (e.g., Zapf 2002). Emotion work includes activi-ties often associated with volunteer work, the private sector, and the public sector (e.g., Aronson 1992; Mirchandani 1998). The notion of emotional labour dates back to Hochschild's (1979, 1983) study of flight attendants and emphasises the role of emotional aspects of work besides physical and cognitive demands. *"The concept of emotion work refers to the quality of interactions between employees and clients. [...] During face-to-face or voice-to-voice interactions, many employees are required to express appropriate emotions as a job requirement."* (Zapf 2002, p. 238). In this regard, for example, teachers must demonstrate empathy and patience towards their students; flight attendants are expected to smile and signal a feeling of safety on board; and doctors must inspire trust in their patients (e.g., Cascio 1995; Mirchandani 1998; Zapf 2002). Many job tasks now require aspects of emotion work; these include jobs that involve caring for others or that involve close contact and managing relationships with others outside and inside the organisation (e.g., Paoli 1997). This development goes hand in hand with changes in work values – as described below – in the shift from a traditional Protestant work ethic.

---

[4] Another example which goes hand in hand with the increase in service jobs is the increasing demand for cognitive work skills, which also reshapes our understanding of 'work' so that it is no longer purely associated with physical work.

3.2 From a Protestant work ethic to a new understanding of the role of work

Traditionally, our commitment to work has been influenced by a dominant Protestant work ethic which holds that *"hard work is intrinsically good and an end in itself"* (Morrow 1983, p. 489; see also Weber 1988). Such a work ethic is primarily shaped by cultural and social influences. The Protestant work ethic in Western societies probably dates back to times when Christian values especially the Calvinist tradition in the 16th century proclaimed hard work as the central value of life. *"It is based on the idea that to work is a moral duty, that it is an obligation to one's family, one's community and to one's religion as well as oneself"* (Applebaum 1992, p. 337). By following a Protestant work ethic that emphasises a strong sense of duty to one's work, work gives meaning to our lives and contributes to our moral worth (e.g., von Rosenstiel 2000; Weber 1988).

Modern work ethics are more liberal and have a more flexible approach to work suited to today's career paths. For most people, hard work per se, as proclaimed by the Protestant work ethic, is no longer an intrinsic motivation or an ultimate life goal. Today, employees look for more in their career paths. Values such as self-fulfilment have replaced the traditional values of the Protestant work ethic. Furthermore, today there is an increasing desire among employees to balance work and personal goals (Klages 1984; Smola and Sutton 2002; von Rosenstiel 2000). Issues such as work-life balance and prevention of burnout-related syndromes become central in societies in which people work more years; career paths do not follow traditional linear paths with life-long relationships with one employer or predetermined careers in one organisation which used to be commonplace (e.g., Applebaum 1992).

Paradoxically, the decrease in physical work and the increase in emotional stress and psychological pressure in the workplace seems to create a greater risk of exhaustion-related syndromes than the hard physical work that in previous centuries used to dominate work life. Work remains an important part of a person's life, even for new generations and younger employees (Smola and Sutton 2002). However, their motives have changed from the Protestant work ethic in favour of a stronger desire for career promotion, self-determined careers, and work as a means to an end – a balanced life and fulfilment of all aspects of life, not just work (e.g., Applebaum 1992; Klages 1984).

3.3 Shifting expectations in the employer-employee relationship

This shift in work values is also represented in modern employer-employee relationships and reciprocal expectations. The traditional 'paternalistic' employer-employee relationship is eroding (Cavanaugh and Noe 1999). In the past, the employer role was often perceived as kind of a caretaker for employees; in modern societies, employees take on the role of taking care of themselves and managing their own careers. Traditional employer role models meant handing over an important portion of employee career planning to the employer. Strong performers were often guaranteed a job in a company until their retirement. Furthermore, the employer helped plan career and promotions within the company. In return, employees were loyal and committed to a specific organisation for most or all of their professional lives.

Although many employers still play an important role as mentors and career coaches for their employees, and promotions often depend on the support of a supervisor who fosters the careers of his/her subordinates, employee expectations are today somewhat lower. Employees take on greater self-responsibility for their careers, replacing the loyalty and commitment devoted to one organisation with a stronger commitment to work performed more independently of the organisation and the employer (Cavanaugh and Noe 1999; Smola and Sutton 2002).

3.4 A female concept of work and the consequences of the integration of women into the workplace

Besides ageing, one of the most influential demographic changes in workforce structures is the increase in female workers. This increase is based on shifts in the social role of women, and is also a result of other demographic developments such as an ageing population, which forces Western economies to fully exploit the potential available workforce including women (Dychtwald et al. 2006; Milliken et al. 1990). The changing nature of women's social roles, particularly their work roles, has not only lead to an overall increase in female work, but also to major changes in the relationship between work experiences and family life-cycles (Milliken et al. 1990; Oppenheimer 1973). Women thereby dominate specific white-collar occupations such as teaching and nursing that specifically rely on emotion work (Mirchandani 1998; Oppenheimer 1973; Pleck 1977).

While the implications of this development affect women's social status, it also broadens the definition of 'work' to include emotional and relational work aspects that are not included in the traditionally taken-for-granted work notions focusing on the physical aspects of work (Mirchandani 1998). Gender segregation in workplaces as well as gender-based monopolisations of certain occupations make it clear that conventional definitions of work are gendered (gender biased) (e.g., Pleck 1977).

There seems to be a 'masculinist work norm' that, among others, emphasises hard physical work and work as a financial means to nurture one's family. This masculine work norm devalues some 'female' activities and certain occupations. Implicitly, based on socialisation in societies with strong traditional family role models, emotion work – which women perform in their family role but also in certain occupations – does not correspond with what we associate with 'real work' (namely hard physical work).

A broader notion of work must therefore include efforts that focus on emotional and relational aspects. Considering the increase in service jobs in Western societies, and the decrease in manufacturing work, a broader notion of work and a redefinition of the common understanding of work are necessary. This shift in job structures favours skills no longer related to the physical work performance but to skills necessary to successfully master the emotional, relational, and knowledge-based aspects of work (often referred to as 'soft skills').

3.5 Generational conflicts at work due to different work values

Besides changing male-female ratios in workplaces, ageing is one of the most important demographic trends influencing workforce structures. Ageing does not seek to be dealt with in terms of increases in age per se. Furthermore, the ratio between younger and older people is shifting. People are not only living longer, but generational patterns are changing dramatically with a growing percentage of the population being 50+ and a decrease in younger generations (e.g., Geissler 2002). As a result, generational workplace conflicts present challenges, especially if employees remain professionally active longer and age differences in workplaces increase.

Generational conflicts arise because work values and beliefs differ between generations and change during the course of one's life. In this vein, for example, with increasing age, the desire to balance work and personal goals seems to increase as well (Kunze et al. 2010; Smola and Sutton 2002; Snape and Redman 2003). It is not simply age that causes conflicts, but generations confronted with one another in the workplace. Misunderstandings, miscommunication, and mixed signals are sources of potential conflict when, for example, baby boomers and generation X-ers work together.[5] While baby boomers tend to show strong support for the assumption that 'working hard makes one a better person', generation X-ers seem ready to quit their job if, for example, they have inherited a lot of money (Smola and Sutton 2002). For the younger generation, work seems to be more a way of self-fulfilment, of exploring one's possibilities, and to manage one's career with greater self-responsibility and self-management than among previous generations (as described in Section 3.2).[6]

Hard work is no longer the primary life goal, and hard work per se is not considered a means to personal satisfaction. Differing goals and values in work and life increase the chance that one generation will have difficulties understanding the other. This conflict potential is exacerbated because many of these assumptions are not explicitly articulated but implicitly guide our behaviour. An increasing awareness of such conflicts as well as specific measures to sensitise employees to them might be a key to master the challenges of a multi-generation ageing workforce.

---

[5] There is no clear agreement among researchers on how generations should be distinguished according to their year of birth. However, baby boomers roughly refer to the generation born between 1946 and 1964, while generation X-ers usually include persons born between 1960 and 1982 (Smola and Sutton 2002).

[6] For a detailed discussion on generational leadership, see Kunze et al. 2011.

4 Consequences of a shifting work concept

4.1 Consequences for individuals in organisations

The changing nature of work profiles from hard physical work to white-collar work necessitates a shift in our personal understandings of work. In an office job, for example, it is sometimes hard to identify the different aspects of work. At the end of a long day with meetings, conversations with colleagues, and various minor activities, for example, one might sometimes have the impression that one does not achieve much during the course of a day, but still feel exhausted and stressed about everything that remains to be done. However, these types of activities comprise a large part of work activities in modern white-collar positions (e.g., Cascio 1995; Mintzberg 1973, 2009). Socialised ideas of work still make it difficult to accept those aspects as work. The fact that in many jobs, employees have no concrete, physical outcomes at day-end might foster impressions such as 'I got nothing done' or that 'I did not work (enough)'.

Hence, a first consequence of the shifting work concept is to accept that, for many employees in Western societies, work is no longer hard physical work with visible results at day-end. White-collar workers must accept that the results of their work are not always immediately visible and measurable. However, the emotional and relational efforts, for example, in meetings or networking with colleagues or company partners are legitimate work activities. Furthermore, these activities have similar effects to hard physical work: they are exhausting, they sap our energy levels, and demand phases of recovery to restore balance (e.g., Ciulla 2000).

A second consequence is the need to manage our professional careers, not only in the sense of how to reach career aspirations and be successful, but also in the sense of how to design a balanced work life. A considerable amount of our life-spans comprise (paid) work. However, the clear lines of traditional life models such as a period dedicated to education (school followed by university or professional apprenticeship), followed by a phase of work life leading to the last stage of retirement, have become blurred. Traditional work careers with life-long loyalty to one employer, with a clear development path within one company administered by that employer no longer represents today's standards. Instead, it falls to employees to manage their careers across the number of organisations for which they will work. Furthermore, concepts such as life-long learning and continuous development of job skills illustrate that life-long relations with one employer are unlikely nowadays, and that a life-long focus on one job is also less common than it used to be in the past.

Increasingly, people are changing professions, returning to university or other professional training facilities and changing their work contexts. A physician, for example, might start working in a management position for a pharmaceutical company and therefore decide to attain an MBA degree. Many examples highlight that longer working periods in biographies are often guided by a search for self-fulfilment, by exploring one's talents in different areas and by designing a balanced, interesting, and challenging career path.

To sum up, it is the responsibility of every professional individual to actively shape his/her own career path according to his/her personal talents and goals. It is also important to manage one's work-life balance, which allows for mastering the challenges of today's career paths, for example, in terms of longer work life periods.

4.2 Consequences for organisations

It is not surprising that, besides personal responsibilities, working environments determine how well an individual can manage his/her professional life. One key factor in this regard is organisational settings that allow for such personal career responsibility. Modern organisations must consider aspects of demographic changes such as an ageing population, more female employees, shifts in the content of work towards white-collar jobs relying on emotional, relational, and knowledge-related skills.

Organisations can respond in a variety of ways. Increasingly, organisations rely on specialised diversity functions or departments that find solutions to manage increasing workplace diversity. Special programmes are designed to foster integration between different groups of workers (e.g., Armstrong-Stassen and Templer 2005; Elliott 1995; Rynes and Rosen 1995). Such programmes must respond to demographic changes, for example, by designing programmes and services for ageing workers and working moms. Furthermore, work-life balance has become increasingly important due to the previously described reasons embedded in trends. Although employees are less confronted with syndromes of physical exhaustion, syndromes of emotional exhaustion have increased (e.g., Applebaum 1992; De Castro et al. 2004).

One significant danger of the workplace changes and the shift in the work concept relates to the negative psychological effects of modern work environments, such as burnout-related syndromes. Many female workers struggle to manage their professional careers in parallel with their family lives. This challenge now also affects many male workers, as traditional family role models change and fathers assume more family life responsibilities. As we usually work longer than previous generations, we must carefully plan our professional careers, be aware of our personal and professional goals and aspirations as well as balance work and life outside the work context.

Although organisations are becoming more aware of such issues, responses are still few and far between and are sometimes insufficient and not innovative enough to really deal with the full dimensions of current and future changes in work environments due to demographic changes. Therefore, organisations should steer clear of one-sided solutions and should design solutions that holistically address the dimensions of demographic change and related challenges (e.g., Dychtwald et al. 2006).

In this regard, these demographic trends should be regarded as opportunities that might yield significant benefits, rather than merely being regarded as threats (e.g., Cascio 1995; Lawrence 1988). The noted changes in the nature of jobs required in Western economies might benefit from the ageing workforce with its accumulation of invaluable knowledge and work experience. Women entering workplaces bring specific skills that suit modern job profiles. For example, the skills related to emotion work are often related to 'natural' female skill sets, since emotion work is a central task of women in their traditional family roles (e.g., Mirchandani 1998). Furthermore, demographic changes in Western countries' workforce structure mirror general population trends. Therefore, the most efficient way to respond to changes in customer structures and requirements is to reflect on changes in demographic patterns in the composition of employees (e.g., Cox and Blake 1991; Loden and Rosener 1991).

In previous economies, an ageing workforce could create problems for countries reliant on blue-collar workers and hard physical work for economic welfare, due to the resulting decreasing productivity. However, due to economic developments in Western societies, in theory, organisations not only suffer less from such productivity losses, they even benefit from the qualities associated with the composition of today's workforce (e.g., Thomas and Ely 2001; Sepheri and Wagner 2000).

5   Conclusion

Clearly, discussions of demographic change should not only focus on the question of an ageing workforce, but must also consider other demographic developments such as an increasingly female workforce. Furthermore, to evaluate the consequences of demographic change, socio-economic developments must be integrated into the discussion.

It is especially the increase in service and knowledge intensive jobs in Western economies that offers opportunities for demographic change. Organisations might benefit from the rich experience and accumulated knowledge of older employees. Female workers might bring specific emotional skills, for example, related to the family work they often pursue alongside their employment. Such emotional skills are key success factors for many service jobs.

In short, this study does not disregard the threats and challenges that economies and organisations face and will face due to demographic developments. Rather, this chapter is aimed at highlighting the opportunities of such developments, and encourages treating the opportunities and threats equally, instead of focusing only on the negative effects of demographic change.

Human resources already are and will certainly be the most important resources of Western economies. As a result, organisations should shift their thinking from 'how can we reduce the inefficiencies of human capital due to demographic changes' towards 'how can we best benefit from the rich pool of human resources that modern populations offer us'.

References

Applebaum, H. (1992). Work and its future. *Futures,* 24(4): 336-350.

Applebaum. H. (1992b). *The concept of work: Ancient, medieval, and modern.* New York: State University of New York Press.

Armstrong-Stassen, M., & Templer, A. (2005). Adapting training for older employees. The Canadian response to an aging workforce. *Journal of Management Development,* 24, 57-67.

Aronson, J. (1992). Women's sense of responsibility for the care of old people: "But who else is going to do it?" *Gender & Society,* 6, 8-29.

Cascio, W. F. (1995). Whither industrial and organizational psychology in a changing world of work? *American Psychologist,* 50(11), 928-939.

Cavanaugh, M. A., & Noe, R. A. (1999). Antecedents and consequences of relational components of the new psychological contract. *Journal of Organizational Behavior,* 20(3), 323-340.

Ciulla, J. B. (2000). *The working life. The promise and betrayal of modern work.* New York: Times Book.

Cox, T. H. Jr. (1993). *Cultural Diversity in Organizations; Theory, research and practice.* San Francisco, CA: Berret-Koehler.

Cox, T. H. Jr., & Blake, S. (1991). Managing Cultural Diversity: Implications for Organizational Competitiveness. *Academy of Management Executive,* 5(3), 45-56.

de Castro, A. B., Agnew, J., Fitzgerald, S. T. (2004). Emotional labor: relevant theory for occupational health practice in post-industrial America. *AAOHN Journal,* 52(3), 109-15.

Dychtwald, K., Erickson, T. J., Morison, R. (2006). *Workforce crisis: How to beat the coming shortage of skills and talent.* Boston: Harvard Business School Press.

Elliott, R. H. (1995). Human resource management's role in the future aging of the workforce. *Review of Public Personnel Administration,* 15, 5-17.

Geissler, R. (2002). *Die Sozialstruktur Deutschlands: Die gesellschaftliche Entwicklung vor und nach der Vereinigung.* Wiesbaden: Westdeutscher Verlag.

Harpaz, I., & Fu, X. (2002). The structure of the meaning of work: A relative stability amidst change. *Human Relations,* 55(6), 639-667.

Hochschild, A. (1979). Emotion work, feeling rules, and social structure. *American Journal of Sociology,* 85, 555-575.

Hochschild, A. (1983). *The managed heart.* Berkeley: University of California Press.

Hope Pelled, L. (1996). Demographic diversity, conflict, and work group outcomes: An intervening process theory. *Organization Science,* 7(6), 615-631.

Johnston, W. B., & Packer, A. H. (1987). *Workforce 2000: Work and workers for the 21st century.* Indianapolis, IN: Hudson Inst.

Klages, H. (1984). *Wertorientierungen im Wandel.* Frankfurt am Main: Campus Verlag.

Kunze, F., Boehm, S., & Bruch, H. (2011). Generational leadership – How to manage five different generations in the workforce. In S. Kunisch, S. Boehm, M. Boppel (Ed.), *From Grey to Silver – Managing the Challenges and Opportunities of Demographic Change* (pp. 89-102). Heidelberg: Springer.

Kunze, F., Boehm, S., Bruch, H. (2010). Age diversity, age discrimination climate and performance consequences – a cross organizational study. *Journal of Organizational Behavior,* 31, 1-27.

Lawrence, B. S. (1988). New wrinkles in the theory of age: Demography, norms, and performance ratings. *Academy of Management Journal,* 31(2), 309-337.

Lawrence, B. S. (1997). The black box of organizational demography. *Organization Science,* 8(1), 1-22.

Loden, M., & Rosener, J. B. (1991). *Workforce America: managing employee diversity as a vital resource.* Homeewood, IL: Business One Irwin.

Miles, D. (1999). Modelling the impact of demographic change upon the economy. *The Economic Journal,* 109(452), 1-36.

Milliken, F. J., Dutton, J. E., Beyer, J. M. (1990). Understanding organizational adaptation to change: The case of work-family issues. *Human Resource Planning,* 13(2), 91-107.

Mintzberg, H. (1973). *The nature of managerial work.* New York: Harper & Row.

Mintzberg, H. (2009). *Managing.* San Francisco: Berrett-Koehler.

Mirchandani, K. (1998). Protecting the boundary: Teleworker insights on the expansive concept of "work". *Gender and Society,* 12(2), 168-187.

Morris, M. G., & Venkatesh, V. (2000). Age differences in technology adoption decisions: Implications for a changing work force. *Personnel Psychology,* 53, 375-403.

Morrow, P. C. (1983). Concept redundancy in organizational research: The case of work commitment. *Academy of Management Review,* 8(3), 486-500.

Morse, N. C., & Weiss, R. (1955). The function and meaning of work and the job. *American Sociological Review,* 20(2), 191-198.

Neubauer, R. (1990). Frauen im Assessment Center – ein Gewinn? *A & O, Zeitschrift für Arbeits- und Organisationspsychologie,* 34, 29-36.

Oppenheimer, V. K. (1973). Demographic influence on female employment and the status of women. *The American Journal of Sociology,* 78(4), 946-961.

Paoli, P. (1997). *Second European survey on the work environment 1995.* Dublin: European Foundation for the Improvement of Living and Working Conditions.

Pleck, J. H. (1977). The work-family role system. *Social Problems,* 24(4), 417-427.

Rynes, S., & Rosen, B. (1995). A field survey of factors affecting the adoption and perceived success of diversity training. *Personnel Psychology,* 46, 613-627.

Sepehri, P., & Wagner, D. (2000). "Managing Diversity" – Eine empirische Bestandsaufnahme. *Personalführung,* 7, 50-59.

Smola, K. W., & Sutton, C. D. (2002). Generational differences: Revisiting generational work values for the new *Millennium. Journal of Organizational Behavior,* 23(4), 363-382.

Snape, E., & Redman, T. (2003). Too old or too young? The impact of perceived age discrimination. *Human Resource Management Journal,* 13, 78-89.

Spenner, K. I. (1983). Decipheric Prometheus: Temporal change in the skill level of work. *American Sociological Review,* 48(6), 824-837.

Thomas, D. A., & Ely, R. J. (2001). *Making differences matter: a new paradigm for managing diversity. Harvard Business Review on managing diversity.* Boston: Harvard Business School Press.

von Rosenstiel, L. (2000). *Grundlagen der Organisationspsychologie.* Stuttgart: Schäffer-Poeschel.

Weber, M. (1988). *Gesammelte Aufsätze der Religionssoziologie.* Nachdruck der Erstauflage 1920. Stuttgart: UTB.

Wölfl, A. (2005). The services economy in OECD countries. *STI Working Paper 2005/3,* OECD, Paris.

Zapf, D. (2002). Emotion work and psychological well-being: A review of the literature and some conceptual considerations. Human Resource Management Review, *12,* 237-268.

Part C

A human resource and leadership perspective – Managing the ageing workforce

Generational leadership –
How to manage five different generations in the workforce

Florian Kunze, Stephan A. Boehm, Heike Bruch

The successful management of demographic change in German companies will mostly depend on their executives' leadership capabilities. Based on the implicit leadership theory of effective leader-subordinate relationships, the perceived leadership behaviour must match individual subordinates' leadership prototypes. As research in sociology and social psychology indicates, these leadership prototypes – consisting of employees' work values and preferences – are influenced by generational experiences as well as by individual employees' age. Building on these arguments, this chapter tries to develop different leadership styles for the five generations currently present in the German workforce: *The Post-War Generation*, the *Economic-Boom Generation*, the *Baby-Boom Generation*, the *Golf Generation*, and the *Internet Generation*. Such adaptive and generation-specific leadership should help spur high levels of work motivation, organisational commitment, and hence lead to top performance by every generation and age group within the company.

* Dr. Florian Kunze, Senior Research Fellow, Institute for Leadership and Human Resources Management, University of St. Gallen.

Dr. Stephan A. Boehm, Senior Lecturer and Director of the Center for Disability and Integration, University of St. Gallen.

Prof. Dr. Heike Bruch, Director, Institute for Leadership and Human Resources Management, University of St. Gallen.

S. Kunisch et al. (eds.), *From Grey to Silver*,
DOI 10.1007/978-3-642-15594-9_8, © Springer-Verlag Berlin Heidelberg 2011

Table of Contents

1 Leadership in light of demographic change

Demographic change is one of the most urgent challenges of our time. Politicians and the media address the projected shrinking and ageing of the German population on a daily basis. Indeed, society and economy are confronted with immense challenges, such as a decline of the German Population by 8.5 million by 2050, which equals the current population of Lower Saxony. Additionally, the population age structure is also changing drastically – the over 40 age group is estimated to become the largest subgroup by 2018 (Destatis, 2006).

Given these developments, the 'war for talents' (Micheals et al. 2001) is going to increase, and almost no company will remain competitive without relying on at least some older personnel. Therefore, companies urgently need advice on how to tailor their Human Resource (HR) and leadership strategies in order to keep employees of all age groups an engaged and motivated workforce in the long term.

A decisive factor in this regard is adjusting leadership behaviour within the company, even though this is often neglected in practice. In Finland, for example, a longitudinal study indicated that leadership is the only significant factor that increases employees' work ability over time (Ilmarinen 2001).

Consequently, this chapter develops a generational leadership approach that tries to account for the five generations currently present in the German workforce. According to implicit leadership theory (Engle and Lord 1997), successful leadership behaviour should be aligned with employees' individual leadership preferences. These leadership preferences are certainly influenced by each employee's age and generational imprinting (e.g., the influence of specific historic events during childhood and adolescence). Therefore, a framework comprising specific strengths and capabilities of the five generations in the German workforce is presented. Based on this framework, five particular leadership styles are deduced.

2 Five different generations in the workforce

A generation is characterised as an identifiable group that shares birth years, birth location, and significant life events at critical developmental stages during childhood and youth (Kupperschmidt 2000). A generational group, often referred to as a cohort, includes those who share historical or social life experiences that distinguish generations from one another (Jurkiewicz and Brown 1998). Based on the categorization by Bruch et al. (2010) and building on Oertel's (2007) primary definition, five different generations are currently present in the German workforce:

- The Post-War Generation (born approximately 1935-1945, 6% of the 2009 workforce).
- The Economic-Boom Generation (born approximately 1946-1955, 18% of the 2009 workforce).
- The Baby-Boom Generation (born approximately 1956-1965, 24% of the 2009 workforce).

- The Golf Generation (born approximately 1966-1980, 31% of the 2009 work-force).
- The Internet Generation (born approximately 1981 onwards, 22% of the 2009 workforce).

While generational affiliations are similar in most industrialised countries, they still differ slightly due to historical, political or societal events (e.g., unlike in the US, the effects of World War II delayed the economic boom in Germany).

The following sections focus on the specific historical and life events that shaped each generation in Germany during their youth and the start of their working life, thus triggering their particular strengths, capabilities and work values. In addition, the current phase of life as well as each generation's potential ageing effects are discussed, since these factors may also influence the leadership preferences of each cohort. These factors are summarized in Table 1.

Table 1. Characteristics of the five generations in the German workforce (source: own illustration).

Generation	Generational characteristics	Phase of life	Ageing effects
Post-War Generation (born 1935-1945)	■ Reliability ■ Loyalty ■ Dutifulness ■ Respect for hierarchy and supervisors ■ Materialistic values	■ Close to retirement ■ Children are grown up ■ Awareness of finiteness of life	■ Critical phase for cognitive and physical capabilities ■ Immense experience-based know-how
Economic-Boom Generation (born 1946-1955)	■ Idealism ■ Sceptical of authority ■ Post-materialistic values ■ Independence and participation important	■ At the peak of working life ■ In the second half of life ■ Hinge or sandwich generation	■ Decline in cognitive and physical capabilities, but great individual differences ■ Immense experienced-based know-how
Baby-Boom Generation (born 1956-1965)	■ Assertiveness ■ Team players ■ Experience with competition and conflicts ■ Environment and emancipation important	■ Largest parent generation ■ Mid-life phase, which allows taking stock of achievements and failures	■ First decline in physical capabilities, which can often be compensated for by experience and dedication
Golf Generation (born 1966-1980)	■ Individualistic and materialistic values ■ Career-oriented ■ Pragmatic and rational ■ Only loyal in the short-term	■ Middle phase of life ■ Established in working life ■ Late family planning	■ Only limited decline in achievement potential ■ Very capable and self-confident
Internet Generation (born from 1981)	■ High willingness to learn ■ Technology affinity ■ Very flexible and mobile ■ Tolerant	■ Start becoming established in working life ■ Phase of independency before starting a family ■ 'Rush hour' of life	■ Physically and cognitively very competent ■ High learning capabilities ■ Limited experience-based know-how

1.1 Post-War Generation

Most members of the *Post-War Generation* are now close to retirement or have already entered retirement. During their childhood and youth, they were mostly influenced by World War II in Germany and the following reconstruction period. Their education at home and in school was based on conservative values and hierarchies and often still included corporal punishment (Schuetze and Geulen 1995). For many people, the direct post-war years were shaped by their daily fight for survival, which triggered this generation's pragmatic and determined behaviour. Which is still prevalent. Furthermore, this generation is characterized as cost-conscious, polite, loyal and assiduous in their working behaviour.

The working environment this generation entered in the 1950s was dominated by strong hierarchies and authorities in industrial factories. The prevailing management principle was Taylorism (Taylor 1977), which had a mechanistic view of the individual employee. Employees were treated as "exchangeable parts of a machine". Informal communication, especially across various hierarchal levels, was limited, and private and business life were strictly separated. Work was treated as a means to an end rather than a means to individual self-fulfilment.

In their current life phase, most members of this generation have a desire for work-load relief and a higher leisure time orientation, which should finally result in their retirement (Oertel 2007). This generation is assumed to have a prevention-oriented focus aimed at preventing physical and psychological losses as well as a financial and social decline.

In the light of ageing-related factors, the Post-War Generation is in a critical phase regarding its work-related capabilities. Members of this generation face increasing physical restrictions in their working life. On the other hand, they possess an immense work-related know-how accumulated during their working life, which enables them to deal with various tasks and situations efficiently.

1.2 Economic-Boom Generation

The *Economic-Boom Generation* consists of employees born between 1946 and 1955, who are now in an advanced stage of their working life. Many of them have reached leadership positions in companies and in society.

During their youth, this generation strongly advocated post-materialistic values and a change in societal circumstances, which cumulated in the "'68 revolution" (Klein 2003). These post-materialistic values developed primarily due to the – seemingly endless – economic boom in the 1950s and 1960s. During these times of full employment and growing wealth for almost everybody, this generation began to orient itself more towards the principle 'work to live' instead of 'live to work'. Consequently, this generation – whose members are more oriented towards self-fulfilment and appreciation in their working life – considers material incentives less important (Oertel 2007).

The working environment responsible for this generations' socialisation shifted from Taylorism to the Human Relations Movement, in which leadership and management focus on the individual employee (Kieser and Walgenbach 2007).

Leadership in companies was hence characterized by an increase in employee participation.

In their current life phase, members of this generation often have to find a balance between the challenges of educating their children and organising care for their elderly parents. Consequently, this generation is often described as a 'hinge or sandwich generation' (e.g., Luescher and Liegle 2003).

As far as their physical and psychological capabilities are concerned, this generation could experience the first cognitive and physical decline, although with immense individual differences. Empirical studies show that individuals' physical and cognitive abilities can remain almost constant or drastically decrease, depending, for example, on their fitness (Illmarinen 2001). In contrast, most Economic-Boom Generation members are able to work efficiently under stress and compensate for small age-related deficits through routines, passion and experience-based know-how.

1.3 Baby-Boom Generation

The *Baby-Boom Generation* has a slightly different origin in Germany than in the USA. In contrast to the USA, where the baby-boom started directly after World War II, Germany's birth rates only started to increase in 1955 due to the tough post-war decade. This development lasted until 1965, when the invention of the birth control pill triggered a sudden drop in birth rates. Today, the Baby Boomers represent the largest population in the German workforce.

The childhood and youth of this generation were shaped by the first massive economic crisis in the German post-war period. Consequently, this generation is also sometimes referred to as the crisis children (Preuss-Lausitz et al. 1994). Thus, members of this generation realised, in contrast to their predecessors, that their future personal and work-related development may also involve risks and uncertainties. This lead to a decrease in societal engagement and less support for the Economic-Boom Generation's post-materialistic goals. Nevertheless, this generation showed a strong and successful shift towards gender equality, and raised awareness of environmental issues.

The working environment at the start of their working life was similar to that of the Economic-Boom Generation. Influenced mainly by an increase in labour unions, participative leadership and employees' greater involvement became more prevalent.

Owing to the cohort's size – they have many siblings, were one of many in kindergarten, in school, and later at work – this generation has always faced competition for scarce resources (Dychtwald 2003). This competition strengthened this generation's assertiveness, but also generated higher levels of social competencies and capacities for teamwork.

Today, members of this generation are in the middle years of their life – a period for taking stock of achievements and failures in their jobs and private lives. Many are currently parents, and sometimes also have to deal with the same 'hinge function' that the Economic-Boom Generation faces.

This generation has not reached a phase of life characterized by physical or cognitive deficits. In fact, many of their members are at the peak of their achievement potential at work, and represent the backbone of the German workforce.

1.4 Golf Generation

The name of the *Golf Generation* originates from a novel written by Florian Illies (2000) in which he compares this generation to the Volkswagen Golf automobile. The book discusses the members of this generation – born between 1966 and the end of the 1970s –, who currently have an established working life and have made notable career progress.

In contrast to the two preceding generations, this generation did not grow up in an environment of steady prosperity increments, increasing social benefits and decreasing working hours. Instead, the 1980s were shaped by an increase in long-term unemployment rates and rising national debts. Moreover, this generation experienced Germany's reunification as young adults (Oertel 2007).

Members of this generation strive for wealth, strong careers, and own security. Compared to the Baby Boomers and the Economic-Boom Generation, this generation is less politicized and more materialistic (Klein 2003). Consequently, the Golf Generation is often described as independent, ambitious, pragmatic, individualistic and reliable.

The working environment that socialised this generation was shaped by a steady decentralisation and lower positions in companies' hierarchies. Triggered by increasing globalised competition and repeated economic crises in the 1970s and 1980s, companies were forced to become more flexible in their structure and organisation. Therefore, team and project-based forms of organisation became increasingly popular (Schreyoegg 2003). Technological change also caused a shift from physically demanding tasks to knowledge-based work that required all employees to continuously learn new skills. Owing to the media revolution, this generation is also the first cohort to socialise using technologies such as personal computers and mobile phones.

Members of this generation are currently in the middle adulthood stage of life. Many of its members have tried to extend their youth as long as possible, and postponed starting a family. After almost a decade of being career-focused, the New Economy crisis at the brink of the new millennium indicated that continuous economic and private growth was not guaranteed.

Ageing effects do not yet impact this generation, although hair loss and/or weight increases are already visible at times. Most of the generation's members possess high physical as well as cognitive capabilities.

1.5 Internet Generation

A new generation emerged in the German-speaking world with the children born in the 1980s, who are referred to as the *Internet Generation* due to the Internet's strong influence on them. Members of the Internet Generation have mostly finished their education, and are thus at the start of their careers.

During their socialisation, this generation was shaped by the end of the East-West conflict and the subsequent hegemony of the Western culture as well as increasing globalisation. The Internet Generation is the first generation to profit from the benefits of globalisation, namely worldwide mobility and interconnectedness. However, this generation is also confronted with the downsides of these developments, such as increased competition in Western economies and in welfare states. In general, members of the Internet Generation are forced to focus their personal and job planning on the short term; clear and predictable career paths over years, and decades are scarce for this generation.

The Internet Generation's working environment is heavily shaped by the Internet's vast and increasing possibilities. This generation takes the ease of communication via email, blogs, and social online networks for granted, in private life as well as at work. Additionally, members of this generation have accepted the disappearing borders between private and work life, and are able to perform multiple tasks simultaneously (Gursoya et al. 2008).

Most of the Internet Generation members are in a period of independence preceding the start of a family. However, most of this generation's members seem to be in the so-called 'rush hour' of life, which is a 5-10 year phase requiring numerous important decisions in both one's private life, and at work (Bertram 2005; Schuler 2006).

Members of the Internet Generation are at the peak of their cognitive, mental, and physical abilities. Consequently, this generation is able to cope with difficult and stressful work situations, as well as able to easily adjust to new tasks, and situations. Their only disadvantage is their lack of experience, which is essential for strategic decision-making, and leading employees.

3   Leadership of five different generations in the workforce

How do these different generational identities impact the leadership relation between supervisors and subordinates? Following an individualised leadership approach (e.g., Dansereau et al. 1995), leadership behaviour should be adjusted to individual employees' needs, and values. Consequently, a supervisor should considers individual employees' strengths, weaknesses and preferences by showing confidence in their integrity, and capabilities. The following sections will thus develop individualised leadership strategies for each of the five generations (Bruch et al. 2010).

Table 2. Generational leadership traits of five generations (source: own illustration)

Generation	Individual Strengths	Communication and Leadership	Performance Assessment
Post-War Generation (born 1935-1945)	▓ Experience ▓ Reliability ▓ Loyalty ▓ Calmness	▓ Personal communication ▓ Hierarchy-focused, involvement of experience for important decision making ▓ Enable a flexible transition to retirement	▓ Individual-focused performance assessment
Economic-Boom Generation (born 1946-1955)	▓ Experience ▓ Social competence ▓ High work ethic	▓ Personal communication ▓ Critical of authority and hierarchy, thus apply participative leadership ▓ Emphasize meaning of tasks	▓ Individual-focused performance assessment
Baby-Boom Generation (born between 1956-1965)	▓ Assertiveness ▓ Social competence ▓ Good team player	▓ Personal and electronic communication ▓ Show future career possibilities to avoid demotivation ▓ Consensus-oriented leadership	▓ Competitive performance assessment
Golf Generation (born 1966-1980)	▓ High willingness to perform ▓ Flexibility ▓ High resistance to stress	▓ Communication through new media ▓ Clear and direct leadership ▓ Emphasize materialistic goals, and incentives	▓ Competitive performance assessment
Internet Generation (born from 1981)	▓ Innovativeness ▓ Flexibility ▓ Multitasking ability	▓ Communication through new media, but personal communication still important ▓ Strong and visionary leadership due to limited work and life experience ▓ Guidance for establishment in working life, and future career progress	▓ Competitive performance assessment

Such *generational leadership* behaviour should create a work environment that enables the sustainable commitment, satisfaction and productive engagement of all five generations in the workforce. This section applies a very broad definition of leadership behaviour that includes all supervisor activities directed towards individual employees' task assignments, professional development, and personal motivation. The following sections draw on *each generation's specific strengths* that should be appreciated, *optimal communication and leadership behaviour* as well as the best way to carry out *performance assessments* of each generation, as shown in Table 2.

3.1 Experience-based leadership for the Post-War Generation

As previously stated, the Post-War Generation was socialised in times of hierarchal and formal organisational structures. That is why they are expected to prefer clear-cut, goal-oriented leadership behaviour. On the other hand, due to their extensive life and work experience, members of this generation like to feel valued. Consequently, they want to be involved in decision-making processes for which they possess relevant knowledge. Moreover, supervisors should recognise their other strengths, such as reliability, loyalty, dutifulness, resistance to stress, and social competence.

Many members of the Post-War Generation no longer have career goals, which implies that they do not feel too much competition from other employees. This should be considered during their performance evaluations that should rather be carried out in an individualistic than in a collectivistic framework. Therefore, their goal accomplishments should be assessed in comparison to their development, and not to that of other team or company members. The Post-War Generation members might prefer personal relationships and direct communication with their supervisors, instead of excessive communication via modern media devices.

When planning this generation's retirement, one has to consider and strive for a smooth transition to retirement as a main objective. This transition phase should also enable the company to retain experienced workers' often valuable implicit knowledge. Good examples of such strategies are phased retirement models, mentoring roles for older workers and senior expert models that allow retired employees to be called back for specific projects.

3.2 Meaningful participative leadership for the Economic-Boom Generation

The Economic-Boom Generation has more diverse leadership preferences than the Post-War Generation. As mentioned before, this generation is characterized by idealism and post-materialistic values that also shape its leadership preferences. Members of this generation tend to have less respect for hierarchies and hence prefer a more participative leadership behaviour. When setting goals and incentives, leaders should try to explain the meaningfulness of the tasks. Consequently, supervisors can highlight how the current assignment is embedded in and fits into a broader organisational context.

The Economic-Boom Generation also lacks an intuitive approach to modern communication technologies. Thus, direct communication should play a major role for this generation as well. With regard to communication content, it seems vital that supervisors emphasize this generation's specific strengths, such as the critical questioning of routines, social competencies, and experience-based knowledge.

Leaders should also bear in mind that this generation sometimes faces the double burden of being responsible for their own children as well as for their parents, who are potentially in need of care. Such a double accountability might be balanced by adjusted working hours. The Post-War Generation's performance assessments should be undertaken with an individualistic rather than a collectivistic focus.

3.3 Development-oriented cooperative leadership for the Baby-Boom Generation

Effective leadership of the Baby Boomers is especially relevant since they are the backbone of today's workforce. Based on its socialisation, this generation is used to competition, and is continuously looking for development opportunities in their working life, which their supervisors should provide. Owing to their competiveness, the Baby Boomers are the first generation that might favour a collectivistic performance assessment that compares their performance with that of relevant colleagues.

In addition to their assertiveness, this cohort possesses immense social competencies, especially in group settings, which their supervisors should take into account. Owing to their experience in diverse group settings, this generation could be applied as moderators between generations in teams or in the company as a whole.

The Baby Boomers are comparable to the Economic-Boom Generation regarding their value structure, however, they are often more pragmatic. They likewise follow post-materialistic goals, but also consider ways to successfully implement their ideas. This also affects their motivational disposition at work, which is shaped by intrinsic values as well as personal advancement at work. As stated before, since they are now in their mid-life, this generation's members are often in a stock-taking phase. Supervisors' relevant leadership activities should include showing employees in this transition period opportunities for further development, either in terms of career advancement or expert career perspectives.

As with the previous generations, communication with Baby Boomers should also include personal communication, although electronic media such as email can be used as complementary means of communication without major problems.

The Baby Boomers are also the first generation that will be affected by the extended working life until the age of 67 and beyond. Therefore, this generation should be sensitized that early retirement options, which have often been the norm for preceding generations, will only be the exception in their case.

3.4 Pragmatic goal-oriented leadership for the Golf Generation

The Golf's Generation leadership preferences differ from both the Economic-Boom and Baby-Boom generations. Its members do not primarily aim for self-fulfilment, but follow a more pragmatic and realistic approach to work. Leaders should consider this when setting incentives, which should also include more materialistic goals (e.g., high financial benefits, high status company cars, etc.).

While the Golf Generation prefers a mainly flat hierarchy at work, it is not as consensus oriented as the two preceding generations. Arsenault (2004) maintains that 'brutal honesty' is this generation's trademark, as it favours direct and clear communication (including electronic forms such as email, etc.) as well as transparent goal setting. Career goals are especially relevant as their careers largely play a key role in this peer group's social acceptance.

Additionally, this generation possesses skills to process enormous amounts of information simultaneously, as well as an international orientation, and good language skills – it was, after all, the first generation to grow up in a more globalised environment. All of these factors should be considered for their leadership, and task assignments.

Supervisors have to keep the Golf Generation's comparatively low loyalty to the firm in mind when dealing with them. Job changes, also across borders, are taken for granted by this cohort. Companies should thus provide their top performers with good career perspectives within the company to avoid opportunistic job changes.

Like the Baby Boomers, this generation also prefers a more competitive, collectivistic performance assessment. Owing to their often extrinsically-driven motivation, they like to be assessed by being compared to their colleagues.

3.5 Vision-oriented leadership for the Internet Generation

The Internet Generation prefers the most direct leadership of all five generations due to their limited work and life experience. Members of this generation want their supervisors to set clear goals, and visions. They do not expect participative leadership behaviour, but rather clear rules, and limits that help them become established in working life.

Additionally, members of this generation are always up for new challenges in their working lives. Hence, they can easily complete demanding and challenging tasks. Furthermore, the youngest generation likes to increase its knowledge, and should thus be provided with sufficient learning opportunities at work.

Since this generation is most familiar with modern communication devices, communication via email seems appropriate. However, direct personal communication is still preferred for discussions of long-term visions and goals.

As with the four other generations, supervisors should show appreciation for the Internet Generation's particular strengths, such as their dynamism, innovativeness, and quick perception. Thus, this generation can be expected to successfully deal with dynamic, changing environments, which should be considered when they are assigned tasks.

Similar to the Golf Generation, members of the Internet Generation show relatively low loyalty to their company. It will be the first generation to experience the labour market's shift from a demand to a supplier market (Flato and Rheinbold-Scheible 2008). Therefore, young professionals from this workgroup are a scare resource, and it is especially urgent for companies' future prosperity that they retain the top performers of this age group in their workforce. One way to achieve this is by setting up mentoring programmes that allow them to get to know experienced and successful executives as role models, and also to enable the transfer of the older generations' experience-based knowledge to the newcomers.

Finally, supervisors should also take into account that the Internet Generation's members are in the 'rush hour' of life in which many important decisions are made – also in their private lives –, and they should adjust their leadership behaviour accordingly.

4 Summary and conclusion

This chapter has outlined the specific characteristics of the five different generations currently present in the German workforce and their specific leadership preferences. In order to have both committed and effective employees, and to remain productive in times of demographic change, companies have to develop individualised leadership behaviours for the five different generations.

As recent surveys show, little effort has been undertaken to prepare and adjust leadership behaviour in keeping with the demographic change. For example, a survey of 77 German companies found that only 25% teach their executives how to deal with experienced workers in this time of demographic change (Bruch et al. 2010), and thus instigate at least some kind of individualised leadership in the company. To develop real generational leadership capabilities, and to avoid the stigmatization and potential discrimination of experienced workers, leadership should, of course, be adjusted to suit all five generations.

While individualised leadership behaviour might seem like the answer, it is important to note that some situations in companies might require a more collectivistic, common leadership style, for example, by fostering common group and organisational goals. A recent empirical study, for example, showed that too strong individualised leadership behaviours might diminish group performance (Wu et al. 2010). Nevertheless, generational leadership styles are highly necessary for productivity with the increasing generational diversity in the workforce.

Most companies focus more on hard measures, such as ergonomic adjustments of workplaces or health-management, to address the demographic change, which are easier to implement than changing the company's leadership culture. However, relying solely on these hard measures will not be sufficient in the long run. It is therefore hoped that this chapter will convince many executives to start thinking about adjusting their individual leadership behaviour to the different generations' needs and preferences, and that companies will consider generational leadership a key pillar of their future leadership development.

References

Arsenault, P. M. (2004). Validating generational differences. *The Leadership and Organization Development Journal*, 25, 124-141.

Bertram, H. (2005). Nachhaltige Familienpolitik im europäischen Vergleich. In: P. A. Berger, Kahlert, H. (Eds.), *Chancen für die Neuordnung der Geschlechterverhältnisse* (pp. 203-236). Frankfurt am Main: Campus Verlag.

Bruch, H., Kunze, F., Boehm., S. (2010). *Generationen erfolgreich Führen. Konzepte und Praxiserfahrungen zum Management des demographischen Wandels.* Wiesbaden: Gabler.

Dansereau, F., Alutto, J. A., Nachman, S., Al-Kelabi, S.A., Yammarino, F.J., Newman, J., Naughton, T., Lee, S., Dumas, M., Kim, K., Keller, T (1995). Individualized leadership: A new multiple-level approach. *Leadership Quarterly*, 6, 413-450.

Destatis (2006). *Bevölkerung Deutschlands bis 2050 – 11. Koordinierte Bevölkerungs-vorausberechnung.* Wiesbaden.

Dychtwald, K. (2003). The age wave is coming, *Public Management,* 85, 6-12.

Engle, E. M., & Lord, R. G. (1997). Implicit Theories, Self-Schemas, and Leader-Member Exchange. 40, 988-1010. *Academy of Management Journal.*

Flato, E., & Reinbold-Scheible, S. (2008). *Zukunftsweisendes Personalmanagement: Herausforderung demografischer Wandel: Fachkräfte gewinnen, Talente halten und Erfahrung nutzen.* München: MI Verlag.

Gursoya, D. A., Maier, T. A., Chi, C.G. (2008). Generational differences: An examination of work values and generational gaps in the hospitality workforce. *International Journal of Hospitality Management,* 27, 448-458.

Illies, F. (2000). *Generation Golf. Eine Inspektion.* Freiburg: Herder.

Ilmarinen, J. E. (2001). Aging Workers. *Occupational and Environmental Medicine,* 58, 546-546.

Jurkiewicz C.E., & Brown R.G. (1998). GenXers vs. boomers vs. matures: Generational comparisons of public employee motivation. *Review of Public Personnel Administration,* 18, 18-37.

Kieser, A., & Walgenbach, P. (2007). *Organisation.* Stuttgart: Schaeffer-Poeschel.

Klein, M. (2003). Gibt es die Generation Golf? *Kölner Zeitschrift für Soziologie und Sozialpsychologie,* 55, 1-28.

Kupperschmidt, B. R. (2000). Multigeneration employees: Strategies for effective management. *The Health Care Manager,* 19, 65-76.

Lueschcer, K & Liegle, L. (2003). *Generationsbeziehungen in Familie und Gesellschaft.* Konstanz: UVK Verlagsgesellschaft.

Michaels, E., Handfield-Jones, H, & Axelrod, B. (2001). *The war for talent.* Boston: Harvard Business School Press.

Oertel, J. (2007). *Generationenmanagement im Unternehmen.* Wiesbaden: Gabler.

Preuss-Lausitz, U., Büchner, P, Fischer-Kowalski, M., Dieter Genien, M., Karsten, E., Kulke, C., Rabe-Kleberg, U., Rolff, H.G., Thunemeyer, B., Schütze, Y., Seidl, P., Zeiher, H., Zimmermann, P. (1994). *Kriegskinder, Konsumkinder, Krisenkinder. Zur Sozialisationsgeschichte seit dem zweiten Weltkrieg.* Weinheim: Beltz Verlag.

Schreyoegg, G. (2003). *Organisation. Grundlagen moderner Organisationsgestaltung.* Wiesbaden: Gabler.

Schuler, K. (2006). *Hilflos in der Rush-Hour.* Die Zeit (25.4.2006).

Schuetze, Y., & Geulen, D. (1995). Die Nachkriegskinder und die Konsumkinder: Kindheitsverläufe zweier Generationen. In U. Preuss-Lausitz et al. (Eds.), *Kriegskinder, Konsumkinder, Krisenkinder. Zur Sozialisationsgeschichte seit dem zweiten Weltkrieg (pp. 29-52).* Weinheim: Beltz Verlag.

Taylor, F. W. (1977). *Die Grundsätze wissenschaftlicher Betriebsführung.* Weinheim: Beltz Verlag (Original 1911).

Wu, J. B., Tsui, A. S., Kinicki, A. J. (2010). Consequences of differentiated leadership in groups. *Academy of Management Journal,* 53, 90-106.

Rationale for and implementation of age-neutral HRM in divergent institutional contexts – examples from Britain and Germany

Heike Schroder, Matt Flynn and Michael Muller-Camen[*]

Owing to demographic change as well as international and national pressures, organisations will have to abandon oftentimes prevalent youth-centric HRM practices in favour of age-neutral HRM that is inclusive of the entire workforce, regardless of age. In order to do so, organisations turn to 'best practice' guides. These, however, do not tend to differentiate recommendations by country and/or sector. Based on research in eight case study organisations in the chemical, steel and retail sectors as well as in public schools in Germany and Britain, this chapter argues that the rationale for and the implementation of age-neutral HRM practices differ by national institutional and sectoral context as well as by the relative influence of social partners. Hence, organisations planning to implement age-neutral HRM should take organisational, institutional and sectoral peculiarities into account when doing so.

[*] Heike Schroder, Ph.D. candidate in HRM, Middlesex University (UK).
Dr. Matt Flynn, Senior Lecturer in HRM, Middlesex University (UK).
Prof. Dr. Michael Muller-Camen, Professor of International Human Resource Management, Middlesex University (UK).

S. Kunisch et al. (eds.), *From Grey to Silver*,
DOI 10.1007/978-3-642-15594-9_9, © Springer-Verlag Berlin Heidelberg 2011

Table of Contents

1   Introduction: From youth-centric to age-neutral HRM

Demographic research shows that in most industrialised countries the average age will increase, while the number of labour market entrants will decline. Furthermore, trends towards early retirement have led to the premature and sometimes permanent labour market exit of a large proportion of those aged 50+ (Auer and Fortuny 2000). Based on these trends, economic forecasts not only predict the future non-sustainability of social security and pension systems (OECD 2006), but also a shortage of skilled labour, and the rapid loss of organisational tacit knowledge due to retirement waves (Strack et al. 2008).

Even though implications of the ageing workforce are widely discussed, negative perceptions of and age discrimination towards older workers remain widespread. Consequently, organisations tend to focus their Human Resource Management (HRM) upon younger workers. Such *youth-centric practices* include the direct and indirect discrimination of older workers in recruitment, training, and career development (Wood et al. 2008, McVittie et al. 2003). Furthermore, some countries and/or sectors still display a strong early retirement culture even though state-financed early retirement pathways have largely been abolished (Muller-Camen et al. 2010). In order to mediate the macro- and microeconomic implications of demographic change, national governments have started to adopt measures to reverse early labour market exit trends and to promote the labour market participation of individuals aged 50+ (Taylor 2004). Furthermore, European governments have employed legal pathways through, for example, the transposition of the European Union (EU) 2000 equal treatment directive into national law to abolish age discrimination.

Hence, organisations have to change their youth-centric HRM to an HRM inclusive of the entire workforce, regardless of age. Such *age-neutral HRM* is holistic, inter-generational and life-phase oriented, and has been discussed in academic (Hedge 2008; Armstrong-Stassen 2008) as well as practitioner-oriented (Vickerstaff 2005; Flynn and McNair 2007) literature. Age-neutral practices promote the avoidance of de-qualification through life-long learning; systematic change in positions through job rotation, and job enrichment; health, and safety management; flexible working hours; and age-mixed teams (Flynn and McNair 2007). These measures do not only aim to enable the labour market participation of older employees, but target the employability, productivity, and well-being of the entire workforce throughout the life course (Armstrong-Stassen 2008). Even though this normative and prescriptive literature offers valuable insights to organisations, most 'best practice' guides suggest universal measures regardless of the national and/or sectoral context (for exceptions, see Vickerstaff 2005). Nevertheless, it is suggested that HRM varies according to the cultural and institutional context within which an organisation operates. Hence, cross-national differences result in nationally distinct HRM (Brewster et al. 2008).

This chapter aims to establish whether, how, and why organisational approaches to age-neutral HRM differ between Britain and Germany.[1] The chapter firstly introduces institutional differences between Germany and Britain. The subsequent sections discuss HR challenges with regard to demographic change and the implementation of related solutions in German and British case study organisations. Lastly, the conclusion section evaluates whether and how these solutions differ, and whether these differences emanate from the institutional context.

2 Institutional context and its effect in shaping organisational age management in Germany and Britain

This section elaborates on institutional differences between Germany and Britain with regard to state intervention, pension systems, labour market structure, education and qualification systems, and the influence of employment relations upon the management of an older workforce.

Table 1: Summary of institutional differences between Germany and Britain (Source: own illustration)

Institutional context	Germany	Britain
State intervention	High	Low
Pension systems	Mainly based on state pension	Combination of state, occupational and private pension
Labour market structure	Mainly external labour market structure	Mainly internal labour market structure
Education systems	Knowledge acquisition mainly focused on early life course	Life-long learning approach
Influence of employment relations	Depending on sector, high on sectoral level	Relatively low, but partly influential on workplace level

2.1 State intervention and the design of pension systems

State intervention regarding labour market structure and outcomes is considered stronger in the German 'coordinated market economy' than in the British 'liberal market economy' (Hall and Soskice 2001). The German government has in the past promoted a 'generational exchange' model to account for discrepancies between older employees' qualification and wage levels, and organisational demands for

---

[1] The project 'Age Diversity at the Workplace' was funded by the British Economic and Social Research Council (ESRC), and led by Michael Muller-Camen, and Matt Flynn at Middlesex University Business School. Between November 2007 and May 2009, 116 semi-structured interviews were conducted with industry experts, HR managers, line managers, employee representatives, and workers aged 50+ in eight organisations in the chemical, steel, and retail sectors as well as in public schools in Britain and Germany. The organisations were selected as they were known for championing age-neutral HRM.

qualified and flexible labour (Blossfeld and Stockmann 1999). This was done by promoting and providing older workers with financially attractive early retirement routes. German politics has thus created incentives for organisations to externalise older employees as a socially acceptable measure to shed labour. Even though such pathways have since been closed, this created the perception among employees that early retirement is a legal and enforceable right (Buchholz 2006).

Contrary to this, British governments have followed neo-liberal principles by leaving the adaptation of older workers to economic and occupational changes to the free market, therefore only marginally influencing the labour market situation of older workers. The 2006 anti-age discrimination legislation, based on the EU 2000 equal treatment directive, signifies a first active step by the government. At the same time the government implemented employees' 'right to request' to work past retirement age which employers may grant, but do not need to justify if they refuse. The previous Labour government had promised to abolish mandatory retirement in 2010. Although there may be some delay, the new coalition government has pledged to carry on with the abolition.

The British pension system provides only basic state pensions while emphasising the importance of private and occupational schemes. Therefore, individuals without sufficient pension entitlements have to remain in the labour force until reaching the national retirement age. Financially attractive early retirement pension schemes, as found in Germany, barely exist in Britain (Golsch et al. 2006).

2.2 Labour market structures and education systems

Britain's external labour market allows for relatively unrestricted mobility between occupations, while Germany is characterised by a state-regulated occupation-specific internal labour market that largely hinders such mobility. These are mirrored in the respective education systems. While Britain promotes flexible educational and vocational pathways through which job-specific qualifications may be gained and updated throughout the life course (Golsch et al. 2006), Germany's education system mostly focuses on knowledge and skills acquisition in the early life course. Furthermore, the high occupational standardisation forces individuals in Germany to choose a career early on without many options to change occupations in later life (Buchholz 2006). Older German employees therefore tend to lack up-to-date occupational knowledge and skills due to the absence of life-long-learning opportunities, while their British counterparts can update these skills more regularly – also in later life – and hence better match the qualifications demanded by the labour market (Schroder et al. 2009).

2.3 Influence of employment relations

Moreover, the influence of employment relations on age management varies between Germany and Britain. While employment relations in the German labour market are highly regulated, the British labour movement lost a significant amount of its influence in the Thatcher era (Gall 2005). Also, there is a pronounced difference regarding the involvement of social partners in HRM. While German labour unions influence HRM through collective agreements on the national or sectoral level, British unions are mostly active at the workplace level (Flynn et al. 2010).

The influence of the German employment relations system is evident in the comparatively strong dismissal protection due to collective-agreement-based seniority regulations. However, this creates an insider-outsider labour market structure that protects older employees, but constrains the labour market re-entry of older unemployed individuals. Instead, unemployment in later life has turned into a pathway to early retirement (Buchholz 2006).

Conversely, Britain offers a less pronounced employment protection and therefore facilitates labour market re-entry in case of old-age unemployment (Hofaecker and Pollnerová 2006). In contrast to Germany, employer and occupation changes are more common in Britain, and old age unemployment does not potentially signify a subsequent economic inactivity (Golsch et al. 2006). The strong labour union influence in Germany has furthermore led to the establishment of seniority pay, which increases wage levels relative to age and tenure. This is not the case in Britain. Instead, the OECD (2006, p. 71) finds a decline in average wages among older British workers.

2.4 Summary

In summary, the two institutional contexts provide divergent frameworks for age management. The German system is highly regulated, and has in the past relied on generational change through attractive exit routes to allow for organisational flexibility. The British system has conversely left the management of older workers to free market principles. While German workers received financial incentives to leave the labour force, British workers, if lacking adequate pension provisions, were forced to remain in the labour market for financial reasons. The following sections present and discuss the rationales for and the implementation of age management strategies in four matched pairs of case study organisations in the chemical, steel and retail sectors as well as public schools in Germany and Britain. Each case study organisation received a pseudonym relating to the country and sector, and will be discussed in turn.

3 Implementation of age management strategies in organisations in Germany

3.1 *German Chemical*

The company *German Chemical* has a strong internal labour market, and experienced workforce cuts and recruitment freezes in the 1980s and 1990s. Hence, the age structure is becoming old-age centred. This is a challenge, as the work environment is designed for a young workforce. Also, the increasing average age means that large proportions of the workforce will soon reach retirement age. As *German Chemical* mainly recruits employees at entry level, the retirement-caused employee outflow will lead to a significant loss of skills, and knowledge. *German Chemical* is therefore expecting a future lack of adequately skilled workers to fill this gap. This is intensified as the company assumes a decline in young labour supply.

The recognition of these challenges by *German Chemical's* board of directors, and employee representatives lead to the development of a comprehensive life-phase-oriented age management concept in 2005, which targets workers of all age groups. The aims of the project are to ensure employability until pension age, to create awareness of demographic change, to enhance recruitment activities to attract the best talent available, to ensure competitive productivity despite the increasing average age, and to maintain a sustainable occupational pension scheme.

The age management concept primarily includes the systematic analysis of all HR processes with regard to their effects on older workers, and foresees the implementation of a comprehensive list of policies that will help achieve these aims. Among these policies are strategies to ensure that all employees have up-to-date qualifications through life-long learning, and that knowledge and skills are passed on through knowledge exchange. Furthermore, the company introduced measures that assess the suitability and safety of specific tasks for different age groups. Owing to its early recognition of the challenges posed by demographic change, *German Chemical* was a role model for a collective agreement in the German chemical industry that came into effect in 2008. In summary, *German Chemical* has proactively implemented age management policies that are highly valued by works council and employees, and that, through employment relations, have influenced the entire sector's approach to demographic change.

3.2 *German Steel*

German Steel has a strong internal labour market, and low labour turnover with most employees leaving the company only when retiring. Owing to unfavourable economic conditions, *German Steel* had to reduce its workforce, and did so mainly through early retirement and recruitment freezes. As a consequence, the average age of the workforce is increasing. The company experiences similar challenges than *German Chemical*: an old-age centred workforce, bulk retirement, loss of accumulated knowledge, and a potential skill shortage especially among engineers. A specific challenge is posed by the prevalence of shift work as the company will have problems managing its productivity if the increasing group of older workers cannot do shift work due to health issues.

The approach chosen by *German Steel* resembles the one in *German Chemical*. *German Steel* recognised the potential importance of demographic change in the early 2000s. Reasons for this comparatively early start were the recognition of emerging health and qualification risks among the ageing workforce, the 'best practice' example of a competitor and the results of a research project by a trade union-funded foundation. In 2005, a holistic age management concept comprising five main aims was presented. These aims concern culture and leadership, employer branding and recruitment, human resource development and training, work organisation, working time and pay, as well as health management, ergonomics and absence management. Specific initiatives include awareness-raising courses for middle managers regarding age-related health problems and their prevention. Also, *German Steel* introduced job enlargement to allow employees to change tasks – if necessary – due to health reasons. Similar to the German chemical industry, the German iron and steel industry negotiated a collective agreement with social partners to implement age management sector-wide. The agreement was implemented in 2006 and therefore preceded the chemical sector agreement. *German Steel* acted as a role model for this agreement and supported its implementation.

3.3 German Retail

German Retail's labour turnover varies by occupation, being the highest among front line staff. Front line staff aged 50+, however, seldom resign voluntarily, unless for health reasons, because they fear old-age unemployment. Nevertheless, the age structure remains balanced due to a large group of those aged 35-59. Therefore, demographic change has only had a medium impact on *German Retail* so far. Even so, the management of the company realised the potential effects from demographic change as the older age group who work flexibly, are used as an asset to fill those work shifts which are not popular with younger workers. For similar reasons, employees have for some time been encouraged to work past retirement age. Consequently, the company realised the potential of health management in allowing older workers in physically strenuous front line positions to stay healthy, to reduce absence rates, and to enable employees to stay past retirement age.

The company therefore decided to participate in a research project partly financed by the German Federal Agency for Occupational Health and Safety and conducted by a German research institute. The project was concerned with extending working life in organisations through health management. The company selected several retail shops to participate in the project. Researchers evaluated occupational health measures and suggested recommendations for an old-age-suitable health management and age-neutral HRM. These recommendations covered workplace design and ergonomics, arrangements for and timing of breaks, job design and changes, reduction of work demands and pressures, health promotion through health awareness courses, HR planning and development, and awareness raising of demographic and health issues. This project was well perceived by the works council and staff members. One middle manager who manages one of the pilot retail shops mentioned that the positive outcomes of the project were that employees were increasingly health-conscious, and that the company had been encouraged to invest in equipment to make the workplace healthier. The outcomes of the research projects mostly focused on health management, but also enabled the implementation of more comprehensive age management strategies.

3.4 German School

The *German School* case study, conducted in a German Federal state, covered three comprehensive schools, and their teaching staff. *German School* is affected by demographic change as the average age of the teaching staff has increased over the past decades. The teaching force is therefore old-age centred with increasing cohorts of young teachers entering the workforce. As with *German Chemical* and *German Steel*, this is due to recruitment freezes in the 1980s and early 1990s, and a lack of alternative career options for German teachers. The old-age-centred age structure is already leading to bulk retirement of teachers. The advantage thereof is generational change in the teaching profession, while the consequential disadvantage is the loss of accumulated knowledge. At the same time, many teachers in *German School* leave the profession early, mainly because of health reasons caused by stress and burn-out. The number of early retirements has decreased, though, as state-financed pathways have been abolished. Hence, schools are left to deal with potentially unhealthy teachers until they reach pension age. At the same time, there is a shortage of young teachers. Therefore, the recruitment of young teachers, health management and the knowledge exchange between young and old teachers are a main concern of *German School*.

In 2003, *German School* started to systematically analyse its age structure. The results have been published on an annual basis, and have been discussed in various Federal state bodies. As the management of the teaching staff has been largely de-centralised to head teachers, concerted state-wide strategies are difficult to implement. Nevertheless, *German School* has started to emphasise health management by offering voluntary health as well as stress and time management courses. Furthermore, head teachers and teachers can seek school-level and individual health advice from the state's teacher training institute. Also, the state participated in a research project on health management which was conducted in 16 pilot schools. The project assessed the health and safety risks associated with the profession. In order to decrease stress levels of older teachers, *German School* is currently planning to re-implement an old-age working time reduction for teachers aged 60+ which had been abolished in the past. The re-implementation decision was based on significant pressure from the teacher trade union, and from older teachers. Teachers themselves can decide on their working time arrangements and can hence reduce their teaching load. This is a self-financed measure but it is considered an important option for teachers who cannot cope with job-related stress anymore. Furthermore, *German School* encourages knowledge exchange by offering courses for head teachers on how to pass their knowledge to their successors. On the school-level, there are various practices to support older teachers, though they appear to be mostly reactive once individual (health) problems have occurred. Nevertheless, most head teachers try to reduce older teachers' work load and amount of responsibility when necessary and feasible. In summary, in supporting older teachers, *German School* experiences problems due to the de-centralisation of HRM. Nevertheless, the state and the school level provide support through training, and individualised solutions to problems.

4 Implementation of age management strategies in organisations in Britain

4.1 UK Chemical

UK Chemical is the subsidiary of a US multinational and mainly employs highly qualified research, technical, and management staff. The age structure of the subsidiary is the youngest of all case study organisations with an average age of 38, although managers noted that the average age of most of its divisions outside Europe is even younger. The company maintains a 'grow from within' strategy that focuses on graduate student recruitment. Older candidates can be recruited, though also at entry level, and are not actively sought after. *UK Chemical* has a defined benefit pension scheme that allows employees to retire early on generous terms. Early retirement has in the past been used to avoid redundancies, and apparently employees do not oppose this strategy as they are able to start second careers. Nevertheless, the decreasing availability of young graduates might impact *UK Chemical's* recruitment strategy in future, requiring the company to look towards graduates who had taken career breaks, and who would be slightly older than its usual recruits. This is, however, not likely to change the company's 'grow from within' strategy. *UK Chemical* is therefore not yet experiencing change pressures due to demographic change.

The introduction of the 2006 anti-age discrimination legislation, however, lead to a review of all HR policies. According to the HR manager, only few processes had to be adapted. Nevertheless, the company's occupational pension scheme was thought to need revising. This is because currently only few employees work past retirement age. If more employees take advantage of their legally instated 'right to request' to work past retirement age, the current scheme might no longer be viable. In order to facilitate the retirement process and knowledge exchange *UK Chemical* introduced a phased retirement option through part-time work prior to full retirement. Also, the company offers flexible working time options to all its employees. Older workers therefore have various options to reduce stress and/or working time. Generally, the company did not offer any specific age-related HR practices, but was concerned about diversity management and equal opportunities for all their staff. Employees felt that there was no age-related discrimination as all employees have equal access to training and career opportunities if they wish to apply, and if their performance justifies the promotion.

4.2 UK Steel

UK Steel is the only major organisation in its sector in Britain. The workforce was decreased by 80% over the last decades in response to market forces and globalisation. This was mainly done through redundancy and early retirement schemes. Employees can retire on a comfortable pension at age 55 and tend to do so. *UK Steel* is strongly unionised, and the trade union is involved in HRM at the work site level. Similar to *German Steel*, demographic change is affecting *UK Steel*, particularly as it has a strong internal labour market. Over the past two decades, *UK Steel* has managed job attrition with recruitment freezes, resulting in an older workforce. In future, labour shortages may necessitate incentives for workers to stay in employment after the age of 55. In the short term, the company expected to face skill shortages in engineering, and programmes were in place to recruit graduates in this field.

Nevertheless, there are currently no programmes specifically targeting older workers. Overall, the company maintains an early retirement culture which is supported by both managers and the trade union. Early retirement was regarded as the 'least painful' approach to job attrition at a time when major job cuts are proposed.

4.3 UK Retail

UK Retail is one of the largest retail organisations in Britain. The company strives to employ a workforce that matches its local customer base. Hence, diversity management, and especially gender diversity, plays a prominent role. However, this increasingly includes age management as the customer base is ageing due to demographic change. Furthermore, the company found that widening the recruitment pool to older candidates helps to decrease turnover, and to attract more suitable candidates. This is because the retail sector is not perceived as an employer of choice. Also, similar to the German case, older workers might be more flexible when required to work evening shifts. Consequently, the workforce of *UK Retail* is relatively age-mixed.

Although the 2006 age discrimination law did not lead to many policy changes, it has drawn attention to the issue of age management. As a consequence, the company monitors its age structure, and introduced a compulsory workshop for middle managers focusing on managing an older workforce. It informs managers about the 2006 age regulations, and aims to raise awareness of and discuss stereotypes related to age. Besides this, the organisation offers further age management tools such as the option to draw the company pension while still working, multi-skilling that facilitates job changes, pre-retirement training, and adjustments to the work environment such as orthopaedic chairs. Overall, the company's age management policies seem primarily driven by recruitment demands and business objectives. The company sees the older workforce as an untapped resource for talent in a high turnover industry.

4.4 UK School

UK School is based on three comprehensive schools in a British local authority (LA). Major challenges are retention management and demographic change. As a large proportion of young teachers either leaves the LA due to high housing prices, or leaves the profession due to the combination of low pay and high stress, *UK School* has a U-shaped age structure, lacking a medium-aged cohort. As older teachers will retire in bulk over the next ten years, *UK School* is hence concerned about skill shortage and succession planning. Furthermore, teachers tend to retire early: the occupational pension which becomes available at age 60 acts as an incentive to do so. In the past, there were additional policies in the pension system to allow for early retirement either through long service or incapacity, although these have been largely restricted. Nevertheless, some teachers request to stay past retirement which is granted if this fits the school's strategy. This is because HR decisions are made on the school level. The LA only acts as an intermediary that checks HR decisions against national guidelines and offers legal advice.

Consequently, after the 2006 age regulations, the LA evaluated school-level HR processes for age discrimination and offered model policies that are conform to the law. As retention management is a national challenge, the national government introduced measures, and incentives – mostly monetary – to increase recruitment numbers, and to encourage teachers to stay in the profession. Furthermore, the government facilitated access to the profession. However, the government did not introduce measures in support of older teachers. On the contrary, early exit pathways were closed or access made more difficult. Contrary to the German case, however, British teachers can theoretically leave the profession and change occupations also in later life due to transferable skills and due to a pension scheme that can be transferred to other private or public sector employers. Meanwhile, individual schools are left to deal with the repercussions of demographic change, and those older teachers who decide to remain in the teaching force. As head teachers are in charge of HRM, approaches to dealing with older teachers vary between schools. Some schools support older teachers with regard to training, flexible working time arrangements, and working past retirement age while others display a more restrictive behaviour towards older teachers, and towards requests to work past retirement age. Hence, school-level decisions were mainly based on business rationales and on head teachers' perceptions of (their) older teachers.

5   Conclusion

All the case study organisations discussed were more or less affected by demographic change. The largest effect was evident in those organisations that already have an old-age-centred age structure, have a strong internal labour market, currently do not plan organisational restructuring, and do not have significant occupational pension schemes. This was the case at *German Chemical, German Steel, German School, UK School* and, to some extent, at *German Retail*. Consequently, these organisations have been the ones with the greatest need to implement age management strategies. Nevertheless, the most substantive strategies appear to have been implemented in *German Chemical* and *German Steel*.

The study therefore established that the national institutional context shapes organisations' HR strategies towards their ageing workforce. While the lack of early retirement schemes and pressures from social partners forced *German Steel* and *German Chemical* to pursue extensive age-neutral HRM, *UK Chemical* and *UK Steel* had more scope to design their HR strategies due to the British free market context. Nevertheless, the examples of the school and retail organisations show that sectoral peculiarities play a significant role as well. Both *UK Retail* and *German Retail* showed similar business rationales and hence similar strategies towards their

Table 2: Summary of age management strategies and respective implementation pressures (Source: own illustration)

Organisation	Germany	Britain
Chemical	▓ Introduction of holistic age-neutral HRM due to skill shortage ▓ Pressures based on organisational, institutional and industrial relations environment	▓ No (old) age-specific HRM strategy, but general diversity management ▓ No institutional and/or industrial relations pressures
Steel	▓ Introduction of holistic age-neutral HRM due to health management and skill shortage ▓ Pressures based on organisational, institutional and industrial relations environment	▓ Maintenance of generous early retirement scheme ▓ No institutional pressures to postpone retirement timing ▓ Only moderate industrial relations pressures on workplace level, mainly to maintain early retirement scheme
Retail	▓ Introduction of age-neutral HRM due to organisational health management concerns relating to retention and absence management, and flexibility. ▓ Pressures mainly based on organisational business objectives ▓ No pressures from institutional and/ or industrial relations environment	▓ Introduction of age-neutral strategy based on diversity management, recruitment, retention and health management ▓ Pressures mainly based on organisational business objectives ▓ No pressures from institutional and/ or industrial relations environment
School	▓ Introduction of age-neutral policies based on health management and skill shortage ▓ Further age-neutral practices at the school level ▓ Based on institutional and industrial relations pressures	▓ Introduction of age-neutral strategy based on health management, skill shortage and succession planning ▓ Age management strategy mainly de-centralised to school level ▓ Implementation thereof within discretion of head teacher based on business rationales ▓ No pressures from institutional and/ or industrial relations environment

older staff. A mixed case is presented by the school case studies. Both *UK School* and *German School* reported similar challenges and solutions. Still, *German School* was bound to the German internal labour market with a lack of alternative career and dismissal options and was therefore responsible for maintaining teachers' productivity and employability. Contrary to this, *UK School* could draw on free market principles as teachers could (theoretically) be dismissed and had the opportunity to change professions also in later life due to life-long-learning opportunities.

Organisations' approaches to demographic change thus vary depending on the institutional context and on the sector in which they operate. In addition, as shown in two German case studies, social partners may influence the rationale, motivation, and design of age-neutral HRM. Hence, it is suggested that organisations willing to implement age-neutral HRM do not solely rely on existing universal 'best practice' literature and recommendations, but establish their approaches according to institutional and sectoral peculiarities. Nevertheless, universal 'best practices' might provide adequate starting points, but should be evaluated for their applicability and usefulness in the organisation-specific context.

References

Armstrong-Stassen, M. (2008). Organisational practices and the post-retirement employment experience of older workers. *Human Resource Management Journal,* 18(1), 36-53.

Auer, P. & Fortuny, M. (2000). Ageing of the labour force in OECD countries: economic and social consequences. *Employment Paper.* Geneva: International Labor Organization.

Blossfeld, H.-P. & Stockmann, R. (1999). The German dual system in comparative perspective. *International Journal of Sociology,* 28(4), 3-28.

Brewster, C., Wood, G. & Brooks, M. (2008). Similarity, isomorphism or duality? Recent survey evidence on the Human Resource Management policies of multinational corporations. *British Journal of Management,* 19(4), 320-342.

Buchholz, S. (2006). Men's late careers and career exits in West Germany. In H.-P. Blossfeld, S. Buchholz & D. Hofäcker (Eds.), *Globalization, uncertainty and late careers in society* (p. 55-78). London: Routledge.

Flynn, M. & McNair, S. (2007). Managing age – A guide to good employment practice. London: Chartered Institute of Personnel Development (CIPD) and Trade Union Congress (TUC).

Flynn, M., Upchurch, M., Muller-Camen, M. & Schroder, H. (2010). Trade union responses to aging workforces: The cases of the UK and Germany. *submitted for review to Industrial Relations,* 1-33.

Gall, G. (2005). The first five years of Britain's third statutory union recognition procedure. *Industrial Law Journal,* 34(4), 345-348.

Golsch, K., Haardt, D. & Jenkins, S. P. (2006). Late careers and career exits in Britain. H.-P. Blossfeld, S. Buchholz & D. Hofäcker (Eds.), *Globalization, uncertainty and late careers in society* (p. 183-210). London: Routledge.

Hall, P. A. & Soskice, D. (2001). Varieties of capitalism: the foundation of comparative advantage. Oxford: Oxford University Press.

Hedge, J. W. (2008). Strategic Human Resource Management and the older worker. *Journal of Workplace Behavioral Health,* 23(1/2), 109-123.

Hofaecker, D. & Pollnerová, S. (2006). Late careers and career exits. An international comparison of trends and institutional background patterns. H.-P. Blossfeld, S. Buchholz & D. Hofäcker (Eds.), *Globalization, uncertainty and late careers in society* (p. 25-54). London: Routledge.

McVittie, C., McKinlay, A. & Widdicombe, S. (2003). Committed to (un)equal opportunities?: "New ageism" and the older worker. *British Journal of Social Psychology,* 42(4), 595-612.

Muller-Camen, M., Croucher, R., Flynn, M. & Schroder, H. (2010). National institutions and employers' age management practices in Britain and Germany: 'Path dependence' and option creation. *Human Relations,* forthcoming.

OECD (2006). Ageing and employment policies: Live longer, work longer. Paris: OECD.

Schroder, H., Hofäcker, D. & Muller-Camen, M. (2009). HRM and the employment of older workers: Germany and Britain compared. *International Journal of Human Resources Development and Management,* 9(2/3), 162-179.

Strack, R., Baier, J. & Fahlander, A. (2008). Managing demographic risk. *Harvard Business Review,* 86(2), 119-128.

Taylor, P. (2004). Age and work: International perspectives. *Social Policy & Society,* 3(2), 163-170.

Vickerstaff, S. A. (2005). Managing the older workforce. *Equal Opportunities Review,* 137, 6-10.

Wood, G., Wilkinson, A. & Harcourt, M. (2008). Age discrimination and working life: Perspectives and contestations – A review of the contemporary literature. *International Journal of Management Reviews,* 10, 425-442.

From grey to silver –
More than a question of age

Eva Bilhuber Galli[*]

Delusions and reality

For companies, the implications of an ageing workforce are multiple and complex. They must consider these challenges, and must quickly find responses to them. In fact, they have started doing so. Many companies have realised that ageing is not necessarily a process towards less productivity. Many older employees have significant experience and know-how in their jobs. However, the challenge for companies is how to effectively unlock and utilise this experience. Many such corporate *silver* and *50+* initiatives exist. These range from flexible retirement models to integration workshops, and they seek to transfer know-how and experience from senior employees to their younger colleagues.

But do these age-related measures really help unlock the potentials of senior employees? Age-related human resource (HR) measures all assume that age is a sufficient category to describe the needs, behaviours, and thinking of a cohort of employees. My personal observations and perceptions lead me to question this assumption. It seems that age is not a good descriptor of what people need, how they behave, and what they think.

Age does not indicate communalities

Elderly employees have very diverse backgrounds. A 50-year-old mechanic and a 50-year-old head of product development may not have much in common besides their age, and the fact that they work for the same company. The heterogeneity of biographies reaches a peak in the middle of the lifecycle. Thus, chronological age and certain biographical experiences can be decreasingly related. Instead, what drives our thinking, activities, and needs is based on our individual life experiences. Thus, chronological age might not represent a homogeneous group of needs. On the contrary, to only use age as the basis for any initiative might fail to address senior employees' diversity of experienced-based and lifestyle-driven needs.

[*] Dr. Eva Bilhuber Galli, management consultant and executive coach, human facts ag.

S. Kunisch et al. (eds.), *From Grey to Silver*,
DOI 10.1007/978-3-642-15594-9_10, © Springer-Verlag Berlin Heidelberg 2011

Age is not what employees want to be recognized for

To categorise employees according to their age with the label *50+* or *silver* might be obvious but superficial. It disregards their heterogeneous needs, behaviours, and experiences. Furthermore, it runs the risk of creating exactly the kind of stigma that senior employees actually seek to avoid. Employees do not want to be recognised as senior due to their age, but due to their distinct experiences, know-how, and performance. An HR manager recently told me that she only experienced resistance from senior employees at the mention of designing 50+ initiatives. It seems that employees do not want to be labelled according to a demographic category that they cannot influence. It seems that they prefer categories they have some say over, i.e. that relate to roles, lifestyles, or performance.

Age is not the ultimate driver of (un)productiveness

Many senior employees have valuable experience and broad know-how. They are open to learning, show interest in new developments, and constantly share and grow their know-how. On the other hand, many senior employees do not develop their know-how, are stubborn, block discussion (with phrases like "we always did it like this"), and are averse to new developments and changes. It seems that age is not a good discriminating factor to categorize employees, as we find these opposing behaviours within one cohort.

A question of learning attitude

If age itself is not a useful category, what could be a better descriptor? In short, learning attitude. People with an attitude of life-long learning accumulate experience and know-how. They are also able to distinguish between what they know and what they do not know, can describe it, and are willing to and capable of sharing it. They display curiosity towards new developments and seek opportunities to grow their wisdom and personalities. They continually integrate new knowledge into their existing knowledge base. They often engage in dialogue with others because they know the value of interactions with others in shaping new insights. In the process, they obtain a deeper level of self-reflection, which is the basis for externalising know-how.

The ageing workforce can therefore be of great value to a company, but only if they are able and willing to engage in these behaviours. Consequently, companies' age management challenge is located in their employees' learning attitude; these attitudes must be addressed regardless of age.

The need for a holistic organisational learning approach

Consequently, corporate age management may start by implementing measures that focus on older employees and build the necessary awareness of differences. However, one should strive for integration, rather than separation. In order to effectively and sustainably deal with the challenge of an ageing workforce, companies should support the life-long learning attitude in everything it does, at every level. At a cultural level, this implies encouraging learning from mistakes, rewarding a learning attitude, and management living a learning attitude. At an individual level, this might imply supporting learning experiences on the job and constantly investing in education and coaching, irrespective of age. Paradoxically, effective age management might imply not talking about age as a differentiator, but valuing different experiences, know-how, backgrounds, and opinions.

If this argument holds true, distinctly age-related management initiatives might be pointless or even counterproductive. By cultivating a learning attitude throughout the organisation and among all employees (irrespective of their age), differences become a source of learning and must be embraced if performance is to be achieved. In such an environment, elderly as well as young employees will welcome one another's differences, and not due to their age differences, but due to their different experiences, know-how, and perspectives.

Age diversity and its performance implications – Analysing a major future workforce trend

Stephan A. Boehm, Miriam K. Baumgaertner, David J. G. Dwertmann, Florian Kunze[*]

Demographic change, increased retirement age, and efforts to shorten the duration of education will lead to a more age-diverse workforce in future. Age diversity's successful management will therefore become an important business issue for company practitioners. Unfortunately, knowledge concerning the outcomes of diversity in general and age diversity in particular lacks consistency. On the basis of the similarity-attraction paradigm, social identity and self-categorisation theory, token status, and inequality, some scholars argue that diversity has negative effects. On the basis of the information/decision-making perspective, other scholars predict that diversity has positive outcomes.

In order to shed light on these conflicting findings, this chapter discusses and analyses the age diversity literature. Consequently, it investigates prior research on the possible moderators and mediators of the age diversity-performance relationship. Following this review, this chapter provides practical recommendations on how to deal with an age-diverse workforce.

[*] Dr. Stephan A. Boehm, Senior Lecturer and Director of the Center for Disability and Integration at the University of St. Gallen, Switzerland.

Miriam K. Baumgaertner, Research Associate and Ph.D. candidate at the Center for Disability and Integration at the University of St. Gallen, Switzerland.

David J. G. Dwertmann, Research Associate and Ph.D. candidate at the Center for Disability and Integration at the University of St. Gallen, Switzerland.

Dr. Florian Kunze, Senior Research Fellow at the Institute for Leadership and Human Resources Management of the University of St. Gallen, Switzerland.

S. Kunisch et al. (eds.), *From Grey to Silver*,
DOI 10.1007/978-3-642-15594-9_11, © Springer-Verlag Berlin Heidelberg 2011

Table of Contents

1   Introduction

Effective management of *diversity* is a critical success factor for companies and will become even more important in future. This not only applies to diversity dimensions such as gender, ethnicity, and nationality, but also to age diversity (Smola and Sutton 2002; Shore et al. 2009). Despite several recent reviews (e.g., van Knippenberg and Schippers 2007; Jackson et al. 2003; Williams and O'Reilly 1998) and meta-analytical analyses of diversity's effects in the workplace (e.g., Joshi and Rho 2009), there is no systematic knowledge on age diversity's potential outcomes in organisational settings.

This seems problematic for a number of reasons. Firstly, *age* is becoming one of the most relevant diversity dimensions. Triggered by demographic change, age diversity in the workplace is increasing more strongly than other diversity dimensions such as gender and nationality. Secondly, companies currently have only a vague idea of how the increase in age diversity will impact their internal processes and states, including their employees' well-being, commitment, and performance. Compared to other diversity dimensions, handling of an age-diverse personnel is a rather new challenge for companies. Consequently, it is not yet an established component of corporate training and development initiatives.

This chapter aims at closing this relevant knowledge gap by providing scholars and practitioners with insights into age diversity's distinct effects and recommendations on how to handle an age-diverse workforce successfully.

2   Increasing age diversity: A major workforce trend

2.1   Reasons for growing age diversity in the workplace

Demographic change is a major workforce trend. However, employees are not only ageing (a mean increase), the variation in age between co-workers is also on the rise (a variance increase).

This growing age diversity is caused by multiple influences. Firstly, the demographic change and the resulting shift in the workforce's distribution will lead to further diversity. To date, most companies in Western Europe have tended to hire mainly young employees. In 2001, more than 50% of German companies had no employees older than 50 (Bellmann and Kistle 2003). In 2006, more than one third of the small and medium-sized companies (SMEs) had not yet employed any older people (Watt 2006). In contrast, older employees have often been offered early retirement. Thus, the age distribution of the employees does not follow a normal distribution. Instead, employees' age distribution is skewed to the right, resulting in a comparatively low mean or average age. Owing to relatively low birth rates, there will be a lack of young employees over the next decades. Therefore, companies will be forced to hire or retain older employees in their workforce (Dychtwald et al. 2004; Tempestet al. 2002), which will lead to more diversity.

Secondly, the increasing number of retired people is starting to be a heavy financial burden on social welfare systems (Hayashi et al. 2009). The ratio between taxes paid and pensions received is shifting, since life expectancy is increasing, and people are receiving pensions for a longer time. This can be balanced out in part if people work for longer and, consequently, pay more taxes. Therefore, to cope with the effects of demographic change, governments have started raising retirement age (e.g., in Germany and Austria). Increased retirement age, which is in fact an extension of the workforce's age range, results in a higher variance and thus diversity.

Thirdly, governments not only try to lengthen the duration of working time at the higher end but also at the lower one. In Europe, for example, university degrees have changed. Countries have started adopting the Anglo-Saxon bachelor and master system. By doing so, they hope to shorten the duration of academic studies (Kaube 2008). In Germany, the high school diploma was shortened by one year as well. Therefore, people can start working earlier than before. Again, this extension of the age range within the workforce increases the age diversity.

2.2 Implications for organisations

All three influences (the demographic change, the extension of older workers' retirement age, and the shortening of young people's education time) will cause an increasing age diversity within the workforce. While these basic trends are equally valid for most Western European countries, Germany is facing particular challenges due to the demographic change. Figure 1 shows the German workforce's projected development until 2050.

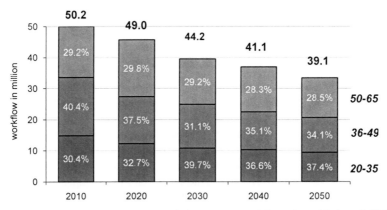

Figure 1: Projected development of the German workforce from 2010 until 2050 (Source: Destatis 2006).

Two major tendencies have become obvious. On the one hand, the overall workforce is continually shrinking from approximately 50 million individuals in 2010 to projected 40 million in 2050. This is different in Switzerland, for example, where the workforce is expected to remain stable over the next 40 years. On the other hand, the group of older employees (aged 50-65) is going to become the largest subgroup within the German workforce. This will be the start of a growing trend towards a greater number of old workers in firms and organisations and hence a growing overall age diversity within the workplace. This second tendency is also affecting Switzerland and other European countries with higher birth or migration rates.

To date, organisations seem to be ill-prepared for an increase in age diversity. They only have a vague idea of the emerging potential challenges and opportunities, and have not yet taken measures regarding age diversity's active management in the workplace (e.g., Goerges 2004; Saba et al. 1998; Shore et al. 2009). This might be due to increased age diversity seeming to have mixed outcomes.

3 Theoretical basis of diversity effects

3.1 Reasons for potentially negative diversity effects

There is an ongoing debate on the effects of diversity in general as well as age diversity in particular. This debate is based on different psychological theories on social interaction processes. Various theories imply that diversity has negative effects. Among these are the similarity-attraction paradigm (Byrne 1971), social identity (Tajfel and Turner 1986), self-categorisation (Turner 1987), token status (Kanter 1977; Young and James 2001), as well as inequality (Blau 1977) theories.

The similarity-attraction paradigm assumes that individuals prefer to interact with others who are similar to them (Byrne 1971). The assumption of similarity can be drawn from various attributes such as demographics (e.g., age, gender, and ethnicity), attitudes, opinions, and beliefs. The psychological rationale for this assumption is that people seem to obtain more affirmative feedback from people who are similar to them, which in turn reduces uncertainty (Hinds et al. 2000; Rand and Wexley 1975). Diversity's similar negative effects might also be based on the social identity (Tajfel and Turner 1986) and self-categorisation (Turner 1987) theories. Both theories state that people form certain in and out-groups based on personally relevant attributes. Again, these attributes may comprise demographics, attitudes, opinions, and beliefs. Groups to which the individual belongs (in-groups) will be perceived as superior to other groups (out-groups). This is due to a basic human need to strengthen one's self-esteem (Hogg and Abrams 1988; Hogg 2001). Consequently, individuals favour members of their in-group, which results in higher levels of trust, cooperation, and communication. Out-group members are seen in a more sceptical light, which could lead to stereotyping and discrimination (Brewer 1979; Brewer and Brown 1998; O'Reilly et al. 1989). In short, 'otherness' is perceived as a deficiency (Loden and Rosener 1991).

In addition, Kanter (1977) describes 'token status'. Based on her assumptions, minorities (usually less than 15% of the total group) are less represented as individuals but rather as members or symbols of their category (Young and James 2001). With regard to age diversity, an example would be a small group of older employees in a primarily young organisation, or vice versa. In a software firm, for example, older members among a predominantly young group might not be perceived as equal colleagues with individual strengths and weaknesses, but rather as members of the same group who all tend to miss a few relevant competencies and attitudes. The consequences of such a token status include stereotyping, unfair performance pressure, and the formation of interpersonal boundaries – which all lead to diversity having negative outcomes.

Finally, the concept of inequality (Blau 1977; Blau and Blau 1982; Blau 1986), which stems from sociological literature, is another model assuming that diversity has negative implications. It focuses on the distribution of goods, mainly income. However, especially in the organisational psychology literature, attention has also been paid to other resources such as power, status, and prestige (Harrison and Klein 2007). Nevertheless, research on inequality is generally limited (Harrison and Klein 2007). Inequality means that relevant resources are allocated unequally across group members. The resulting different levels of power or influence can lead to negative outcomes such as communication problems or intra-group conflicts (Smith et al. 1994). Keltner and colleagues (2003, p. 277) conclude that powerful members in teams *"talk more, interrupt others more, are more likely to speak out of turn, and are more directive of others' verbal contributions than are low power individuals"*.

3.2 Reasons for potentially positive diversity effects

Contrary to prior rationales, scholars also argue in favour of positive diversity effects. This assumption is based on the *information/decision-making perspective* (van Knippenberg and Schippers 2007, p. 518; Hoffman et al. 1962), which emphasises the greater information richness in diverse surroundings. This richness, which focuses on cognitive resources, may be based on a variety of demographic attributes like age, gender, and ethnicity, which foster different experiences and knowledge bases. In addition, individuals with different backgrounds may have productive external and internal networks, leading to complementing information (Austin 2003; Beckman and Haunschild 2002). This information richness is assumed to be especially rewarding when dealing with non-routine problems (Carpenter 2002) and when striving for creative solutions (Burt 2002; Jackson et al. 1995). Moreover, groupthink (Janis 1972) might be successfully prevented as heterogeneous groups tend to discuss problem solutions in more detail and with more divergent perspectives (Fiol 1994).

4   Summary of knowledge on age diversity

4.1 Outcomes of age diversity

The diversity research field is characterised by different theoretical perspectives predicting diversity's either positive or negative results. These theoretical arguments have also been applied to predict age diversity's outcomes or effects (see Table 1 for an overview). On the one hand, individuals are likely to develop stronger personal ties with employees who are more or less the same age, since they *"share comparable experiences and therefore develop like attitudes and beliefs"* (Lawrence 1988, p. 313). With employees of different age groups, such personal connections are likely to be less pronounced, paving the way for the social identity processes (Tajfel and Turner 1986) and self-categorisation (Turner 1987) described above. Such a formation of age-related in and out-groups may, in turn, lead to more conflicts between employees of different age groups and to heightened levels of strain, conflict, and perceived discrimination within age heterogeneous workgroups and organisations (Kunze et al. 2010).

Table 1: Overview of age diversity outcomes (source: own illustration)

Outcomes	Description	Study
Team performance in working teams	▨ Negative relationship between age diversity and performance in working teams	Wegge et al. 2008 Timmerman 2000 Ely 2004 Leonard et al. 2004
Team performance in top management teams	▨ Positive relationship between age diversity and performance in top management teams	Kilduff et al. 2000
	▨ No relationship between age diversity and performance in top management teams	Bunderson and Sutcliffe 2002 Simons et al. 1999
	▨ Negative relationship between age diversity and performance in top management teams	West et al. 1999
Cognitive diversity	▨ Negative relationship between age diversity and cognitive diversity	Kilduff et al. 2000
Turnover	▨ Positive relationship between age diversity and turnover	Cummings et al. 1993 Jackson et al. 1991 Milliken and Martins 1996 O'Reilly et al. 1989 Wiersema and Bird 1993
	▨ Employees who differ most from the rest of their working group are those most likely to turn over	O'Reilly et al. 1989 Wagner et al. 1984
	▨ Not diversity but isolation from co-workers and customers is associated with increased turnover	Leonard and Levine 2006
Absenteeism	▨ Positive relationship between age diversity and absenteeism	Cummings et al. 1993
Innovation	▨ No relationship between age diversity and innovation	Bantel and Jackson 1989 O'Reilly et al. 1993 O'Reilly et al. 1997 Wiersema and Bantel 1992
	▨ Negative relationship between age diversity and innovation	Zajac et al. 1991
Conflict	▨ Positive relationship between age diversity and emotional conflict	Jehn et al.1997
	▨ No relationship between age diversity and task conflict	Pelled et al. 1999 Pelled et al. 2001
	▨ Negative relationship between age diversity and affective conflict	Pelled 1993 Pelled et al. 1999
Communication	▨ Negative relationship between age diversity and professional communication	Zenger and Lawrence 1989

On the other hand, drawing on the information/decision-making perspective, one could also expect age dissimilar groups to have positive outcomes, with different perspectives, experiences, and information leading to a broader knowledge base and, consequently, to more creative, innovative, and productive team processes. However, which theoretical positions are supported by empirical studies' findings?

Various potential outcome variables have been investigated in respect of age diversity, including team performance, cognitive diversity, turnover, innovation, and group processes such as conflict and communication. They have revealed an unclear pattern.

Team performance

Empirical studies' findings on age diversity's performance consequences are not consistent. There is no strong evidence for age diversity's effects on performance (Williams and O'Reilly 1998). Primarily, the positive expectations drawn from the information/decision-making perspective were not supported by empirical investigations. In contrast, most studies reveal a negative relationship between age diversity and performance (Wegge et al. 2008). Timmerman (2000) showed age diversity to be negatively related to performance in professional basketball teams. Ely (2004) reported similar results in a sample of 486 branches of a financial service company. Furthermore, Leonard and colleagues (2004) reported that, in a sample of 700 retail stores, age heterogeneity had similar negative effects on sales figures.

However, focusing on top management teams solely, Kilduff and colleagues (2000) found age heterogeneity to be the only demographic diversity measure to positively affect overall performance. In their experimental study, diversity in a top management team had significantly positive effects on organisational performance. Nonetheless, even top management team research is characterised by mixed findings. For example, Bunderson and Sutcliffe (2002) as well as Simons and colleagues (1999) found no link between age diversity and performance. Furthermore, West and colleagues' longitudinal study (1999) of 42 UK manufacturing organisations showed that age diversity in top management teams is a negative predictor of company performance.

Cognitive diversity

Kilduff and colleagues (2000) examined the relationship between demographic and cognitive diversity, testing whether age diversity predicts cognitive diversity. Contrary to their expectations, the authors found that age diverse teams are not more cognitively diverse even though they perform better. The authors conclude that *"the link between demographic and cognitive diversity may be more complex than generally assumed (...)"* (Kilduff et al. 2000, p. 22). They further argue that *"Age diversity does matter, but not because it predicts cognitive diversity. Teams heterogeneous on demographic variables may be better able to build on the diverse experience base of the team to validate diverse cognitions, and thus take advantage of innovative suggestions"* (p. 32).

Turnover

Most studies investigating the relationship between age diversity and turnover found a positive association between the two constructs, meaning that higher age diversity typically leads to higher turnover among employees (e.g., Jackson et al. 1991; O'Reilly et al. 1989; Wiersema and Bird 1993). Furthermore, Wagner and colleagues (1984) showed that the employees who differ most from the rest of their working group are most likely to turn over. This was confirmed by O'Reilly and colleagues (1989). Milliken and Martins (1996, p. 408) state that: *"Not surprisingly, the people who are different from their group members in terms of age are more likely to turn over"*. In addition, Cummings and colleagues (1993) discovered that, in addition to turnover, absenteeism is more likely for those who differ most from their group in terms of age. However, these findings are not supported by Tsui and colleagues' (1992) study. Moreover, Leonard and Levine (2006) found that, not diversity, but isolation from co-workers and customers was often associated with increased turnover.

Innovation

Most studies found age diversity and innovation to be uncorrelated. Bantel and Jackson (1989) tested two conflicting hypotheses on the association between age heterogeneity and innovativeness among top management team members. They concluded that age diversity predicted neither total, technical, nor administrative innovation. Other studies by Wiersema and Bantel (1992), O'Reilly et al. (1997) as well as by O'Reilly and colleagues (1993) also found no association between age diversity and innovation. Zajac and colleagues (1991) investigated innovation across 53 internal corporate joint ventures among physicians. They found age diversity to be negatively related to innovativeness.

Conflict

As described earlier, social categorisation (Tajfel 1974; Tajfel and Turner 1986) may lead to stereotyping and subgroup formation that may produce conflict as well as less cooperation. There are mixed results concerning the relationship between age diversity and conflict. Generally, research differentiates between task-related/ substantive and emotion-based/affective conflict (Pelled 1996; Pelled et al. 2001; Pelled et al. 1999). Compared to task-related conflict, emotion-based conflict is assumed to affect performance less favourably (Dos Reis et al. 2007). Contrary to her hypothesis, Pelled (1993) found age diversity to be negatively related to affective conflict. Pelled and colleagues (1999) found no association between age diversity and task conflict, and a negative link between the former and emotional conflict. Task routineness and group longevity moderated these relationships. Hambrick (1994) explained the rationale behind the relationship between age heterogeneity and less emotional conflict. Since age is related to career, people compare themselves with individuals of a similar age. Accordingly, rivalry is more likely to occur between employees of the same age (e.g., Hambrick 1994). These findings indicate that *"any tendency for age differences to trigger emotional conflict appears to be overshadowed by the tendency for age similarity to trigger social comparison and, ultimately, emotional conflict"* (Pelled et al. 1999, p. 21).

However, other studies found opposing results: Jehn and colleagues (1997), for example, found age diversity to be positively related to relationship conflict. In line with these findings, Pelled and colleagues (2001) found individual dissimilarity in age to be positively associated with emotional conflict in a Mexican employee sample. Consequently, culture may also be a moderator in the age diversity-conflict relationship.

Communication

With regard to communication, Zenger and Lawrence (1989) investigated the relationship between organisational demography and communication frequency. They found age diversity to be a negative determinant of professional communication in technical project groups.

4.2 Explanations for inconsistencies in findings

In general, reasons for these inconsistent results can be subsumed under one of three categories: (1) diversity's different *outcome measures,* (2) diversity's different *conceptualisations,* and (3) diversity's *context factors.* The first category refers to the diverse measurement outcomes. It seems logical that age diversity's effects may vary according to the outcome variable targeted in a study (e.g., team performance versus turnover) or might even be influenced by the same outcome variable's operationalisation (e.g., self-rated, peer-rated or objective performance). The previous section focused on this topic by summarising research on various outcome measures. The other two categories are explained in the following section.

When researching age diversity, the construct conceptualisation should determine its measurement. Harrison and Klein (2007) argue that failure to do so leads to ambiguous empirical findings. They describe three distinctive types of diversity, namely separation, variety, and disparity. In turn, these types of diversity may have different consequences. Firstly, separation represents differences in opinion such as opposing views and disagreement. There is separation if individuals differ in terms of attitudes or values. Secondly, variety refers to differences in knowledge and experiences among group members, resulting in an increased pool of information on which a group can draw. The third type of diversity, which is called disparity, describes *"differences in concentration of valued social assets or resources such as pay and status among unit members"* (Harrison and Klein 2007, p. 1200). These findings are also consistent with the third section of this chapter's propositions. Processes, such as similarity attraction, self-categorisation, and token status are typically attributed to separation; inequality is attributed to disparity (both with negative effects), and the information/decision-making perspective corresponds to variety (with diversity having positive effects on potential outcomes).

The third aspect contributing to the mixed empirical results on age diversity relates to the phenomenon of opening the *"black box of organizational demography"* (Lawrence 1997, p. 1; Pelled et al. 1999). Researchers have largely focused on the direct effects between demographic characteristics and outcome variables, without paying too much attention to the intervening factors. In recent studies, the need to develop more complex theories and undertake research on the moderating variables that may explain diversity effects has become apparent (e.g., Van Knippenberg and Schippers 2007). Thus, considering aspects like the working context or the importance of social interaction should be the main effort when studying diversity. Shore and colleagues (2009) state, for example, that *"older employees are likely to have knowledge and experience that is useful within groups, but such human capital may only be utilized in an environment in which positive relations among members are conducive to appreciating different types of contributions"* (p. 121).

4.3 Diversity context factors

An overview of the context factors influencing the relationship between age diversity and performance is presented in Table 2.

Table 2: Overview of age diversity context factors (source: own illustration).

Context factor	Description	Study
Cooperation and teamwork	▪ Higher levels of cooperation lead to performance losses ▪ Lower levels of cooperation and teamwork lead to performance gains or no relationship	Ely 2004
Task complexity	▪ Diverse groups perform complex tasks better than homogeneous ones (but not routine tasks)	Bowers et al. 2000 Wegge et al. 2008
Leadership	▪ The better the leader-member exchange relationship, the weaker the diversity-turnover relationship	Nishii and Mayer 2009
	▪ Age diversity is negatively related to team performance when transformational leadership is low but not related to team performance when transformational leadership is high	Kearney and Gebert 2009
	▪ Transformational leadership is a positive context factor for the relationship between age diversity and performance	Kunze and Bruch 2010
Faultlines	▪ Certain combinations of different dimensions lead to more negative diversity effects	Bezrukova et al. 2009 Homan et al. 2008 Lau and Murninghan 1998 Lau and Murninghan 2005 Migdal et al. 1998

Team processes: Cooperation and teamwork

Ely (2004) investigated 486 retail bank branches and found team processes to be a significant moderator in the relationship between age diversity and performance. Contrary to her expectations, she discovered that cooperation and teamwork have a counterintuitive effect on performance losses, whereas lower levels of cooperation and teamwork were related to either performance gains or no relationship between diversity and performance. High cooperation and teamwork were associated with a negative relationship between age diversity and the attainment of goals set regarding revenue from new sales and total performance. Ely (2004) concluded that *"[m]anagers should take from this research a degree of caution in the way they address differences. While one would be hard pressed to suggest that enabling teamwork and cooperation is not a worthy goal in any team, managers should take care that such processes do not inadvertently suppress differences from which the workgroup could otherwise benefit"* (p. 777). The results of this study indicate that the complexity of team processes has not yet been comprehensively understood.

Task complexity

In their meta-analysis, Bowers and colleagues (2000) showed that diverse groups only performed complex tasks better than homogeneous ones. A recent study by Wegge and colleagues (2008) confirmed this boundary condition in a European sample of the public administration sector by showing that age diversity is positively correlated with performance in complex task, but not in routine ones. The authors could also replicate this finding a year later. They explained their line of reasoning by proposing that *"task complexity (defined in terms of strong demands for complex decision making) is critical for obtaining a positive relationship between age composition in teams and team performance. That is, in complex group decision-making tasks, older workers may have the knowledge (and time) to help younger workers, thereby facilitating each group member's individual work. In contrast, when the group task is routine and does not benefit from knowledge sharing, there should be no advantage for age diversity"* (Wegge et al. 2008, p. 1303).

Leadership

The successful development of a team in general and of a diverse team in particular is a leadership challenge. Thus, one may think that leaders' influence on diverse teams' outcomes is well researched. However, little is known about leadership's role in the relationship between age diversity and performance. To our knowledge, only three studies have examined leadership as a boundary condition of age diversity effects. Nishii and Mayer (2009) examined leader-member exchange as a moderator of the relationships between demographic (i.e. race, age, and gender) and tenure diversity, and group turnover. The authors showed that leaders can have a positive impact on group diversity's effect on turnover. The better the relationship between leaders and subordinates, the weaker the diversity-turnover relationship.

Kearney and Gebert (2009) discovered that age diversity was not related to team performance when transformational leadership was high, but negatively related to team performance when transformational leadership was low. The authors conclude that *"transformational leadership could be a key factor in fostering performance and preventing process losses in diverse teams"* (Kearney and Gebert 2009, p. 88).

Furthermore, Kunze and Bruch (2010) researched the effects of the relationship between age-based faultlines (e.g., faultlines that foster sub-group formation of age in alignment with other demographic characteristics) and transformational leadership on productive energy. Transformational leadership was once again identified as a positive moderator of the relationship between age diversity and team outcome. Consequently, the authors conclude that transformational leadership may enable productivity and performance increases in teams with strong age-based faultlines.

Interaction of age with other demographic characteristics

A more recent stream of reasoning follows the idea that diversity processes may not occur as a result of a single demographic attribute, but as consequence of a bundle of demographic characteristics (Bezrukova et al. 2009; Lau and Murnighan 2005). *"Diversity research needs to move beyond conceptualizations and operationalizations of diversity simply as dispersion on a single dimension of diversity. Rather, it should conceptualize diversity as a combination of different dimensions of differentiation, take asymmetries into account, and be open to nonlinear effects"* (van Knippenberg and Schippers 2007, p. 534).

In this vein, the faultlines concept has recently been the focus of research attention. This concept, introduced by Lau and Murninghan (1998), describes hypothetical dividing lines within teams. These faultlines are based on visible attributes such as demographics. The authors describe faultlines as *"an alignment of several characteristics that heightens the possibility of internal subgroup dynamics"* (Lau and Murninghan 1998, p. 327). For example, in a team of four members, Case 1 is the team consisting of two 60-year-old men, and two 25-year-old women. Case 2 is the team consisting of one 60-year-old man, and one 60-year-old woman, and one 25-year-old man, and one 25-year-old woman. It is not difficult to imagine that the team in Case 1 is potentially divided by a stronger faultline than the team in Case 2. The combination of age and gender in Case 1 may easily lead to the formation of two opposing subgroups ('old men' versus 'young women') within the team. In Case 2, on the other hand, while the level of diversity is the same, the potential for the formation of such in and out-groups is much smaller as age and gender are distributed equally.

In most cases, the literature has found faultlines to be negative for team outcomes, which is in line with Lau and Murninghan's (1998) proposition that faultlines reflect a group's potential to split into subgroups, leading to less positive interaction and conflict. The authors state *"that strong faultlines may lead to recurring and salient subgroups, which then may become a more likely basis for self-identity and social categorization"* (Lau and Murninghan 1998, p. 336). Homan and colleagues (2008) mention two main reasons for faultlines' negative effects. Firstly, cross-cutting categories make social categorisation more complex leading to a decreased probability to differentiate between in and out-group. Secondly, if employees belong to multiple groups at the same time, perceptions of subgroup differences and categorisations decrease. In line with these arguments, in their meta-analysis, Migdal and colleagues (1998) showed that intergroup bias is reduced when diversity attributes diverge which, in turn, reduces conflict.

5 Practical implications and recommendations

The presented research findings have several practical implications for companies on the organisational and supervisor levels. An overview is presented in Table 3.

Table 3: Overview of practical implications (source: own illustration).

Level	Action to be taken	Description & Examples
Organisational level	Deliberate team composition	■ Age diverse teams for complex, non-routine tasks ■ Avoiding faultlines ■ Younger employees learn from older ones and vice versa ■ Mentoring and knowledge management ■ Setting up heterogeneous teams with a clear business objective (facilitating inter-generational knowledge-transfer, capturing new markets, developing innovative products, etc.) and communicating it
Organisational level	Diversity trainings (age awareness seminars)	■ Age awareness seminars
Supervisor level	Transformational leadership	■ Creating a common social identity ■ Acting as an appropriate role model ■ Fostering the acceptance of common goals ■ Identifying and articulating a clear vision for the future ■ Setting high performance expectations ■ Providing individualised support ■ Providing intellectual stimulation for follower
Supervisor level	Enhanced interaction	■ Assigning tasks to a whole team ■ Architectural considerations ■ 'Off-site' activities

5.1 Organisational level

Deliberate team composition

The teams' composition within organisations determines whether age diversity has positive or negative effects (Bruch et al. 2010). Organisations can group their employees in age homogeneous teams, age heterogeneous teams or even randomly. While 'preventing' diversity's possible negative effects by forming age homogeneous teams, organisations also miss out on the chance of younger employees learning from their older and more experienced colleagues, and vice versa. Especially in challenging work environments, effective mentoring and knowledge management can be crucial success factors (Allen et al. 2006; Grover and Davenport 2001). However, as prior research outlined in the fourth part of this chapter indicates, the formation of age diverse teams runs some risks.

These risks, namely discrimination (Goldman et al. 2006; Kunze et al. 2010) and decreased communication, can dramatically increase, if organisations do not consider certain aspects. Firstly, companies should set up age heterogeneous teams with a clear business objective and also communicate these ideas to the team members. Among such objectives might be the facilitation of inter-generational knowledge transfer, the capturing of new markets (e.g., silver markets with more mature consumers), and the development of innovative products that call for the competencies of the different age groups within an organisation. In all of these cases, the reason for being in an age-heterogeneous team becomes very obvious for the team members, and they know that their particular skills and experiences are equally needed and valued. The formation of age-related in and out-groups is very unlikely when inter-generational cooperation is one of the team's key targets.

Secondly, companies should strive to form age-heterogeneous teams, especially to fulfil non-routine tasks. As described above, Bowers and colleagues (2000) showed that complex tasks are more suited for age-diverse teams as they can exert their special skills, and competencies.

Thirdly, as described in the previous section, organisations should be aware of potential faultlines in age-heterogeneous teams. In practice, management and HR should take care that age heterogeneity does not coincide with other variables such as gender, nationality, and functional background. In such cases, it is likely that in and out-groups will form, thereby triggering conflict and reduced levels of cooperation.

Diversity trainings

An often neglected aspect of diversity implications in general and age diversity implications in particular is that people in organisations are unaware of the opportunities and pitfalls (Kunze et al. 2010). Therefore, an important step in managing an age-diverse workforce is to raise awareness of the issue (Kunze and Bruch 2010). This holds true for all employees, especially supervisors. As will be outlined in the next section, supervisors can make a meaningful contribution to the prevention of discrimination, and the facilitation of interaction among subordinates. One way to sensitise both employees and supervisors is through special age awareness seminars (Armstrong-Stassen and Templer 2005; Rynes and Rosen 1995).

5.2 Supervisor level

Transformational leadership

Discrimination within teams, resulting from diversity (i.e. faultlines), can be prevented by creating a common identity among team members (Bezrukova et al. 2009). One way to do so is by enhancing the unit attachment and team cohesiveness through the use of transformational leadership (House and Shamir 1993; Jung and Sosik 2002). Bass (1985) created a transformational leader construct, namely someone who can, according to Antonakis and colleagues (2003), act *"proactive, raise follower awareness for transcendent collective interests, and help followers to achieve extraordinary goals"*. According to Podsakoff and colleagues (1996), transformational leadership comprises a combination of six key behaviours, namely: (1) acting as an appropriate role model, (2) fostering the acceptance of common goals, (3) identifying and articulating a clear vision for the future, (4) setting high performance expectations, (5) providing individualised support and (6) intellectual stimulation for followers. By following these guidelines, leaders can create a new predominant social identity (team membership). Hereby, team members perceive each other as in-group members, regardless of their demographic attributes such as age.

Transformational leadership's general positive effects on performance were confirmed in meta-analytic studies by Lowe and colleagues (1996), and Patterson and colleagues (1995). More interestingly for the purpose of this chapter, Kearney and Gebert (2009) as well as Kunze and Bruch (2010) have recently discovered that transformational leadership has positive effects on the relationship between age diversity and performance.

Enhanced interaction

Another way of supporting the formation of a common identity is by enhancing the interaction between team members (Gaertner and Dovidio 2000). In addition to interaction's positive effects on group performance (Chatman and Spataro 2005; Wageman 1995), the resulting common identity can prevent discrimination (Pettigrew 1998).

Supervisors can facilitate the interaction between group members in multiple ways. Firstly, tasks can be assigned to the whole team or groups instead of individuals. Secondly, architectural considerations can improve contact. Open team offices, shared coffee corners, and group work rooms can make a substantial contribution (Bruch et al. 2010). Thirdly, so-called 'off-site' activities can improve team spirit. Outdoor-training events are a well-known example. These outdoor team activities may serve especially well in age diverse teams since older employees tend to prefer experience and behaviour-based forms of learning (Bruch et al. 2010).

6   Conclusion

The future workforce will be increasingly age diverse. This shift in the workforce composition will have a strong influence on organisational and workgroup diversity. However, the outcomes of this change are less clear. On the one hand, different theories predict that age diversity can have either positive or negative effects. On the other hand, many scientific studies do not explicitly address which processes are expected to take place and why.

Therefore, empirical findings are also mixed. Scholars have only recently started taking contextual factors and boundary conditions into account. Previous research found some results to be more stable than others (e.g., the positive effects of diversity in complex task situations). Based on a diversity research review, practical recommendations are also offered in this chapter. By being aware of the possible risks and opportunities resulting from age diversity, practitioners can take action on different organisational levels to improve their company's efficiency, which should lead to a strategic advantage in future.

References

Allen, T. D., Eby, L. T., & Lentz, E. (2006). The relationship between formal mentoring program characteristics and perceived program effectiveness. *Personnel Psychology*, 59(1), 125-153.

Antonakis, J., Avolio, B.J., & Sivasubramaniam, N. (2003). Context and leadership: An examination of nine-factor full-range leadership theory using the Multifactor Leadership Questionnaire (MLQ Form 5X). *Leadership Quarterly*, 14(3), 261-295.

Armstrong-Stassen, M., & Templer, A. (2005). Adapting training for older employees: The Canadian response to an aging workforce. *Journal of Management Development*, 24(1), 57-67.

Austin, M.P. (2003). Antenatal screening and early intervention for "perinatal" distess, depression and anxiety: where to from here? *Arch Womens Ment Health*, 7(1), 1-6.

Bantel, K., & Jackson, S. (1989). Top management and innovation in banking: does the composition of the team make a difference?. *Strategic Management Journal*, 10, 107-124.

Bass, B.M. (1985). *Leadership and performance beyond expectations*. New York: Free Press.

Beckman, C.M., & Haunschild, P.R. (2002). Network learning: The effects of heterogeneity of partners' experience on corporate acquisitions. *Administrative Science Quarterly*, 47(1), 92-124.

Bellman, E. & Kistler, W. J. (2003). Betriebliche Sicht- und Verhaltensweisen gegenüber aelteren Arbeitnehmern. *Aus Politik und Zeitgeschichte*, 20, 26-34.

Bezrukova,K., Jehn, K.A., Zanutto, E.L., & Thatcher, S.M.B. (2009). Do workgroup faultiness help or hurt? A moderated model of faultiness, team identification, and group performance. *Organization Science*, 20(1), 35-50.

Blau, F. (1977). *Equal pay in the office lexington*. Mass.: D.C. Heath.

Blau, P.M. (1986). *Exchange and power in social life*. New York: Wiley.

Blau, J.R. & Blau, P.M. (1982). The cost of inequality: Metropolitan structure and violent crime. *American Sociological Review*, 47(1), 114-129.

Brewer, M.B. (1979). In-group bias in the minimal intergroup situation: A cognitive-motivational analysis. *Psychological Bulletin*, 86(2), 307-324.

Brewer, M.B., & Brown, R.J. (1998). *Intergroup relations. The handbook of social psychology*. Boston: McGraw-Hill.

Bruch, H., Kunze, F., & Boehm, S. (2010). *Generationen erfolgreich führen: Konzepte und Praxiserfahrung zum Management des demographischen Wandels*. Wiesbaden: GWV Fachverlage GmbH.

Bunderson, J.S., & Sutcliffe, K.M. (2002). Comparing alternative conceptualizations of functional diversity in management teams: Process and performance effects. *Academy of Management Journal*, 45(5), 875-893.

Burt, R.S. (2002). Bridge decay. *Social Networks*, 24(4), 333-363.

Byrne, D. (1971). *The attraction paradigm*. New York: Academic Press.

Carpenter, S.R. (2002). Ecological futures: Building an ecology of the long now. *Ecology*, 83(8), 2069-2083.

Chatman, J.A., & Spataro, S.E. (2005). Using self-categorization theory to understand relational demography-based variations in people's responsiveness to organizational culture. *Academy of Management Journal*, 48(2), 321-331.

Cummings, A., Zhou, J., & Oldham, G. (1993). *Demographic differences and employee work outcomes: Effects on multiple comparison groups*. Paper presented at the annual meeting of the Academy of Management, Atlanta, GA.

Destatis. 2006. *Bevölkerung Deutschlands bis 2050 – 11. Koordinierte Bevölkerungsvorausberechnung.* Wiesbaden.

Dos Reis, C.R.D.A., Castillo, M.Á.S., & Dobón, S.R. (2007). *Diversity and business performance: 50 years of research.* Heidelberg: Springer.

Dychtwald, K., Erickson, T., & Morison, B. (2004). It's time to retire retirement. *Harvard Business Review, 82,* 48-57.

Ely, R.J. (2004). A field study of group diversity, participation in diversity education programs and performance. *Journal of Organizational Behavior,* 25(6), 755-780.

Fiol, C. M. (1994). Consensus, diversity, and learning in organizations. *Organization Science,* 5(3), 403-420.

Gaertner, S.L., & Dovidio, J.F. (2000). *Reducing intergroup bias: The common ingroup identity model.* Philadelphia: Psychology Press.

Grover, V., & Davenport, T.H. (2001). General perspective on knowledge management: Forstering a research agenda. *Journal of Management Information System,* 18(1), 5-21.

Goldman, B.M., Gutek, B.A., Stein, J.H., & Lewis, K. (2006). Employment discrimination in organizations: Antecedents and consequences. *Journal of Management,* 32(6), 786-830.

Görges, M. (2004). *Gesellschaftliche Alterung als Herausforderung für betriebliche Arbeitsmärkte.* Münster: Universität Münster.

Hambrick, D.C. (1994). Top management groups: A conceptual integration and reconsideration of the 'team' label. In B. M. Staw & L. L. Cummings (Eds), *Research in organizational behavior* (pp. 171-213). Greenwich, CT: JAI Press.

Harrison, D.A., & Klein, K.J. (2007). What's the difference? Diversity constructs as separation, variety, or disparity in organizations. *Academy of Management Review,* 32(4), 1199-1228.

Hayashi, C., Olkkonen, H., Sikken, B.J., & Jermo, J. (2009). Transforming pensions and healthcare: Opportunities and collaborative strategies. Mercer perspectives.http://www.mercer.com/attachment.dyn?idContent=1355455&filePath=%2fattachments%2fEnglish%2f02664-RE_WEF_Perspective_PW.pdf&fileType=DB&siteLanguage=100. Accessed 14 June 2010.

Hinds, P.J., Carley, K.M., Krackhardt, D., & Wholey, D. (2000). Choosing work group members: Balancing similarity, competence, and familiarity. *Organizational Behavior and Human Decision Processes,* 81(2), 226-251.

Hoffman, L.R., Harburg, E., & Maier, N.R.F. (1962). Differences and disagreement as factors in creative group problem solving. *The Journal of Abnormal and Social Psychology,* 64(3), 206-214.

Hogg, M.A. (2001). A social identity theory of leadership. *Personality & Social Psychology Review,* 5(3), 184-200.

Hogg, M.A., and Abrams, D. (1988). *Social identifications: A social psychology of intergroup relations and group processes.* London and New York: Routledge.

Homan, A.C., Hollenbeck, J.R., Humphrey, S.E., Van Knippenberg, D., Ilgen, R.D., & Van Kleef, G.A. (2008). Facing differences with an open mind: Openness to experience, salience of intragroup differences, and performance of diverse work groups. *Academy of Management Journal,* 51(6), 1204-1222.

House, R., & Shamir, B. (1993). Toward the integration of transformational charismatic and visionary theories. In M. M. Chemers & R. Ayman (Eds.), *Leadership theory and research: Perspectives and directions* (pp. 167-188). San Diego: Academic Press.

Jackson, S.E., Brett, J.F., Sessa, V.I., Cooper, D.M., Julin, J.A., & Peyronnin, K. (1991). Some differences make a difference – individual dissimilarity and group heterogeneity as correlates of recruitment, promotions, and turnover. *Journal of Applied Psychology,* 76(5), 675-689.

Jackson, S.E., Joshi, A., & Erhardt, N.L. (2003). Recent research on team and organizational diversity: SWOT analysis and implications. *Journal of Management*, 29(6), 810-830.

Jackson, S.E., May, K.E., & Whitney, K. (1995). Understanding the dynamics of diversity in decision-making teams. In R. A. Guzzo & E. Sales (Eds.), *Team decision-making effectiveness in organizations* (pp. 204-261). San Francisco: Jossey-Bass.

Janis, I.L. (1972). *Victims of groupthink: A psychological study of foreign-policy decisions and fiascoes*. Boston: Houghton Mifflin.

Jehn, K.A., Chadwick, C., & Thatcher, S.M.B. (1997). To agree or not to agree: the effects of value congruence, individual demographic dissimilarity, and conflict on workgroups outcomes. *International Journal of Conflict Management*, 8(4), 287-305.

Jung, D.I., & Sosik, J.J. (2002). Transformational leadership in work groups. *Small Group Research*, 33(3), 313-336.

Kanter, R.M. (1977). *Men and woman of the corporation*. New York: Basic Books.

Kaube, J. (2008). Schneller am Markt? Frankfurter Allgemeine Zeitung. http://www.faz.net/ s/RubC3FFBF288EDC421F93E22EFA74003C4D/ Doc~E1D95D73DFD714F029496E13A338C03D6~ATpl~Ecommon~Scontent.html. Accessed 14 June 2010.

Kearney, E., & Gebert, D. (2009). Managing diversity and enhancing team outcomes: The promise of transformational leadership. *Journal of Applied Psychology*, 94(1), 77-89.

Keltner, D., Gruenfeld, D.H., & Anderson, C. (2003). Power, approach, and inhibition. *Psychological Review*, 110(2), 265-284.

Kilduff, M., Angelmar, R., Mehra, A. (2000). Top management team-diversity and firm performance: examining the role of cognitions. *Organization Science*, 11(1), 21-34.

Kunze, F., Boehm, S., & Bruch, H. (2010). Age diversity, age discrimination climate, and performance consequences – A cross-organizational study. *Journal of Organizational Behavior*, 31(6), 1-30.

Kunze, F., & Bruch, H. (2010). Age-based faultiness and perceived productive energy: The moderation of transformational leadership. *Small Group Research*, 41(4), 1-27.

Lau, D.C., & Murninghan, J.K. (1998). Demographic diversity and faultiness: The compositional dynamics of organizational groups. *Academy of Management Review*, 23(2), 325-340.

Lau, D.C., & Murnighan, J.K. (2005). Interactions within groups and subgroups: The effects of demographic faultiness. *Academy of Management Journal*, 47(4), 645-659.

Lawrence, B.S. (1996). Organizational age norms: Why is it so hard to know one when you see one? *The Gerontologist*, 36(2): 209-220.

Lawrence, B.S. (1997). The black box of organizational demography. *Organization Science*, 8(1), 1-22.

Leonard, J., & Levine, D. (2006). The effect of diversity on turnover: a large case study. *Industrial & Labor Relations Review*, 59(4), 547-572.

Leonard, J. S., Levine, D. I., & Joshi, A. (2004). Do birds of a feather shop together? The effects on performance of employees' similarity with one another and with customers. *Journal of Organizational Behavior*, 25(6), 731-754.

Loden, M., & Rosener, J.B. (1991). *Workforce America: Managing employee diversity as a vital resource*. Homewood, IL: Business One Irwin.

Lowe, K.B., Kroeck, K.G., & Sivasubramaniam, N. (1996). Effectiveness correlates of transformational and transactional leadership: A meta-analytic review of the MLQ literature. *Leadership Quarterly*, 7(3), 385-425.

Migdal, M., Hewstone, M., & Mullen, B. (1998). The effects of crossed categorization in intergroup evaluations: A meta-analysis. *British Journal of Social Psychology*, 37(3), 303-324.

Milliken, F.J., & Martins, L.L. (1996). Searching for common threads: understanding the multiple effects of diversity in organizational groups. *Academy of Management Review*, 21(2), 402-433.

Nishii, L.H., & Mayer, D.M. (2009). Do inclusive leaders help to reduce turnover in diverse groups? The moderating role of leader-member exchange in the diversity to turnover relationship. *Journal of Applied Psychology*, 94(6), 1412-1426.

O'Reilly, C.A., Caldwell, D.F., & Barnett, W.P. (1989). Work group demography, social integration, and turnover. *Administrative Science Quarterly*, 34(1), 21-37.

O'Reilly, C.A., Snyder, R., & Boothe, J. (1993). Effects of executive team demography on organizational change. In G. Huber & W. Glick (Eds.), *Organizational change and redesign* (pp. 147-175). New York: Oxford University Press.

O'Reilly, C.A., Williams, K.Y., & Barsade, S. (1997). Group demography and innovation: Does diversity help? In E. Mannix & M. Neale (Eds.), *Research in the management of groups and teams* (pp. 183-207). Greenwich, CT: JAI Press.

Patterson, C., Fuller, J.B., Kester, K., & Stringer, D.Y. (1995). *A meta-analytic examination of leadership style and selected compliance outcomes*. Paper presented to the Society for Industrial and Organizational Psychology, Orlando, FL.

Pelled, L.H. (1993). *Work group diversity and its consequences: The role of substantive and affective conflict*. Stanford, CA: Doctoral Dissertation, Stanford University.

Pelled, L.H. (1996). Demografic diversity, conflict, and work group outcomes: An intervening process theory. *Organization Science*, 7(6), 615-631.

Pelled, L.H., Eisenhardt, K.M., & Xin, K.R. (1999). Exploring the black box: An analysis of work group diversity, conflict, and performance. *Administrative Science Quarterly*, 44(1), 1-28.

Pelled, L.H., Xin, K.R., & Weiss, A.M. (2001). No es como mí: relational demography and conflict in a Mexican production facility. *Journal of Occupational and Organizational Psychology*, 74(1), 63-84.

Pettigrew, T.F. (1998). Intergroup contact theory. *Annual Review of Psychology*, 49(1), 65-85.

Podsakoff, P.M., MacKenzie, S.B., & Bommer, W.H. (1996). Transformational leader behaviors and substitutes for leadership as determinants of employee satisfaction, commitment, trust, and organizational citizenship behaviors. *Journal of Management*, 22(2), 259-298.

Rand, T.M., & Wexley, K.N. (1975). A demonstration of the Byrne similarity hypothesis in simulated employment interviews. *Psychological Reports*, 36, 535-544.

Rynes, S., & Rosen, B. (1995). A field survey of factors affecting the adoption and perceived success of diversity training. *Personnel Psychology*, 48(2), 247-270.

Saba, T., Guerin, G., & Wils, T. (1998). Managing older professionals in public agencies in Quebec. *Public Productivity & Management Review*, 22(1), 15-34.

Shore, L.M., Chung-Herrera, B.G., Dean, M.A., Erhart, K.H., Jung, D.I., Randel, A.E., & Singh, G. (2009). Diversity in organizations: Where are we now and where are we going? *Human Resource Management Review*, 19(2), 117-133.

Simons, T., Pelled, L.H., & Smith, K.A. (1999). Making use of difference: Diversity, debate, and decision comprehensiveness in top management teams. *Academy of Management Journal*, 42(6), 662-673.

Smith, K. G., Smith, K. A., Olian, J. D., Sims Jr, H. P., O'Bannon, D. P., & Scully, J. A. (1994). Top management team demography and process: The role of social integration and communication. *Administrative Science Quarterly*, 39(3), 412-438.

Smola, K.W. & Sutton, C.D. (2002). Generational differences: revisiting generational work values for the new millennium. *Journal of Organizational Behavior*, 23(4), 363-382.

Tajfel, H. (1974). Social identity and intergroup behavior. *Social Science Information*, 13(2), 65-93.

Tajfel, H., & Turner, J.C. (1986). The social identity theory of intergroup conflict. In S. Wochel & W.G. Austin (Eds.), *Psychology of intergroup relations* (pp. 7-24). Chicago: Nelson-Hall.

Tempest, S., Barnatt, C., & Coupland, C. (2002). Grey advantage – new strategies for the old. *Long Range Planning*, 35, 475-492.

Timmerman, T.A. (2000). Racial diversity, age diversity, interdependence and team performance. *Small Group Research*, 31(5), 592-606.

Tsui, A., Egan, T., & O'Reilly, C. (1992). Being different: relational demography and organizational attachment. *Administrative Science Quarterly*, 29(4), 897-901.

Turner, M.G. (1987). Spatial simulation of landscape changes in Georgia: A comparison of 3 transition models. *Landscape Ecology*, 1(1), 29-36.

Van Knippenberg, D.L., & Schippers, M.C. (2007). Work group diversity. *Annual Review of Psychology*, 58, 515-541.

Wageman, R. (1995). Interdependence of group effectiveness. *Administrative Science Quarterly*, 40(1), 145-180.

Wagner, G.W., Pfeffer, J., & O'Reilly, C.A. (1984). Organizational demography and turnover in top-management groups. *Administrative Science Quarterly*, 29(1), 74-92.

Wegge, J., Roth, C., Neubach, B., Schmidt, K.H., & Kanfer, R. (2008). Age and gender diversity as determinants of performance and health in a public organization: The role of task complexity and group size. *Journal of Applied Psychology*, 93(6), 1301-1313.

West, M., Patterson, M., Dawson, J., & Nickell, S. (1999). *The effectiveness of top management groups in manufacturing organizations*. CEP Discussion Paper No. 0436. London, England: Centre for Economic Performance, London School of Economics.

Wiersema, M.F., & Bantel, K.A. (1992). Top management team demography and corporate strategic change. *Academy of Management Journal*, 35(1), 91-121.

Wiersema, M.F., & Bird, A. (1993). Organizational demography in Japanese firms – group heterogeneity, individual dissimilarity, and top management team turnover. *Academy of Management Journal*, 36(5), 996-1025.

Williams, K., & O'Reilly, C. (1998). Demography and diversity in organizations: A review of 40 years of research. *Research in Organizational Behavior*, 20, 77-140.

Young, J.L., & James, E.H. (2001). Token majority: The work attitudes of the male flight attendants. *Sex Roles*, 45, 299-319.

Zajac, E., Golden, B., & Shortell, S. (1991). New organizational forms for enhancing innovation: The case of internal corporate joint ventures. *Management Science*, 37(2), 170-184.

Zenger, T.R., & Lawrence, B.S. (1989). Organizational demography: The differential effects of age and tenure distributions on technical communication. *Academy of Management Journal*, 32(2), 353-376.

Stepping down but not out – Characteristics of post-executive careers in Switzerland

Peder Greve, Winfried Ruigrok[*][1]

This chapter sheds light on retirement behaviour in the executive labour market segment, presenting characteristics and trends in the market for executives' post-career activities and employing Switzerland as a case in point. The observations are based on a dataset comprising the 104 executives who retired from top management positions at 50 of the largest publicly listed Swiss companies and left the executive labour market between 2006 and 2008. The findings show that there is an emerging market for post-executive activities in Switzerland, and that the type, intensity, and location of activities pursued in the post-executive labour market are related to the demographic characteristics and career profiles of retiring executives.

[*] Dr. Peder Greve, Research Fellow at the Research Institute for International Management at the University of St. Gallen.
Prof. Winfried Ruigrok, Ph.D., is a professor of International Management and the Academic Director of the MBA programme at the University of St. Gallen, Switzerland.

[1] Acknowledgements: We thank Ksenia Kozhukovskaya for contributing to this chapter by sharing data collected for her master thesis at the University of St. Gallen.

S. Kunisch et al. (eds.), *From Grey to Silver*,
DOI 10.1007/978-3-642-15594-9_12, © Springer-Verlag Berlin Heidelberg 2011

Table of Contents

1   Introduction

A key current policy concern in developed economies is how to deal with the stagnant labour market participation of older individuals in a highly skilled work-force. Switzerland is a typical case in point. Highly skilled individuals retire early in Switzerland, both by international standards and relative to lower-skilled workers in Switzerland (Buetler et al. 2005). These concerns are further exacerbated by de-clining birth rates and increasing life expectancy.

At the same time, according to the 'Survey of Health, Ageing and Retirement in Europe' (SHARE), Switzerland has an exceptionally high activity rate among retirees. This is potentially related to the low retirement age of the highly skilled. For motivated, highly experienced, and well-educated individuals, the transition to formal retirement does not necessarily imply a sudden withdrawal from market or non-market work. Many highly skilled workers remain economically active after having reached the end of their primary career by participating in post-career activ-ities of various types and intensities (Kim and Feldman 2000). Indeed, the range and quality of post-retirement opportunities are likely to critically influence the decision to retire from the highly skilled segment of the labour market. For highly skilled and highly experienced individuals, the set of possible post-career activities include positions as a non-executive director (*Verwaltungsrat*), as an internal or external consultant, or as a manager at a non-profit organisation.[2]

Whereas extensive knowledge exists on the antecedents and consequences of top managers' human and social capital (for reviews, see, e.g., Carpenter et al. 2004; Certo et al. 2006; Hambrick 2007), little is yet known about the extent to which retir-ing top managers' experience, skills, and networks continue to be utilised following retirement from the *executive labour market*. By actively participating in market and non-market activities, former executives, senior managers, and other high-level pro-fessionals can exploit the potential of their specialist knowledge, vast experience, and valuable networks for a number of years following retirement. *Post-executive activities* enable companies and other organisations to effectively utilise the full eco-nomic value of top managers' accumulated human and social capital beyond their primary careers.

This chapter outlines the characteristics of *post-executive careers* and examines the possible determinants of different post-executive career paths and activity levels. Firstly, the chapter provides an overview of the factors that inform the deci-sion to retire from the executive labour market and enter the market for post-career activities. Secondly, it outlines the role of human and social capital as potential determinants of the type, intensity, and location of post-executive activities. Thirdly, this chapter provides an overview of the prevalent characteristics of post-executive careers in Switzerland based on data from the period 2006-2008. Finally, emerging trends are discussed, followed by a brief review of some of the key oppor-tunities and challenges for future research in this area.

---

[2]   The activities pursued following retirement are referred to as *post-executive activities* and the sequence of such activities as *post-executive careers*.

2   Entering a post-executive career

2.1 The retirement decision

As executives and senior managers of large companies leave their positions, they face two main options: (1) to pursue further opportunities in the managerial labour market, or (2) exit the managerial labour market and enter the market for post-executive activities. The former refers to movement within the executive labour market and has been addressed extensively in past research on executive turnover and top management careers. On the other hand, the latter alternative refers to departing top managers who retire from their primary managerial careers. These individuals enter the market for post-executive activities, in which they face opportunities to pursue a post-executive career. Such opportunities enable retiring executives to experience a smooth transition from full-time work to complete retirement, analogous to the notion of flexible retirement arrangements (see, e.g., Blau 1994). Entry into the market for post-executive activities can be described as a type of *bridge employment*, i.e. the positions held and activities performed after career employment and prior to full retirement (Ruhm 1990), for the most highly skilled segment of the labour force.

    A manager's decision to retire and enter the market for post-executive activities is closely tied in with labour supply considerations. Economic theories of labour supply and retirement decisions explain retirement behaviour as a combined function of older workers' decreasing productivity, rigidities in wage-setting mechanisms, and the existence of age and health-related benefit schemes (e.g., French 2005; Lazear 1979; Stock and Wise 1990). Ageing managers who become eligible for pensions and related benefits face increasing financial incentives to end their managerial careers. This is due to the large, implicit taxes on continued work imposed by pension systems, making formal retirement an increasingly attractive option (Gruber and Wise 1998). The availability of post-executive career opportunities following retirement provides additional impetus to stimulate the managerial labour market exit decision.

    At the same time, companies are inherently encouraged to stimulate the early retirement of older managers, as a result of how incentives are structured over an employee's working life. At a young age, employees exhibit a high willingness to sacrifice current wages for learning opportunities due to the length of time that they have to recoup investments in human capital (Ben-Porath 1967). Older employees, on the other hand, expect to be compensated on the basis of their seniority and experience, resulting in a negative marginal product for the company due to incrementally increasing wage costs and diminishing productivity (Lazear 1979). Thus, as highly paid executives approach the upper age cohorts, they become increasingly expensive for the company relative to their productive contribution. As companies are unable to adjust salaries downward to account for older managers' decreasing productivity, they would benefit from designing attractive, early retirement schemes to facilitate the replacement of ageing managers with younger and more cost-efficient alternatives.

The decision to retire from the managerial labour market and enter the market for post-career activities is primarily driven by post-retirement welfare prospects and the rate of individual productivity decline (Feldman 1994). Furthermore, it has been shown that employees' socio-demographic traits, endogenous experiences, and career paths partially explain individual preferences in the retirement process (Blau 1994; Kim and Feldman 2000). The executive labour market segment offers a particularly attractive context for studying managers' retirement decisions. The highly skilled and highly experienced individuals who make up this segment of the labour force are likely to face particularly high levels of discretion in the retirement decision process (as the financial constraints on their retirement decision are likely to be lower) as well as a more attractive set of opportunities in the market for post-career activities. The combination of these features implies that arguably the most highly skilled, knowledgeable, and resource-rich segment of the workforce faces the strongest incentives to retire at an early age. This highlights the need to ensure that the productive capacities of these individuals are retained in the extended labour market at the post-retirement stage in order to mitigate the extent of knowledge and resource redundancies upon retirement.

2.2 Determinants of post-executive careers

Retiring managers need to make two interdependent decisions: (1) when to retire, and (2) what to do after retirement. These decisions need to be made jointly and are interdependent to the extent that the attractiveness of subsequent opportunity structures is related to the optimal retirement timing. Unique opportunity structures accrue to individuals from their accumulated human and social capital configurations, which are attributable to individual experience profiles, network positions, and other background characteristics. These opportunity structures influence decisions pertaining to the type and intensity of subsequent post-executive activities. Thus, it is likely that the nature and scope of post-executive careers are at least partially path-dependent.

Human and social capital theories are employed to explain the opportunity structures faced by retiring executives. By investing in education, training, and on-the-job experiences throughout their careers, managers become increasingly valuable repositories of knowledge and experience as their careers progress (Becker 1975; Bird 1994). High educational achievements (e.g., a Ph.D.) and vast international experience are examples of how top managers can raise the marketable value of their *human capital* during the course of their careers. Individual managers' investments in human capital are valued in external and internal labour markets. The value assigned to a particular investment depends on the extent to which the investment is relatively generic or (firm-)specific as well as the extent to which the investment reveals information about the manager's true underlying abilities to current and potential employers.

The managerial labour market distributes managerial candidates within and across companies on the basis of the perceived value of their accumulated human capital configurations (e.g., Fama 1980; Harris and Helfat 1997; Murphy and

Zabojnik 2004; Rosen 1992). Highly skilled and highly experienced individuals who retire from the managerial labour market will have made extensive human capital investments during their careers and, in the process, will have revealed a substantial amount of information about their actual abilities to internal and external labour markets. These individuals' accumulated human capital (as well as information about it) will subsequently be transferred to the market for post-executive activities and serve as key determinants of their post-executive careers.

At the same time, managers are embedded in social structures both within and beyond the companies for which they work. This implies that other market actors' awareness of the existence and value of managers' human capital increases incrementally with career progress (Granovetter 1992). The value of such awareness can be translated into the concept of *social capital*, defined as the total value of goodwill towards a particular individual within that individual's overall social structure (Adler and Kwon 2002). A distinctive aspect of social capital is that it exists between people (i.e. it is embedded in the structure of relationships) and serves to facilitate economic activity by effectively channelling information throughout social structures (Coleman 1988).

Unlike human capital, which allows people to purposefully invest in their own skills and abilities and to expect predictable returns on such investments, the social structural positions that individuals accrue from participation in economic activities are spill-over effects that they accumulate at no intrinsic cost (Granovetter 1992). The value of a particular network position depends on the overall social structure surrounding the sphere of primary contacts, with a greater value attached to structural network positions that provide access to a heterogeneous sphere with few redundant linkages (Burt 1992). This implies that social capital is not only dependent on the size and quality of personal networks, but also on their density. Several studies emphasise the prevalence of network ties in the process of appointing individuals to post-executive roles (e.g., Mizruchi 1996; Westphal 1999), suggesting that social structures directly affect appointments to post-executive positions. Top managers with vast experience are likely to generate more opportunities, but may not be in a sufficiently strong position to capitalise on all the available options. While a narrow and focused experience base may generate fewer opportunities, it will increase the likelihood that such opportunities will subsequently materialise.

As retiring executives exit the managerial labour market and enter the market for post-executive activities, they transfer their human and social capital profiles in the process. Each executive retiree possesses a combination of specific and generic human and social capital that becomes available in the market for post-executive activities and generates a set of opportunities. On the basis of the perceived attractiveness of these opportunities, the retiring executives choose their preferred type and level of involvement in post-executive activities. The nature and intensity of a post-executive career will therefore be jointly determined by the attractiveness of individual executive retirees' human and social capital profiles in markets for different types of post-executive activities, as well as the extent to which they perceive the post-executive opportunities that accrue to them as more attractive than full retirement.

3 Post-executive careers in Switzerland

3.1 Overview of post-executive activities

The observations presented in this chapter are based on a dataset comprising information on the 104 individuals who retired from executive positions at the 50 largest publicly listed Swiss companies (as of year-end 2005) during the period between 1 January 2006 and 31 December 2008. A detailed description of the data and definitions used in this chapter can be found in the Appendix.

Table 1: Types of post-executive activities (Source: own data)

Type of activity	Type of organisation	Number of activities
Board membership	Company	84
	Non-profit	23
	Educational	12
	Professional/Industry association	9
	Governmental	3
	Cultural	1
	Pension fund	1
	Political	1
Management	SME	12
	Non-profit	4
	Professional/Industry association	1
Consulting	Within company	6
	Professional service firm	3
Teaching	Educational	2
Miscellaneous	Company	4
	Professional/Industry association	2
	Educational	1
	Governmental	1
Total		170

There are four main types of post-executive activities conducted by the executives retiring from the 50 largest companies in Switzerland (see Table 1). The 81 executives for whom complete records could be retrieved pursued a total of 170 unique activities in the post-executive labour market. This amounts to an average of 2.10 post-executive activities for each retired executive. The most active retired executive in the sample pursued 10 different post-executive activities during the period examined. The 60 executives who remained active in the post-executive labour market pursued an average of 2.83 activities.

Post-executive activities were unevenly distributed across the different types of activities (as shown in Table 1). The vast majority of post-executive activities involved different types of board memberships. Company board memberships were most prevalent, followed by board memberships at non-profit organisations, educational institutions, and professional associations/industry organisations. Besides board memberships, some retiring executives took on smaller-scale management positions, primarily at small and medium-sized enterprises (SME) and non-profit organisations, or continued to be active in different types of consulting roles. Involvement in other activities such as teaching, politics, and government roles was largely limited to individual cases.

Of the 60 executives who continued to be active in the post-executive labour market 27 retained an association with the company from which they retired. In the majority of cases (14), these individuals became members of the company's board of directors following retirement. A few others took on internal consulting roles (5), became involved in the management of internal ventures (4), or became board members at one of the company's subsidiaries (3).

Table 2: Location of post-executive activities (Source: own data)

Location	Count
Switzerland	122
US	21
UK	6
Germany	5
South Africa	4
The Netherlands	3
Belgium	2
France	2
Austria	1
Japan	1
Liechtenstein	1
Luxembourg	1
Spain	1
Total	**170**

Of the 170 post-executive activities pursued by the 81 retired executives for whom data were available, 122 activities were located in Switzerland and 48 in other countries (see Table 2). Post-executive activities were pursued in 12 different countries other than Switzerland. The most prevalent locations of post-executive activities outside Switzerland were the US, followed by the UK, Germany, South Africa, and the Netherlands.

The 60 executives who pursued opportunities in the post-executive labour market comprised 36 Swiss nationals and 24 foreigners. 7 of the 36 Swiss nationals pursued at least one post-executive activity outside Switzerland following retirement. Of the 24 foreigners, 12 retained at least one post-executive activity within Switzerland at the post-retirement stage.

3.2 Post-executive career paths

To shed light on the emerging patterns between top managers' backgrounds and their post-executive career paths, the type, intensity, and location of post-executive activities are broken down by the demographic characteristics and background profiles of the 81 retiring executives (see Tables 3a and 3b). Several post-executive career patterns can be observed in the data.

Firstly, younger executive retirees are more likely to remain active in the post-executive labour market than executives who retire at an older age (see Table 3a). Whereas nearly half of executives who retired after 60 did not pursue any post-executive activities, all retirees below 50 subsequently moved to the post-executive labour market. Secondly, in accordance with data from the SHARE survey, Swiss executives are more likely to pursue post-executive opportunities after retirement than non-Swiss executives. Thirdly, retiring executives with high education levels and international career experience appear somewhat more likely to engage in post-executive activities than executive retirees with a lower education and domestic work experience.

Furthermore, Table 3a displays the retiring executives' participation in the three main types of post-executive activities (see also Table 1 above), namely board memberships, small-scale management positions, and consulting roles. A clear pattern is emerging with regard to the age of executive retirees and the type of activity pursued. Executives who retired before 55 typically stepped down by taking on smaller-scale managerial positions (e.g., at SMEs or non-profit organisations) or consulting activities. Many of these executives also assumed board memberships. However, board appointments accrue to executives in the upper age cohorts to a much greater extent than to their younger counterparts. Furthermore, retiring Swiss executives typically take on more board memberships than foreigners. Meanwhile, non-Swiss executives more frequently assume consulting roles following retirement.

Table 3a: Breakdown of post-executive activities by individual background characteristics: active versus inactive; activity types (Source: own data)

Characteristics		Post-executive career		Activity types		
Type	Category	Active	Inactive	Board	Management	Consulting
Age at retirement	60+	12	10	41	0	0
	55-59	21	8	61	2	4
	50-54	12	3	20	5	3
	-49	15	0	12	8	2
Nationality	Swiss	36	10	90	10	2
	Foreign	24	11	44	7	7
Gender[a]	Male	57	21	132	16	8
	Female	3	0	2	1	1
Education	Ph.D.	16	7	58	4	0
	Master	29	6	54	7	8
	Bachelor	10	6	15	2	1
	Other	4	2	6	2	0
International career	Yes	27	8	67	6	5
	No	14	6	40	2	2

a) As the sample contains only three females, we simply report the means for males and females for illustrative purposes, without commenting specifically on any observed differences.

With regard to educational backgrounds, retiring executives with a Ph.D. appear to be particularly attractive as candidates for board appointments. Executives with Master's level degrees, on the other hand, are much more inclined to take on managerial or consulting roles after retirement (possibly as a reaction to fewer board membership opportunities). Executives who have completed Bachelor-level education or lower are relatively less involved in post-executive activities following retirement.

International career experience does not appear to increase the attractiveness of retiring executives in the market for post-executive activities. On the contrary, the data suggest that executives who have not worked abroad are somewhat more likely to have multiple board memberships than the executives who have gathered international work experience during their careers.

Distinct patterns emerge with regard to the intensity and location of post-executive activities (see Table 3b). Firstly, executives in the upper age cohorts appear to pursue a greater number of post-executive activities simultaneously – more so than their younger counterparts. This may be partly due to the fact that different types of post-executive activities are not equally time-consuming. Indeed, younger retirees' post-executive activities more frequently involve management and consulting activities (Table 3a), which are likely to be more time-consuming than, for example, board memberships. At the same time, retiring executives at the largest Swiss companies tend to pursue high-intensity post-executive careers, even if they retire after 55.

Table 3b: Breakdown of post-executive activities by individual background characteristics: activity intensity; location of activities (Source: own data)

Characteristics		Intensity	Location	
Type	Category	Average # of activities	Switzerland	Abroad
Age at retirement	60+	3.75	33	12
	55-59	3.24	46	22
	50-54	2.67	28	4
	-49	1.67	15	10
Nationality	Swiss	3.11	99	13
	Foreign	2.42	23	35
Gender	Male	2.89	117	48
	Female	1.67	5	0
Education	Ph.D.	4.25	50	18
	Master	2.55	47	27
	Bachelor	1.80	16	2
	Other	2.25	8	1
International career	Yes	3.15	54	29
	No	3.36	45	2

Furthermore, in line with previous observations, retiring Swiss executives pursue more intensive post-executive careers than their non-Swiss counterparts. With regard to education, retiring executives with a Ph.D. pursue the highest average number of post-executive activities, followed by executives with Master's level degrees. In terms of experiential backgrounds, retiring executives without international career experience are on average slightly more intensively involved in post-executive activities than those with international career backgrounds.

The latter finding suggests that in addition to the influence of top managers' human capital configurations, the density of social networks may indeed play a role in the development of individual opportunity structures in the post-executive labour market. Top managers without international career experience are likely to have developed strong and dense domestic networks during the course of their careers, potentially generating a set of higher-quality (domestic) opportunities than executives with more dispersed backgrounds and networks.

The prevalent patterns of the location of post-executive activities are largely in line with expectations. Unsurprisingly, Swiss nationals are more likely to pursue post-executive activities within Switzerland, whereas foreigners pursue a greater proportion of their post-executive activities abroad. Along similar lines, post-executive opportunities abroad are particularly likely to accrue to retiring executives who are highly educated and have international career experience. Meanwhile, there is no obvious reason why executives who retire between 50 and 54 are less likely to pursue post-executive opportunities abroad than executive retirees in the three other age cohorts.

4   Conclusion and future research

There is a vibrant market for post-executive activities in Switzerland. The vast majority of top executives at large Swiss companies who leave their positions and exit the executive labour market seek to make a gradual transition into full retirement by pursuing opportunities in the market for post-executive activities. This enables companies and other organisations to extract the full benefits of such individuals' human and social capital, while also offering a platform for retiring executives to manage the transition to a lower level of activity.

Several patterns can be observed with regard to the nature of post-executive career paths and the emergence of a market for different types of post-executive activities in Switzerland: (1) the type, intensity, and location of post-executive activities depend on the educational and career backgrounds of the retiring executives as well as the timing of retirement; (2) Swiss nationals are particularly likely to participate in post-executive activities relative to foreign nationals; (3) the market for post-executive activities is not highly international, albeit there are some international post-executive opportunities for executives with international career experience; and (4) the market for company board memberships still dominates the market for post-executive activities.

The post-executive labour market offers a broad array of opportunities, enabling highly skilled, highly experienced, and well-networked individuals to leave the managerial labour market without creating knowledge redundancies that carry a high opportunity cost. While many companies and organisations already make effective use of the experience and resources of post-executives, particularly in the role of board members, there is also an abundance of unused opportunities. Very few retiring executives take on consulting roles, which could effectively further the use of their industry and company-specific human capital. In addition, companies could, for example, more frequently deploy post-executive knowledge and resources in the development and expansion of new ventures or in an advisory capacity at poorly functioning subsidiaries. More generally, there are vast opportunities for other types of organisations (e.g., non-profit organisations, industry associations, and educational institutions) to tap into post-executives' human and social capital.

Future studies in this area need to develop an in-depth understanding of the drivers of retirement from the executive labour market and the triggers of different post-executive career paths. Research should go beyond the descriptive analysis of career profiles in this study and include other potential driving forces such as financial incentives as well as individual health and welfare prospects. Both theoretical and empirical models will need to take into account that the transition from an executive career to the post-executive labour market involves two simultaneous decisions, i.e. when to retire and what to do next. Finally, future research must qualitatively address the extent to which knowledge is diffused, and how resources are utilised by post-executives in different roles. This is important in order to identify the most effective and value-adding types of post-executive careers and to develop recommendations that encourage the best possible use of post-executive experience for the long-term benefit of the economy and society.

Appendix: Data

The observations are based on a dataset of the 104 individuals who retired from executive positions at the 50 largest publicly listed Swiss companies (as of year-end 2005) during the period between 1 January 2006 and 31 December 2008. Of the 104 retiring executives, 21 were found to have fully withdrawn from professional activities, including post-executive labour market activities. 71 remained active in post-executive positions. We were able to identify the full extent of 60 of the 71 individuals' post-executive activities. 12 of the 104 retiring executives were excluded from the subsequent analyses due to inconclusive information.

The data includes all post-executive activities and positions that could be identified in an extensive search of the public domain (Internet) and various biographical databases (e.g., LexisNexis, Munzinger Online) between the date of retirement and March 2009. In addition, information on post-executive activities was extracted from press releases and other company statements announcing the retirement of executives. Data were collected on the basis that visibility equals significance, meaning that any post-executive activities that could not be identified via publicly available sources are not included in the study.

As outlined above (see chapter 2.1), a distinction was made between executives who leave their position but remain active in the executive labour market (i.e. take up a new executive position at another large company) and executives who retire from the executive labour market, and enter the post-executive labour market. Entry into the post-executive labour market was defined as retirement from an executive position at one of the 50 companies in the study without taking up a new executive position at another company with more than 250 full-time employees within the data collection period. Companies with less than 250 full-time employees are defined as SMEs according to the European Union.

Active positions in consulting, teaching, government, politics, non-profit organisations, and professional associations were all recorded as post-executive activities if any such roles were held following retirement from the executive labour market. Entry into a management position at an SME is likely to be part of a stepping-down process rather than a career move and was therefore recorded as a de facto retirement, and entry into the post-executive labour market.

References

Adler, P. S., & Kwon, S.-W. (2002). Social capital: Prospects for a new concept. *Academy of Management Review*, 27, 17-40.

Becker, G. S. (1975). *Human capital: A theoretical and empirical analysis, with special reference to education*. New York: Columbia University Press.

Ben-Porath, Y. (1967). The production of human capital and the life cycle of earnings. *Journal of Political Economy*, 75, 352-365.

Bird, A. (1994). Careers as repositories of knowledge: A new perspective on boundaryless careers. *Journal of Organizational Behavior*, 15, 325-344.

Blau, D. M. (1994). Labour force dynamics of older men. *Econometrica*, 62, 117-156.

Burt, R. S. (1992). *Structural holes: The social structure of competition*. Cambridge/London: Harvard University Press.

Bütler, M., Huguenin, O., & Teppa, F. (2005). What triggers early retirement? Results from Swiss pension funds. DNB Working Paper 41/2005.

Carpenter, M. A., Geletkanycz, M. A., & Sanders, W. G. (2004). Upper echelons research revisited: Antecedents, elements, and consequences of top management team composition. *Journal of Management*, 30, 749-778.

Certo, S. T., Lester, R. H., Dalton, C. M., & Dalton, D. R. (2006). Top management teams, strategy and financial performance: a meta-analytic examination. *Journal of Management Studies*, 43, 813-839.

Coleman, J. S. (1988). Social capital in the creation of human capital. *American Journal of Sociology*, 94, S95-S120.

Fama, E. F. (1980). Agency problems and the theory of the firm. *Journal of Political Economy*, 88, 288-307.

Feldman, D. C. (1994). The decision to retire early: A review and conceptualization. *Academy of Management Review*, 19, 285-311.

French, E. (2005). The effects of health, wealth, and wages on labour supply and retirement behaviour. *Review of Economic Studies*, 72, 395-427.

Granovetter, M. (1992). The sociological and economic approaches to labor market analysis: A social structural view. In M. Granovetter & R. Swedberg (Eds.), *The Sociology of Economic Life* (pp. 233-263). Boulder, CO: Westview Press.

Gruber, J., & Wise, D. (1998). Social security and retirement: An international comparison. *American Economic Review*, 88, 158-163.

Hambrick, D. C. (2007). Upper echelons theory: an update. *Academy of Management Review,* 32, 334-343.

Harris, D., & Helfat, C. (1997). Specificity of CEO human capital and compensation. *Strategic Management Journal*, 18, 895-920.

Kim, S., & Feldman, D. C. (2000). Working in retirement: The antecedents of bridge employment and its consequences for quality of life in retirement. *Academy of Management Journal*, 43, 1195-1210.

Lazear, E. P. (1979). Why is there mandatory retirement? *Journal of Political Economy*, 87, 1261-1284.

Mizruchi, M. S. (1996). What do interlocks do? An analysis, critique, and assessment of research on interlocking directorates. *Annual Review of Sociology*, 22, 271-298.

Murphy, K. J., & Zabojnik, J. (2004). CEO pay and appointments: A market-based explanation for recent trends. *American Economic Review*, 94, 192-196.

Rosen, S. (1992). Contracts and the market for executives. In L. Werin & H. Wijkander (Eds.), *Contract economics* (pp. 181-211). Oxford, UK: Blackwell.

Ruhm, C. J. (1990). Bridge jobs and partial retirement. *Journal of Labor Economics*, 8, 482-501.

Stock, J. H., & Wise, D. A. (1990). Pensions, the option value of work, and retirement. *Econometrica*, 58, 1151-1180.

Westphal, J. D. (1999). Collaboration in the boardroom: Behavioral and performance consequences of CEO-board social ties. *Academy of Management Journal*, 42, 7-24.

Consenec – A well-proven model

Kurt Hoerhager[*]

A new career at 60

A very successful family corporation wanted to enter a new technology sector. The corporation has a tradition of working with high technology, and has already produced a series of innovative developments and patents. The technical know-how and the market knowledge necessary for the planned new growth were therefore already available within the corporation.

The management decided to appoint an experienced manager to lead this important strategic project. He was given the task of supporting the team made up of managers from the development, production, sales, and marketing areas in drawing up a critical assessment of the corporation's position and a sound business and action plan. On the basis of his many years of professional experience, he was expected to lead the as-is analysis as well as the decision-making process as a critical and inspiring facilitator. The choice ultimately fell on a Senior Consultant from the Consenec AG corporation.

More freedom – less stress

Until recently, the consultant who accepted the mandate had been a member of the senior executive staff of ABB Switzerland, and, according to plan, had transferred to Consenec on reaching the age of 60. He had started his professional career as a development engineer and held various management functions at home and abroad over the course of the years.

He is happy with this career change, because the new consultant role means less stress and more personal freedom as he is free to choose both his time commitment and the working location. He is therefore able to reduce his working hours as he approaches retirement, but can also remain active beyond retirement age if he chooses. In his consultant work, he intends to focus on the moderation of strategy and organisational development. These subjects have been of special interest to him ever since he was a manager, and he received continual training in these fields.

From manager to consultant

Many people find it difficult to step into a new career as a consultant. The transition from being a 'doer', who is a principal actor in his unit, to a 'consultant', who mainly listens and recommends, is greater than generally assumed. In a two-day

---

[*] Kurt Hoerhager, CEO, Consenec AG.

S. Kunisch et al. (eds.), *From Grey to Silver*,
DOI 10.1007/978-3-642-15594-9_13, © Springer-Verlag Berlin Heidelberg 2011

workshop ('From manager to consultant'), the managers are helped to prepare themselves for their new role. Most of them manage this very well, and soon appreciate the variety of opportunities that their new career at Consenec AG offers.

The Consenec model

As can be seen from its operation, Consenec AG is a consulting firm with a very special business model. The company was originally founded as ABB Consulting AG in 1993. Some years later, together with ALSTOM (Switzerland) and Bombardier (Switzerland), ABB (Switzerland) founded Consenec AG. The model is basically open to other corporations.

Consenec AG's approximately 40 consultants are all former managers from the three founding corporations, ABB, ALSTOM, and Bombardier. Within these corporations, the top managers were transferred to Consenec AG on reaching the age of 60 to make their know-how, experience, and management skills available to the sponsoring corporations, as well as other firms.

Rejuvenation – Retention of know-how – Preparation for retirement

Simultaneously, the three sponsoring corporations achieved three goals with the Consenec model: the rejuvenation of the senior management and the possibility of continuing to make use of its former managers' wealth of experience and know-how. Moreover, the managers are provided with a great deal of freedom in the planning of the final part of their professional career and in step-by-step preparing themselves for retirement – a perspective that is very much appreciated when one considers what the top management has to currently bear.

Consenec AG has been a model for success since its very beginning. The fact that the fundamental rules have been retained throughout all the economic cycles since the inception of the corporation has certainly contributed to this. The Consenec model is therefore valued by the sponsor corporations' organisations as a valuable and lasting cultural element.

Obligatory transfer as a precondition for success

In order to join Consenec, employees have to reach a specific level in the respective sponsoring corporation's hierarchy by the age of 55. Once they have met this entry criterion, they retain the right to be transferred until the obligatory Consenec entry age of 60. Experience has shown that an obligatory transfer is a crucial principle for ensuring the consulting firm's quality and acceptance.

Consultants receive a basic remuneration that corresponds to approximately half their previous salaries, even if they do not carry out any work. This also offers a certain level of security when the employee is unable to carry out consultancy mandates for whatever reason. With full employment, the person in question will again receive his or her original remuneration. Each consultant's daily consultancy fee is proportional to his or her previous salary, and they can determine their own time-commitment and place of work. Consultants will also decide in which field they wish to be active and may acquire their own contracts. From an organisational point of view, the consultants are supported by a professional back office, while regular workshops help them with specific training.

Stepwise reduction of workload

On entering Consenec, most consultants work 80-100% of the time, and systematically reduce their workload until they retire. Around two-thirds of the orders originate from the three sponsoring corporations, with the remainder coming from a broad international client base in both industry and administration. Some of the consultants even decide to continue their work as a consultant at Consenec after their retirement.

Consenec has two basic types of mandates, which also differ considerably with regard to their duration. Approximately two-thirds of the orders are actually consulting or facilitator mandates, which generally last for a few days. The rest are temporary management contracts, which can last from a few weeks to months. They usually comprise deployment in turn-around situations at business units or acting in a temporary bridging capacity while management positions are being filled.

Considerable organisational effort

The organisational effort required for the smooth operation of such a Senior Consulting unit can be easily underestimated. At the very least, thousands of offers and contracts have to be processed and invoiced every year. Because the consultants are free to choose their place of work, and as some of them work on the client's premises, communication is of decisive importance.

Therefore, Consenec operates its own internal platform on the Internet, which enables the consultants to access documents and information from wherever they may be. Consenec maintains a homepage (www.consenec.ch) in which the consultants introduce themselves and present their specific range of services, and where they can be contacted directly.

Over the years, Consenec has become a valued cultural element for the sponsoring corporations and the participating executives. Above all, the clients value the professional network and the consultants' experience and professional methods.

Prerequisites created for future success

After the inquiry from the family corporation mentioned at the beginning, Consenec considered which consultants would be most suitable for this task. An initial, non-binding meeting was agreed upon in order to clarify the as-is situation, the objectives, and the possible procedure. At the first meeting, the client was in favour of the proposed consultant and, working with him, drew up an initial two-day business development workshop for the management team.

Once this workshop had been carried out successfully, they agreed to plan a business strategy and a detailed action plan with the same team in two additional workshops. The consultant prepared and facilitated these workshops and documented the results. The client particularly valued his practical approach and the clearly structured process.

These consultants' ability to understand practical problems through their many years of professional experience, to question fixed opinions, and to introduce new ideas has helped the management team to make a successful start in a new technology sector.

Part D

An innovation and marketing perspective – Extending the customer base

Using innovation contests to master challenges of demographic change – Insights from research and practice

Angelika C. Bullinger, Matthias Rass, Sabrina Adamczyk[*1]

Demographic change poses new challenges to both companies and society as a whole. On the one hand, an ageing population increasingly demands products and services that meet the specific needs of elderly consumers. On the other hand, the workforce necessary to devise and manufacture these products and services has to be recruited from a shrinking basis. At the same time, important knowledge and experience are often lost with senior experts' retirement. Nevertheless, this development also generates opportunities to meet these challenges. Innovation contests seem to be a very suitable method for finding solutions to these challenges – by integrating those affected by demographic change into the development of innovative products and services.

This chapter illustrates the use of innovation contests throughout history to the present and provides an overview of online innovation contests' design elements. Moreover, it presents two vivid examples of successful innovation platforms that search for innovative solutions *for* and *with* the ageing society, and finally derives implications for practical implementation.

[*] Dr. Angelika C. Bullinger, assistant professor, Chair for Information Systems I – Innovation & Value Creation, University of Erlangen-Nuremberg.
Matthias Rass, doctoral candidate and research associate, Chair for Information Systems I – Innovation & Value Creation, University of Erlangen-Nuremberg.
Sabrina Adamczyk, doctoral candidate and research associate, Chair for Information Systems I – Innovation & Value Creation, University of Erlangen-Nuremberg.
[1] Acknowledgements: We thank all inside and outside innovators who are part of our ongoing innovation research journey and gratefully acknowledge support by the German Federal Ministry of Education and Research (projects: OFFIES 2020+, 03SF0371B and EIVE, 01FG09006).

S. Kunisch et al. (eds.), *From Grey to Silver*,
DOI 10.1007/978-3-642-15594-9_14, © Springer-Verlag Berlin Heidelberg 2011

Table of Contents

1 Introduction: Challenges and opportunities of an ageing society

From a company perspective, the ability to generate innovative products and services is a critical success factor in a dynamic market environment (Christensen 1997). Intensified global competition, technological advance, and the emergence of the knowledge economy force companies to focus more strongly on innovation. The ability to bring novel products and services to the market is necessary to improve an organisation's competitiveness or just maintain its current position (Lawson and Samson 2001). Moreover, from a macro-economic perspective, innovation is crucial for economic welfare and societal advance (von Hayek 1968, 1971).

In this context, demographic change poses new challenges to both companies and the society as a whole. Western countries specifically face decreasing birth rates and an increasing life expectancy (United Nations 2002, 2007). This development leads to the dual challenge concerning not only innovation but also innovation management. On the one hand, there is an increasing demand among the ageing population for products and services that meet elderly consumers' specific needs. On the other hand, the workforce required to devise and manufacture these products and services has to be recruited from a shrinking basis. In sum, a comparatively young workforce has to produce innovative solutions for an increasing customer base of elderly people, while important knowledge and experience are often lost with senior experts' retirement.

The loss of expert knowledge is particularly dangerous as innovative capability strongly depends on employees' ability to deploy knowledge resources (Subramaniam and Youndt 2005). Accordingly, the innovation process has been described as a *knowledge management process* (Madhavan and Grover 1998) and innovative companies as *knowledge creating companies* (Nonaka and Takeuchi 1995; Subramaniam and Youndt 2005). More specifically, a company's ability to deploy *external knowledge resources* is considered crucial (Cohen and Levinthal 1990).

Thus, parallel to companies' increasing need to innovate, there is a change in managing innovation: the opening of traditionally closed innovation processes to the environment and the integration of external actors. This approach is often referred to as *Open Innovation* (Chesbrough 2003; von Hippel 2005). Especially customers and users can be a valuable external knowledge resource (Enkel et al. 2005; Neyer et al. 2009; Thomke and von Hippel 2002). Open innovation goes beyond obtaining information from (potential) customers by using common methods of market research. In contrast to these traditional methods, which are usually concluded before the innovation process starts, open innovation approaches have the potential to integrate so-called *outside innovators* (Neyer et al. 2009) into every innovation process step. Typically, open innovation focuses on the early stages, like idea generation and conceptualisation, but in the later stages, such as development and prototyping, integration is also possible. This kind of customer integration helps a company gather the necessary information as well as solution information (Reichwald and Piller 2009; von Hippel 1978, 1994).

Among the many-faceted tools that enable open innovation (e.g., lead user method and online tool kits), the *innovation contest* seems particularly promising and interesting. Innovation contests are increasingly used in practice, and are also attracting growing academic attention (Bullinger and Moeslein 2010; Ebner et al. 2010; Piller and Walcher 2006). Innovation contests have proved useful in different contexts and might be an appropriate means to deal with the mentioned challenges.

2 Background: Innovation contests

2.1 Innovation contests in history and today

Competition can be found in various aspects of life: in the evolution of creatures as well as in sports, business, arts, and science (von Hayek 1971). It is the underlying principle of the free market economy. In 'The Wealth of Nations', Adam Smith concludes that in a competitive environment, individuals' endeavour to maximize utility is conducive to societal welfare (Smith 2009). Similarly, von Hayek (1968) considers competition beneficial for the development of innovations and technological as well as societal progress.

Besides a competitive economic system, history has many examples in which a call for solutions in the form of a competition lead to a variety of answers, even from unexpected (external) sources. For instance, in 1418, a competition was held to find an innovative construction method for the cupola of Santa Maria del Fiore in Florence, Italy. The winning design – that enabled the erection of a dome hailed as one of the greatest architectural achievements of its time – was submitted by a man who had originally been a goldsmith. This *outside innovator* started developing an interest in architecture and thus submitted the radically new design (King 2008; Zucconi 1995). Another example can be found half a millennium later, when in 1919, the *Orteig Prize* was offered for the first nonstop aircraft flight between New York and Paris. This competition and the particular engineering achievement fuelled the development of the then still new aviation industry.

Since the beginning of the Internet age and especially with more and more users actively participating in and contributing to the so-called *Web 2.0* (O'Reilly 2007), organising an innovation contest has become more profitable and feasible, even for individual companies (Bullinger and Moeslein 2010). Thus, over the past years, a great number of these contests has taken place. For example, *Swarovski* used contests to find creative jewellery[2] and watch[3] designs, *Osram* searched for new ideas and designs for LED light solutions[4], and *BMW* called for innovative motorcycle concepts[5] and urban mobility services for the future[6]. *InnoCentive*[7] organised a mul-

---

[2] http://www.enlightened-jewellery-design-competition.com.
[3] http://www.enlightened-watch-design-contest.com.
[4] http://www.led-emotionalize.com.
[5] https://www.atizo.com/projects/ideaproject/24/detail.
[6] http://www.bmwgroup-ideacontest.com.
[7] http://www.innocentive.com.

titude of Internet-based contests for its customers, which were intended to bring together *seekers* and *solvers*. However, the company ended up creating a business model based on these contests. The challenges posed by these modern contests range from ideas that can be devised by normal users to high-end solutions that require expert knowledge (Bullinger and Moeslein 2010; Hallerstede et al. 2010).

However, as illustrated with the historic examples, innovation contests' potential goes beyond individual companies' interests. In addition, they are able to generate solutions to the specific problems of our time. In 2009, the *Save Our Energy* contest[8] aimed at finding energy-efficient concepts for Munich, Germany in 2020 (Adamczyk et al. 2010). In 2010, the *Dell Social Innovation Competition*[9] addressed social problems, for example, in the fields of poverty, human rights, peace, and security, health, education as well as environmental challenges. That same year, the *Go London Social Innovation Competition*[10] intended to spur physical activity and make London a more liveable and healthy city. Likewise, in 2010, *InnoCentive* started a challenge to find solutions to the oil spill caused by the explosion of an offshore oil platform in the Gulf of Mexico.[11] While the operating company's every attempt to stop the oil spill failed, *InnoCentive's* oil spill challenge became the challenge with the highest user activity on the website with almost 2,000 solvers actively participating (as of 31 May 2010).

Innovation contests have been used to integrate a variety of diverse external actors and to initiate knowledge transfer. This approach to harnessing a wide knowledge base has often found solutions to problems affecting the whole society. Demographic change is one of the most important societal challenges of our time, and innovation contests seem to be a good method for finding solutions – by integrating those affected into the problem solving process.

2.1 Design elements of innovation contests

An innovation contest[12] can be defined as a web-based competition of innovators from all over the world who use their skills, experience, and creativity to provide a solution for a particular contest challenge defined by an organiser (Bullinger and Moeslein 2010). In terms of online innovation contests, the corresponding online platform's design is central to the activity. On the basis of a set of various design elements, innovation contests can be designed according to their underlying purpose.

---

[8] http://www.save-our-energy.de.
[9] http://www.dellsocialinnovationcompetition.com.
[10] http://go.london.nhs.uk.
[11] https://gw.innocentive.com/ar/challenge/overview/9383447.
[12] We use 'innovation contest' (IC) instead of 'idea contest' to illustrate that a contest is able and suited to cover the entire innovation process from idea creation and concept generation to selection and implementation (Tidd et al. 1997).

Table 1. Design elements of an innovation contest (Source: Bullinger and Moeslein 2010)

Design element (synonyms): definition	Attributes					
1 Media (-): environment of IC	Online		Mixed		Offline	
2 Organiser (-): entity initiating IC	Company		Public organisation	Non-profit	Individual	
3 Task/topic specificity (*problem specification*): solution space of IC	Low (Open task)		Defined		High (Specific task)	
4 Degree of elaboration (*elaborateness, eligibility, degree of idea elaboration*): required level of detail for submission to IC	Idea	Sketch	Concept	Proto-type	Solution	Evolving
5 Target group (*target audience, target participants, composition of group*): description of participants of IC	Specified			Unspecified		
6 Participation as (*eligibility*): number of persons forming one entity of participant	Individual		Team		Both	
7 Contest period (*timeline*): runtime of IC	Very short-term		Short-term	Long-term	Very long-term	
8 Reward/motivation (-): incentives used to encourage participation	Monetary		Non-monetary		Mixed	
9 Community functionality (*community application, communication possibility, tools*): functionalities for interaction within participants	Given			Not given		
10 Evaluation (*ranking*): method to determine ranking of submissions to IC	Jury evaluation		Peer review	Self assessment	Mixed	

There are basically ten innovation contest design elements (see Table 1). As far as *media* are concerned, innovation contests can be run online, offline or in a mixed mode (Boudreau et al. 2008; Brabham 2009). They are run by an *organiser*, which encompasses companies, public organisations, individuals and non-profit organisations, for example, museums (Ebner et al. 2010; Klein and Lechner 2009).

Usually, the organiser dedicates the contest to a specific topic of which the details vary strongly. The topic indicates the *specificity of the task/topic* (ranging from low if the task is very open to high if the task is highly specific) and the desired *degree of elaboration*. The contest might call for simple textual descriptions of rough ideas, sketches, more elaborated concepts, or even prototypes and fully functional solutions (Ebner et al. 2010; Klein and Lechner 2009; Smith et al. 2003). Another option is to refine potential innovations in a number of contests.

By defining the topic, the organiser also indicates the interested participant *target group*. Two types of target groups can be distinguished: an unspecified target group, i.e. participation is open to everybody, and a specified target group when participation is, for example, limited to a country or qualified by age or interest (Brabham 2009; Carvalho 2009; Randolph and Owen 2008). In addition, the organiser indicates whether *participation* is possible for individuals, teams or both (Boudreau et al. 2008; Carvalho 2009; Smith et al. 2003).

Each innovation contest runs for a limited *period of time*. Contest periods range from very short term (some hours to a maximum of 14 days), short term (15 days to 6 weeks) to long term (6 weeks to 4 month) or even very long term (more than 4 months/ongoing) (Boudreau et al. 2008; Ebner et al. 2010; Plaisant and Grinstein 2007).

The organiser establishes a *reward system* to motivate the target group to participate (Boudreau et al. 2008; Ogawa and Piller 2006; Randolph and Owen 2008). Motivation can be induced via extrinsic motivators (awards and prizes), intrinsic motivators (reputation in the relevant community) or a mixed mode. The literature reports that extrinsic motivators cover both monetary awards (prize money) and non-monetary awards (e.g., valuable goods and services or part-time jobs with the organizer) (Brabham 2009; Piller and Walcher 2006; Randolph and Owen 2008). Intrinsic motivation is stressed in combination with social motivation. It includes motivators like community feedback, building a reputation among relevant peers or self-realisation – all of which the organiser can support, for example, through community applications (Fueller 2006).

Community functionalities foster intrinsic and social motivation, and support the contest and its participants (Brabham 2009; Piller and Walcher 2006). They enhance information exchange, topic related discussion, and – if allowed – the collaborative design of products. Social software applications are well suited to foster community building, for example, a *Facebook*[13] contest's fan page, messaging services and personal profiles on the innovation contest or a *Twitter*[14] account for the contest providing news on new submissions or participants.

Once submissions are made, their *evaluation* can be done in accordance with three basic pathways which can be freely combined: self-assessment by the participant, peer review by the innovation contest's other participants, and evaluation by a jury of experts (Carvalho 2009; Ebner et al. 2010; Klein and Lechner 2009).

Innovation contests can be designed in different ways by using a variety of design elements. They could be a good instrument for finding solutions to the challenges of demographic change. Therefore, the choice of design elements is crucial, and an innovation contest's design should be well thought through.

3 Examples: Successfully innovating in an ageing society

In research and practice, innovation contests have become an elaborate instrument to integrate different groups of outside innovators, such as users, customers, and citizens involved in a corporate innovation process. Innovation contests could be

---

[13] http://www.facebook.com.
[14] http://twitter.com.

applied in a multitude of subjects, such as developing products or services for elderly people, termed as innovating *for* the ageing society. However, there is also the possibility of innovating *with* the ageing society and hence the possibility of utilising seniors' knowledge and experience to find innovative solutions. Moreover, a combination of innovating *for* or *with* elderly people is possible.

In the following section, two vivid examples of successful innovation platforms searching for innovative solutions *for* and *with* the ageing society are presented. In particular, *Einfach telefonieren*[15] (approximately: easy mobile phoning) is an innovation contest focusing on senior mobile phones users. *YourEncore*[16] is an expert-focused innovation platform exclusively for retired scientists and engineers worldwide.

3.1 Innovating *for* the ageing society: *Einfach telefonieren*

Einfach telefonieren is a German innovation contest calling for innovative solutions for the further development of mobile phones. The innovation contest as well as the embedded innovation community is *open to anyone*, i.e. no particular knowledge is required for participation. The innovation contest, which ran between March and June 2010, was targeted at *senior users* with an interest in mobile phones.

A *for-profit* (Emporia Telecom Produktions- und Vertriebs GmbH & Co. KG) and a *non-profit organisation* (Deutsche Seniorenliga e.V.) formed an alliance and jointly arranged the *web-based* innovation contest; the organisers were supported by a specialised intermediary responsible for realising the platform. A standard software solution was used and customized to the innovation contest's specific requirements.

A *jury of five experts* helped select the winning ideas. The jury consisted of two partners in the mobile communications industry, one partner who is in charge of an association for elderly people, and two who work in academia in the areas of technology and innovation management and design.

The organisers requested *product innovations striving to enhance the mobile phone* and *offered prizes,* such as three weekend trips for two to the German capital and ten mobile phones. Users were only allowed to hand in innovative solutions *individually* by either describing the solution and uploading a design, or by using a configuration tool to make up the perfect mobile phone. The possibility to give and gain *peer feedback* in terms of community evaluations and comments was offered. In addition, the organisers provided the users with a *personal messaging function*.

During the *14 weeks* of runtime 166 participants submitted 265 potential innovations. Solutions ranged from very simple ideas such as customizing the font size to more advanced concepts like mobile phones combining functionalities such as an emergency button, a GPS, a measuring device for diabetes or a voice recorder.

---

[15] http://www.einfachtelefonieren.de.
[16] http://www.yourencore.com.

3.2 Innovating *with* the ageing society: *YourEncore*

YourEncore helps companies accelerate innovation by connecting them with retired scientists and engineers to leverage their expertise. Founded in 2003 by a *management team of seven people*, *YourEncore* is an innovation platform that recruits and manages a community of highly qualified technical professionals. These experts' skills and experience are matched with member companies' needs to help them achieve exceptional, innovative results.

As *YourEncore* is a closed innovation platform, only users with a set of certain skills and experience can register. In particular, *YourEncore* seeks to enrol *retired* and *highly experienced people* such as scientists, engineers, product developers, medical professionals, market research experts, quality control, and assurance specialists, and business development managers.

The American innovation platform helps client companies, such as *Procter & Gamble, Eli Lilly, Boeing and General Mills*, recover knowledge from retired employees that would otherwise be lost. Companies undertake collaborations to solve challenging problems, using expertise from a variety of industries. *YourEncore projects* are *highly specific*, and compass assignments such as the facilitation of out-licensing safety and environmental studies.

The contests' run time typically ranges from a *single day to several months*, and the degree of elaboration differs strongly depending on the assignment. The assigned expert users work either *alone* or in a *team* to solve the problem, and are *rewarded monetarily* for their efforts. The *management team* as well as the *client company monitor* the project progress, and *evaluate* the project outcome.

The innovation community features *forums, question posting, wikis, user advisory boards* and many other ways in which client companies can interact with users and users among each other. Within the innovation community, users are allocated to sub-communities based on their skills and experience. There are five large sub-communities in the industry areas: life science, food science, consumer goods, aerospace, and high-tech.

Launched in 2003, *YourEncore* currently encompasses a worldwide network of about 6,000 scientists and researchers. With some very successful projects, this community of experts has served around 65 client companies to date.

4 Conclusion: Using innovation contests to master innovation in times of demographic change

In sum, it is important to note that demographic change induces relevant changes to a society. On the one hand, an ageing society demands innovative solutions for its specific needs. On the other hand, a gap arises between the working force's decreasing potential, and the increase in non-working and merely consuming citizens. Moreover, the financial crisis that began in 2007 worsened this situation. The global economic downturn caused most companies to cut costs, often by decimating their workforces by laying off senior employees – thus losing a valuable source of innovation. Many companies have suffered since releasing some of their most experienced people, while recruiting qualified new employees is difficult.

However, demographic change also generates opportunities to meet these challenges. So far, many of these opportunities have been ignored. Elderly people comprise a large, often misunderstood, consumer group that represents a lost working force worth reintegrating to capture useful knowledge and experience. Innovation contests are a suitable method of integrating senior customers as well as retired experts into the innovation process and hence for innovating *for* and *with* the ageing society.

Innovation contests give elderly people the opportunity to participate in the development of new products and services either for themselves or for others, but within their former field of work. By contributing to innovation activities, they are able to express their needs but also to apply their knowledge, skills, and experience to provide potential solutions. Companies and other institutions have very successfully used web-based innovation contests in different contexts to innovate *for* or *with* senior citizens. This seems to be a very promising method for integrating several kinds of external actors, especially elderly people, and benefitting from their knowledge.

Striving towards innovative solutions, online innovation platforms, such as *Einfach telefonieren* or *YourEncore*, have an opportunity to attract senior users, and to integrate them into the innovation process. Such platforms hold many advantages for the ageing society, and can provide an environment in which the growing number of seniors can continue doing the work they enjoy. These platforms provide elderly people with the possibility to stay connected to their field of work, to collaborate with other people with different experience and perspectives, to continue contributing to innovation, to remain intellectually challenged and at the same time maintain a flexible schedule. The collaboration of people with diverse backgrounds and skills on these platforms can lead to unique solutions and exceptional results. These results can help companies and other institutions remain innovative in times of demographic change, and can contribute to the prosperity of society as a whole.

References

Adamczyk, S., Bullinger, A.C., & Moeslein, K.M. (2010). Call for attention – attracting and activating innovators. *R&D Management Conference*.

Boudreau, K. J., Lacetera, N., & Lakhani, K.R. (2008). Incentives versus diversity: Re-examing the link between competition and innovation. *Wharton Technology Conference*.

Brabham, D.C. (2009). Moving the crowd at Threadless: Motivations for participation in a crowdsourcing application. *Association for Education in Journalism and Mass Communication Conference*.

Bullinger, A.C., & Moeslein, K.M. (2010). Online innovation contests – Where are we? *16th Americas Conference on Information Systems (Lima)*.

Carvalho, A. (2009). *In search of excellence – Innovation contests to foster innovation and entrepreneurship in Portugal*. CEFAGE-UE Working Paper.

Chesbrough, H.W. (2003). *Open innovation: The new imperative for creating and profiting from technology.* Boston: Harvard Business School Press.

Christensen, C.M. (1997). *The innovator's dilemma: when new technologies cause great firms to fail.* Boston: Harvard Business School Press.

Cohen, W.M., & Levinthal, D.A. (1990). Absorptive capacity: A new perspective on learning and innovation. *Administrative Science Quarterly,* 35(1), 128-152.

Ebner, W., Leimeister, J.M., & Krcmar, H. (2010). Community engineering for innovations: The ideas competition as a method to nurture a virtual community for innovations. *R&D Management Journal* 40(4), 342-356.

Enkel, E., Perez-Freije, J., & Gassmann, O. (2005). Minimizing market risks through customer integration in new product development: Learning from bad practice. *Creativity & Innovation Management,* 14(4), 425-437.

Fueller, J. (2006). Why consumers engage in virtual new product developments initiated by producers. *Advances in Consumer Research,* 33(1), 639-646.

Hallerstede, S.H., Neyer, A.-K., Bullinger, A.C., & Moeslein, K.M. (2010). Normalo? Tüftler? Profi? Eine Typologisierung von Innovationswettbewerben. *Multikonferenz Wirtschaftsinformatik.*

King, R. (2008). *Brunelleschi's Dome: The story of the great cathedral in florence.* London: Vintage Books.

Klein, D., & Lechner, U. (2009). The ideas competition as tool of change management – Participatory behaviour and cultural perception. *ISPIM Conference,* Vienna.

Lawson, B., & Samson, D. (2001). Developing innovation capability in organisations: A dynamic capabilities approach. *International Journal of Innovation Management,* 5(3), 377-400.

Madhavan, R., & Grover, R. (1998). From embedded knowledge to embodied knowledge: New product development as knowledge management. *Journal of Marketing,* 62(4), 1-12.

Neyer, A.-K., Bullinger, A.C., & Moeslein, K.M. (2009). Integrating inside and outside innovators: a sociotechnical systems perspective. *R&D Management Journal,* 39(4), 410-419.

Nonaka, I.A., & Takeuchi, H.A. (1995). *The knowledge-creating company: How Japanese companies create the dynamics of innovation.* New York: Oxford University Press.

Ogawa, S., & Piller, F.T. (2006). Reducing the risks of new product development. *MIT Sloan Management Review,* 47(2), 65-71.

O'Reilly, T. (2007). What is Web 2.0: Design patterns and business models for the next generation of software. *Communications & Strategies,* 1(1), 17.

Piller, F.T., & Walcher, D. (2006). Toolkits for idea competitions: a novel method to integrate users in new product development. *R&D Management,* 36(3), 307-318.

Plaisant, C., & Grinstein, G. (2007). Promoting Insight Based Evaluation of Visualizations: From Contest to Benchmark Repository. *IEEE Transactions on Visualization and Computer Graphics,* 1-18.

Randolph, G.B., & Owen, D.O. (2008). Attracting communities and students to IT with a community service web contest. *Special Interest Group for Information and Technology Education Conference.*

Reichwald, R., & Piller, F. (2009). *Interaktive Wertschoepfung: Open Innovation, Individualisierung und neue Formen der Arbeitsteilung* (2nd ed.). Wiesbaden: Gabler Verlag/ GWV Fachverlage.

Smith, A. (2009). *An inquiry into the nature and causes of the wealth of nations (Reproduction):* BiblioLife.

Smith, A., Banzaert, A., & Susnowitz, S. (2003). *The MIT ideas competition: promoting innovation for public service.* 33rd Annual Frontiers in Education, 2003.

Subramaniam, M., & Youndt, M.A. (2005). The influence of intellectual capital on the types of innovative capabilities. *Academy of Management Journal,* 48(3), 450-463.

Thomke, S., & Von Hippel, E. (2002). Customers as innovators: A new way to create value. *Harvard Business Review,* 80(4), 74-81.

Tidd, J., Bessant, J., & Pavitt, K. (1997). *Managing innovation. Integrating technological, market, and organizational change.* Chichester: Wiley.

United Nations (2002). *World population ageing: 1950-2050.* New York: United Nations Publications.

United Nations (2007). *World population ageing 2007.* New York: United Nations Publications.

Von Hayek, F.A. (1968). *Der Wettbewerb als Entdeckungsverfahren.* Institut für Weltwirtschaft an der Universität Kiel, Kiel.

Von Hayek, F.A. (1971). *Die Verfassung der Freiheit.* Tübingen: Mohr.

Von Hippel, E. (1978). Successful industrial products from customer ideas. *Journal of Marketing,* 42(1), 39-49.

Von Hippel, E. (1994). "Sticky Information" and the locus of problem solving: Implications for innovation. *Management Science,* 40(4), 429-439.

Von Hippel, E. (2005). *Democratizing innovation.* Cambridge, Mass.: MIT Press.

Zucconi, G. (1995). *Florence: an architectural guide.* Verona: Arsenale Editrice.

We could have known better –
Consumer-oriented marketing in Germany's ageing market

Frank Leyhausen, Alexander Vossen[*]

On the basis of Germany's ageing population, companies are increasing their focus on the growing mature population group (roughly, 50+), which has significant purchase potential as well as modern values. However, the majority of elderly consumers believe that the economy does not cater sufficiently to their specific needs. Tomorrow's successful products and services must have user friendliness and likeability as core properties. This target group must be addressed in appropriate ways, which calls for companies to synchronise product development and communication activities.

One way to address these challenges can be found in the open innovation paradigm, which seeks to integrate external knowledge into the new product or service development process. This chapter focusses on the usage of so-called *idea contests* to gather information to develop products or services that fit. It also presents a case study of open innovation during the development of mobile phones for elderly people.

[*] Frank Leyhausen, Partner, MedCom International.
Alexander Vossen, Research Associate, Technology and Innovation Management Group at RWTH Aachen University.

S. Kunisch et al. (eds.), *From Grey to Silver*,
DOI 10.1007/978-3-642-15594-9_15, © Springer-Verlag Berlin Heidelberg 2011

Table of Contents

1 Introduction

The fact that Germany's population is ageing has become general knowledge. The opportunities and challenges of a mature consumer base have been foremost in certain consultants and marketers' minds, but are the 50+ generations aware that they are special?

The term *50+ market* seems to have appeared out of the blue. But why 50+, rather than 60+ or even 65+ – the general retirement age in Germany? Many marketers have only just become aware that they have only focused on the 18-49 age group, and have all but ignored the ageing population, although this group holds nearly half of Germany's total purchasing power – approximately 610 billion EUR (GfK GeoMarketing GmbH 2008).

However, there is little experience in Germany on how to cluster or address the 50+ group. According to a recent survey, 75% of participating advertising agencies do not divide the 50+ cluster into more specific groups (Deutsche Seniorenliga e.V. 2010).

The German 50+ group comprises approximately 30 million men and women who have spent a large part of their lives in a divided nation, giving them a specific set of experiences. Besides the influence that living in a capitalist or socialist society has had on their lifestyle and values, these people are also influenced by their date of birth: members of the 50+ cluster were born between 1910 and 1960. While some of them experienced two world wars as well as economic crises, others are part of the generation of so-called baby boomers, many of whom were influenced by the hippy movement, Woodstock, and the idea of sexual liberation.

The global 50+ cluster is thus fundamentally diverse. There is a need for more precise clusters of people with relatively homogenous needs and attitudes. It is clear that age alone is a weak attribute for defining a consumer cluster; age is also a weak indicator of personal self-definition.

Literal age is not central to the self-definition of the 50+ cluster. In general, a person's actual age is ten years higher than his or her *felt* age. In general, people, especially seniors, mainly define themselves by means of their psychophysical condition, their attitudes towards life, and their consumption behaviour.

Besides most people feeling younger than their actual age, *senior* is generally considered a negative term in Germany, in contrast with the UK and the US, for example. In Germany, the public perception of age is still driven by negative stereotypes. To be old is to be thought of as conservative, incapacitated, in need of care, and – often – lonely. Age seems to offer few prospects.

Unlike Germans, the Americans even put 'just retired' stickers on their cars or join retirement communities. Very few German seniors are actually proud of being seniors or retirees, and *old* is always used to describe other people (even if they are of the same age group), never oneself.

2 Different product or service design strategies for elder markets

2.1 Categories of mature people

What are the differences between a healthy 55-year-old man and his 39-year-old tennis partner? The differences are actually slight. Both can be active, healthy, employed, and equipped with state-of-the-art gadgets. There is no age threshold between *young* and *old*. One differentiator for classification is: *from go-go to no-know*.

The first and youngest cluster of mature people (predominantly 50-65) can be called the *go-gos* – people who have the same needs and interests as their friends in their forties. However, most go-gos have something in common that differentiates them from their younger friends – their mature parents. Even when go-gos feel young at heart, they witness their parents or parents-in-law becoming older and often needing care. Go-gos are the first cohort to experience longevity. They witness the gift of a longer life as well as the decline in health, the burden of chronic illness, and are likely to witness someone becoming a multi-morbid or moribund patient. Go-gos experience ageing via their parents and older family members as well as through their own declining health status. While this makes them sensitive to the topic of age/ageing, it may not, subjectively, make them feel old.

The primary reason why people feel they are ageing is the deterioration in their psychophysical condition; this awareness places them in the second cluster, the so-called *slow-gos*. The slow-gos are limited in their mobility and/or sensory perception. Almost 50% of Germany's 65+ population suffers from hearing loss (Hesse and Laubert 2005). Hearing loss, limited vision, and a hip replacement present challenges in their day-to-day lives. Slow-gos are primarily found in the age group 65-75. While they don't need daily care, they do need assistance in some situations. Many are still members of their communities and live active lives. Common German stereotypes of people in this group are people with walkers or grandfathers with bad hearing at a family dinner.

The third cluster comprises people whose personal psychophysical conditions have deteriorated further – the *no-gos*: people who need care several times a week, even several times a day. Most no-gos receive care from their family in their own homes. Less than 20% of people in Germany who need care live in nursing homes.

The fourth cluster should really be a subgroup of the no-gos, but due to the prevalence of and increase in dementia, they comprise a separate cluster, called *no-knows*. In Germany, more than one million patients suffer from dementia; this figure is rising and is likely to continue to do so. These people are vulnerable and need extraordinary support and medical treatment.

Along the path from *go-go* to *no-know*, the core focus of the need definition is the personal psychophysical condition rather than actual age. In marketers' minds, the go-gos are the most desired customers as they have significant purchasing power, are in good shape and in a good state of mind, and enjoy quality of life.

2.2 Three product and communication strategies

How does one approach people who do not identify with their actual age? There is no one answer to this question across all industries. Companies must figure out how to position or alter their product lines and communication efforts. Generally, there are three product and communication strategy approaches (Deutsche Bank Research 2003): (1) one for all, (2) diverse communication, and (3) differentation.

2.2.1 One for all

Companies can sell and communicate their products and services, irrespective of all their (prospective) clients' needs and ages. Such an offer must be very easy to understand and have one value proposition. Electricity is a good example. People generally have the same needs in terms of electricity usage. However, there are very few products and services that can be marketed in this way. Most products and services must take another approach.

2.2.2 Diverse communication

Companies can sell the same product or service to all age groups, but they need differentiated communication to meet different levels of knowledge and/or client category concerns. This type of product and communication mix is often applicable in the field of technology products. Owing to their different individual and professional experiences, different age groups have different understandings of (new) technologies and technical products. Therefore, companies must approach different user groups differently; such groups are not only defined by age.

For example, if a company intends to sell a new type of digital camera, it is likely to consider the following: on the one hand, it must communicate with the experienced user group by focusing on the new camera's technically unique selling proposition (USP). On the other hand, it might consider that there are many people who have never owned a digital camera. These people need to be inspired or even convinced that digital imaging holds many advantages for them, and that this specific product is the one to choose. Without basic digital imaging information – which reduces uncertainty – this consumer type would be unable to understand the camera's advantages and would therefore be unwilling to spend money on a product they do not understand.

Consequently, a different communication need arises. In addition to classic product promotion for experienced users, there must be an informative and/or educational campaign for new users. This type of *support economy* reduces the concerns of non-experienced people; in the technical field, this comprises mostly seniors. Research shows that one-third of Germans have not purchased digital cameras or other technical products due to a lack of product understanding (Research International Deutschland 2004).

Companies must increase their general information and education efforts about innovations if they want to sell to new users. Best practise in Germany shows that general information material with very little commercial content help (ageing) new users explore a new field. Hands-on training can also help beginners become experts, while enhancing word of mouth marketing among seniors. Such communication focused on specific client categories' demands will be the most-needed solution in the next decade.

2.2.3 Differentiation

There are areas in which a specific version of a product for special age needs makes sense. If their sensory skills or visual perceptions have declined, most people are willing to use special products like phones with larger keys, or hand-rails on bathtubs. However, these tend to reflect the needs of people in their seventies, rather than in their fifties.

Another specific version field type is skin care. Most women and some men realise that at a certain age, the skin needs different treatment and accept their aged skin and/or seek to combat the ageing process. Companies can make special products available and communicate in ways that address the needs of an ageing market.

2.3   Differentiation of needs of mature people

All of these three strategies focus on needs, rather than age. While there is a strong connection between ageing and changing needs, age itself does not define a market. The differentiation of needs according to gender will become a new driver.

Marketing to meet mature women's specific needs will become more important in an ageing world because the number of ageing women will increase. Ageing women have, for example, a specific approach to technical and financial services. Mature women have often not controlled the family's financial matters like mortgages or pension planning. On losing their husbands, they may suddenly become responsible for these matters. This new situation generates new customer needs, which represent opportunities. Therefore, communication as well as personal service must address newly widowed women. There are specific target groups of mature women who share the same needs and can be addressed accordingly.

3   Successful differentiation: Need-based product development

3.1 Integrating seniors into the development process

A successful differentiation strategy requires developing special new 'elderly' products or services. In order to develop these, mainly younger product designers seek to understand the different needs by placing themselves in an ageing person's position (e.g., by using special age-imitating 'age suits') for a better impression of specific needs and design aspects. While using an age suit will give one a good idea of an ageing person's limited physical capabilities, it cannot convey the mental challenges.

The inefficiency of this approach seems clear. These designers may know how to design a product or service, but may lack knowledge of which product to design.

As Piller and Ihl (2009) note, every development task requires two kinds of information, namely *solution* information (information on how to solve problems arising from production or providing the offering) and *need* information (information on a target group's existing needs to ensure new product or service fit and success). Both kinds of information are available from the elderly.

In terms of solution information, most industries lack the 50+ market's wisdom and experience. The growing number of retired experts with a vast amount of solution information calls for new ways of involving ageing, experienced people in product/service design to benefit from their expertise. As for need information, integrating the elderly more closely into the development process would result in better fitting offerings, since the 50+ market is especially challenged by new products and services' high failure rates due to unmet customer needs.

Companies and industries therefore need to find additional ways of gathering both types of information. One possible way could be the frequently discussed concepts of *open innovation* (Chesbrough 2003) and *user innovation* (von Hippel 2005), which offer new ways to access, assimilate, and benefit from such external knowledge. Within these concepts, one way to access both kinds of information with externals is so-called idea contests. Idea contests are suitable for a broad range of problems (Piller and Walcher 2006) – from gathering ideas for new products or services and improving current offerings to an open call to solve specific (technical) problems (innovation contests; e.g., Terwiesch and Xu 2008). At a basic level, the functionality of an Internet-based idea contest, which is referred to in this chapter, consists of three features: (1) the possibility of submitting an idea for a new product or service, (2) the possibility of evaluating other people's ideas, and (3) the possibility of commenting on and improving others' ideas.

3.2 Example: Idea contest for user-friendly mobile phones[1]

As noted, new ways of involving older people in new product and service development are needed to face the challenges of an ageing society. The Ministry of Economic Affairs and Energy of North Rhine-Westphalia, along with the European Union, founded the research project *OpenISA – Open Innovation for health related services in the silver market* to address this problem.

The project seeks to develop an interdisciplinary open innovation platform to involve older people in the development of specific products or services for them. The platform is a Web-based community space for users, producers, and providers of specific age-related products and services. Several idea contests will be conducted to gather specific information for specific project priorities.

The first contest was conducted in the spring of 2010 with Emporia Telecom, an Austrian mobile phone manufacturer, to develop age-specific mobile phones (in terms of functionality and design). There were several reasons for focussing on

---

[1] The research project *OpenISA- Open Innovation for health related services in the silver market* was founded by The Ministry of Economic Affairs and Energy of North Rhine-Westphalia and the European Union within the "Ziel2.NRW" initiative (EFRE) 2007 to 2013.

mobile phones in our first contest. Firstly, they represent an important enabler technology for health-related services (so-called telemedicine applications), for which elder customers are a major target group. Secondly, they represent a typical product for which manufacturers tend to choose a differentiation strategy. The contest sought to examine whether mobile phones require a differentiation strategy and, if so, what the functions and designs would look like.

The contest, which is still in progress, has already yielded some interesting first results. Shortly after the contest was launched with a media conference, the first users registered and submitted ideas for the future senior mobile. In terms of registered users and posted ideas on the first day of the contest, the initial feedback has lead to the conclusion that senior customers are very willing to communicate with specific providers and producers. With very little effort, Emporia Telecom was able to generate several wholly new product ideas, extending its view of its own products.

During the first week, the contest had 1,088 visitors, of which 498 returned to the site at least once. In total, these people spent over 161 hours browsing and participating in the contest. Having been run for two months, the contest has had more than 6,000 visitors, who have spent more than 743 hours browsing and participating. 146 users have registered for the contest, shared more than 200 ideas, and posted almost 400 comments on and 1,300 evaluations of those ideas.

Besides providing ideas for developing novel functions or services, the users have also 'developed' highly acceptable products. The other participants (who correspond to the target group) have given any submitted idea an average evaluation of 4,22 on a 1-5 scale   (502 evaluations). The participants were asked for their purchase intentions, which also yielded a very high average: 3,95 on a 1-5 scale (466 evaluations).

The hosts generally view the contest as very successful. Many interesting ideas have been generated, some of which are very detailed. Figure 1 illustrates the contest's ideas development and the registered user numbers over time.

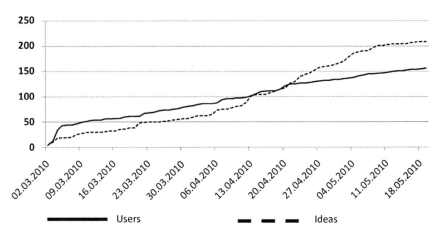

Figure 1: Members and ideas over time (source: authors)

While these first results do not yet show the best strategy for involving senior citizens in new product development (NPD) or new service development (NSD), they nevertheless serve as proof of the concept. Senior citizens are more than willing to participate, companies need to facilitate this valuable source of ideas. The number of seniors who preferred to join the contest offline was very low (less than 2% of the submitted ideas). This supports the argument that Internet use is a major driver of individual seniors' participation, rather than a barrier. Another finding was teamwork's positive effect in this age group. Several groups of seniors gathered to collaborate on an idea submitted by one group member. The participating groups had all been established as local senior special interest groups mainly working on local issues prior to the contest.

In short, by using idea contests, companies can harness many additional R&D 'personnel' from diverse backgrounds at low cost. The submitters of the top three ideas will be awarded a weekend trip to the IFA[2] consumer electronic exhibition for two people. Additionally, ten emporia mobiles will be raffled among the contest participants.

4   Conclusion

To be successful in the *silver markets*, companies must differentiate between clusters within the 50+ age group. These clusters must focus on specific needs, rather than age, and should become the baseline for R&D and communication activities.

This chapter showed different product or service design strategies for specific need-based clusters and provided examples of a successful implementation. For companies choosing a differentiation strategy, it introduced a method (idea contests) that will undoubtedly reduce product/service failure rate by proactively integrating seniors' knowledge, and experience into the innovation process. The elderly are more than happy to share their experience of existing products as well as their ideas and suggestions for new developments. Depending on the cluster definitions, the idea contest concept must be customized to specific group needs.

While idea contests and similar methods might not completely substitute internal R&D, the combination of external need information obtained from the elderly and a well-trained R&D team's capability seems likely to lead to a better understanding of the older generations' limited physical possibilities.

References

Chesbrough, H. (2003). *Open innovation: the new imperative for creating and profiting from technology.* Boston, MA: Harvard Business School Press.

Deutsche Bank Research (2003). The silver test. Deutsche Bank Research, http://www.dbresearch.de/PROD/DBR_INTERNET_DE-PROD/PROD0000000000066853.pdf.

---

[2]   Internationale Funkausstellung Berlin, the International Radio Exhibition Berlin.

Deutsche Seniorenliga e.V. (2010). Der Markt der Best Ager. *Befragung Deutscher Werbe-agenturen*, www.deutsche-seniorenliga-de. Accessed June 2010.

GfK GeoMarketing GmbH (2008). GfK purchasing power study. http://www.gfk.com/group/investor/key_figures_and_publications/investor_relations_news/news/002428/index.de.html.

Hesse, G. & Laubert, A. (2005). Hearing loss in the elderly – characteristics and location. *Deutsches Ärzteblatt*, 102(42), pp. 2864-2868.

Piller F. & Ihl, C. (2009). Open innovation with customers – Foundations, competences and international trends. Expert study commissioned by the European Union, the German Federal Ministry of Research and the Europäischer Sozialfond ESF. Published as part of the project "International Monitoring". Aachen: RWTH ZLW-IMA 2009.

Piller, F., Walcher, D. (2006). Toolkits for idea competitions: A novel method to integrate users in new product development. *R&D Management*, 36(3), 307-318.

Research International Deutschland (2004). Deutsche Konsumenten fühlen sich beim Kauf von technischen Produkten überfordert. *Survey by Research International Deutschland*.

Terwiesch, C. & Xu, Y. (2008). Innovation contests, open innovation, and multiagent problem solving. *Management Science*, 54(9), 1529-1543.

von Hippel, E. (2005). *Democratizing innovation*. Cambridge, MA: MIT Press.

How Swisscom copes with the challenges of demographic change

Guenter Pfeiffer[*]

Why age management? – Customer focus!

An ageing society simply results in an ageing customer base. Swisscom is the leading provider of telecommunications services in Switzerland, covering all market segments and age groups. Therefore, our approach to age management is primarily a market-driven and human-centric one.

We intend to address age-specific customer needs by designing the entire customer experience from the product design to the sales environment and services accordingly. Obviously, customers, particularly 'silver' customers, demand simple, easy-to-use products that support them in their daily life (e.g., easy to read displays and keyboards, intuitive user guidance, security, and health-related services). When asking for support in our shops or calling the service centres, these customers like to be on par with the agent. Thus, the employee structure at all customer touch points should reflect our customer structure. An age mix that matches the customer-base structure and their needs improves the quality of the service and customer loyalty. Current age management initiatives focus on Swisscom shops and customer contact centre helpdesks.

Furthermore, the telecommunications industry faces a technological shift, changing processes and shifting business models. Older and long-serving employees are disproportionately affected by these changes. Public awareness of an ageing workforce's employment is also increasing, and laying off older people is becoming less acceptable. New approaches to restructuring, redeployment, and age management that go beyond the usual instruments of part-time models and flexible retirement schemes are required.

What should the focus be? – Self-motivated people's motivation, creativity and experience!

In order to identify initiatives and projects that support age management, that have a positive business impact and are visible internally, a working group comprising the upper line management's older members was formed in November 2009. The group was empowered to come up with ideas on how to deploy older employees internally and externally. The question and mandate created energy and commit-

[*] Dr. Guenter Pfeiffer, Chief Personnel Officer and member of the Swisscom Group executive board.

S. Kunisch et al. (eds.), *From Grey to Silver*,
DOI 10.1007/978-3-642-15594-9_16, © Springer-Verlag Berlin Heidelberg 2011

ment in the working group, who developed some 70 ideas in design workshops by the end of 2009. Of the 70 ideas, four were selected for prototyping following the question: How can Swisscom develop attractive assignments – which simultaneously generate added value for customers and Swisscom – for its older employees, especially those about to lose their jobs?

The prototypes were presented to members of the Group Executive Board to test the business relevance, and to obtain support for the pilots to be carried out in their organisation as well as for a regular roll-out and sustainable implementation if the pilots proved to be a success. Three pilot projects were specified, managers and participants were identified, and responsibility for the projects was handed over to the line management in the Spring of 2010. The existing work group acted as the commissioning party and monitored the project results, facilitated learning across the projects and coordinated different divisions. In June 2010, the first pilot *silver customer contact centre* (silver CUC) started, followed shortly after by *silver shops*.

The silver CUC, realised in the current team structures, is staffed by experienced Swisscom employees over 50 years of age, who serve customers over 60 in a client relationship with a long history. When calling the standard helpline number, those customers are identified as 'silver customers' and the call is automatically routed to the silver CUC. The silver CUC employees participate voluntarily in the pilot. As long-serving customer agents, they are familiar with age-specific issues and requests. However, they may also take more time to consult the silver clients and solve their problems. Ultimately, customer satisfaction and loyalty should improve in this market segment through this segment-specific service approach. Furthermore, we gain insights into skills required in the silver CUC, average handling times, change in employee satisfaction through empowerment and reduced workload pressure and impact on the standard CUC operations.

The silver shop basically follows the same idea: Older customers with different service expectations benefit from working with older employees with whom they have a long-term relationship and who understand their needs. As in the silver CUC, we leave the shop team composition intact but enhance the shop staff with experienced silver colleagues. We identified different job profiles to cope with the new silver colleagues' different skill sets: Welcome managers (host, concierge), consultants (pre and after sales), support (back office) and sales agents. Compared to standard shop staff, the silver colleagues work on qualitative objectives which have less time pressure, thus creating leeway for part-time assignments.

How to implement successfully? – Learning through visible initiatives!

Our age management projects are still in a phase of continuous learning and optimisation. However, preliminary results indicate certain critical success factors. One of the most important factors is creating a win-win situation for the company and senior staff facing change. This is crucial to achieve commitment from both the line management and silver employees. The project ideas gained support easily as a positive business impact was intuitively obvious. Project implementation was easiest when existing processes, and teams could be used without major adjustments. Achieving a better age mix in already existing teams seems to be superior to special silver entities or locations.

Our existing job creation company, WorkLink, plays an important role as our internal marketplace and links internal demand and supply. During the early test phase, we had to cope with prejudices and obstacles such as that silver staff would be less stress resistant, unable to handle a full shop shift and lacking competencies to use modern IT applications. These issues could be partly resolved by allowing the silver colleagues, and teams to find solutions themselves.

The specific working environment and processes' bottom-up design turned out to be a powerful approach to develop appropriate solutions within the age management framework, which was previously defined top-down. However, continuous internal communication and organisational development are required to achieve sustainable results.

At the end of the day, our customers will determine whether this approach to age management will be successful.

Japan's growing silver market –
An attractive business opportunity for foreign companies?

Florian Kohlbacher, Pascal Gudorf, Cornelius Herstatt[*]

Japan is often considered a *lead market* for *silver* products as it is the country that has experienced the most dramatic demographic change. It has been labelled the most advanced in terms of product development and innovation, with – at least according to the stereotypical view – very affluent, free-spending, and demanding customers. The deeply rooted changes in the structure of Japan's population raise a number of critical questions that companies need to address. The impact of demographic change on human resource management, marketing management, sales, and other business functions is tremendous.

This chapter discusses whether Japan offers an attractive business opportunity in the silver industry with regard to new solutions (technologies, products, and services) corresponding to demand shifts rooted in Japan's demographic changes. Specifically, it discusses if and how foreign companies (in this case, German companies) are attracted to and leverage this innovation potential by investing in the building of local R&D and sales activities. The arguments are corroborated and exemplified by quantitative and qualitative empirical data from German companies doing business in Japan.

[*] Dr. Florian Kohlbacher, Senior Research Fellow and Head of Business & Economics Section, German Institute for Japanese Studies (DIJ) Tokyo, Japan.
Pascal Gudorf, Communications Manager, German Chamber of Commerce and Industry in Japan in Tokyo, Japan.
Prof. Dr. Cornelius Herstatt, Director, Institute for Technology and Innovation Management at Hamburg University of Technology (TUHH), Germany.

S. Kunisch et al. (eds.), *From Grey to Silver*,
DOI 10.1007/978-3-642-15594-9_17, © Springer-Verlag Berlin Heidelberg 2011

Table of Contents

1   Introduction

Attractive *lead markets* can be found in countries in which an innovation is first widely adopted and accepted, and eventually also diffuses from there to other countries (Beise 2001, 2004). Among other factors, demand and demand structure are important drivers in the development of lead markets. Mega-trends like demographic change cause new demand or shifts in existing demand, and can thus create and influence lead markets and their business potential in the countries in question.

Japan is the country most severely affected by the current demographic shift (Coulmas 2007; Coulmas et al. 2008), and also the most advanced country in terms of product development and innovation, with – at least according to the stereotypical view – very affluent, free-spending as well as demanding customers (Herstatt et al. 2006; McCreery 2000). Japan's population began to shrink in 2005, and as of December 2009, people aged 65+ accounted for 22.8% of the population, with those aged 50 and over constituting more than 43.4% of the population (MIC 2010).

The deeply rooted changes in the structure of Japan's population raise a number of critical questions that companies need to address. The demographic change's impact on human resource management, marketing management, sales, and other business functions is tremendous. Demographic change will definitely be one of the challenges that both domestic and multinational companies will need to face now and in future. Although in the current global economic and financial crisis, many companies deal with topics that seem more urgent, companies doing business in Japan need to address the challenges of demographic change if they want to be successful in this market in the long run. At the same time, engaging in a rapidly ageing market like Japan also provides the opportunity to learn from successful examples and solutions early on, and to apply them to the global market situation. Demographic change reflects a global mega-trend affecting not only most of the industrialised nations, but also several of the emerging markets. Indeed, the experiences encountered in the Japanese lead market (Kohlbacher and Herstatt 2008a; Kohlbacher et al. 2010b) may not only provide valuable insights into the societal implications of demographic change, but also uncover trends, opportunities, and innovative approaches for other developing markets.

The goal of this chapter is to discuss whether Japan can offer an attractive business opportunity in the silver product industry with regard to new solutions (technologies, products, and services) corresponding to demand shifts rooted in Japan's demographic changes. Specifically, the purpose is to discuss if and how foreign companies (in this case, German companies) are attracted and leverage this innovation potential by investing in the building of local R&D and sales activities. The arguments are corroborated and exemplified by quantitative and qualitative empirical data from German companies doing business in Japan.

2 Demographic challenges and opportunities

2.1 Rapid demographic change in Japan

Japan leads the world in terms of demographic changes. In 2005, Japan's population, along with its workforce, declined for the first time. If no measures are taken to increase the number of seniors and women working, the working population will decline dramatically. According to a Cabinet Office white book (2009), the labour force population of 66.5 million in 2008 will decline to 42.28 million by 2050. By 2030, a decline of more than 10 million is feared. The outlook for Japan is indeed gloomy by international standards, as shown by the percentage changes in Japan's population, especially its working age population (aged 20-64) (see Figure 1).

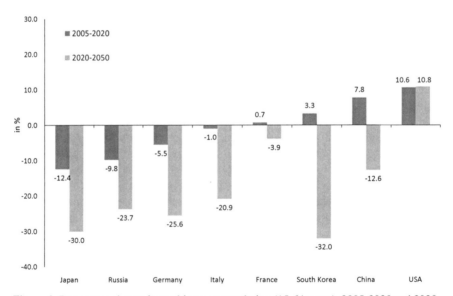

Figure 1. Percentage change in working-age population (15-64 years), 2005-2020 and 2020-2050 (medium variant) (Source: UN Population Division DESA 2009)

Predictions indicate that one quarter of all Japanese people will be over 64 by 2015, and one-third by 2025. At present, one in four women is 65 and older (25.5%), while the corresponding percentage for men is 20.0% (MIC 2010). Overall, the ratio between the 65+ population and the total population is the highest in Japan, and is forecasted to continue increasing and to remain ahead of the rest of the world. The number of senior people in Japan will increase further, while the population will in general decline to about 95 million by 2050 due to the low birth rate. No other country has ever experienced such a population decline combined with such rapid population ageing (Clark et al. 2010: 208).

These rapid demographic changes bear vast macro-level consequences for Japan's economy as well as micro-level consequences for firms and other organisations (Conrad et al. 2008; Kohlbacher and Herstatt 2008b). Indeed, projections and simulations show that while Japan's GDP growth can be sustained until 2019, its GDP will then begin to decline, and GDP per capita will decline after 2024 due to the smaller workforce (Clark et al. 2010, p. 216). On the micro level, challenges and threats include a potential labour shortage and knowledge loss as well as a shrinking customer base, but there are also potential chances and new business opportunities, for example, the so-called *growth market age* or *silver market* (Kohlbacher forthcoming).

2.2 Silver market potential

Demographic change will also shift market segments: a declining youth segment can be anticipated, in contrast with the continuously growing senior segment (Kohlbacher 2007; Kohlbacher and Herstatt 2008b). In fact, many market participants are concerned about the shrinking customer base of young, dynamic buyers as well as the demands of an older target group, which are still not very well understood. Demographic change could therefore cause problems for companies that do not adjust their product range and do not address new target groups.

2.2.1 Demand side

The number of potential customers is not the sole determinant of new business opportunities, however: purchasing power and consumer behaviour play a significant role and could compensate for the decline in customer numbers (Kohlbacher forthcoming). Seniors tend to spend their accumulated income and wealth instead of concentrating on savings and investments (Gassmann and Keupp 2005). Japanese private households with heads aged 50+ spend considerably more money per head than the younger age groups[1] (Figure 2).

---

[1] These figures need to be interpreted with caution. First of all, they are averages and do not say anything about the exact distribution within the whole population (which is all the more important due to the rising social inequalities in Japan). Secondly, the data are aggregated on the household level and do not reveal who actually controls and spends the money. Nevertheless, these figures provide a good overview of the financial situation of the silver generation in Japan.

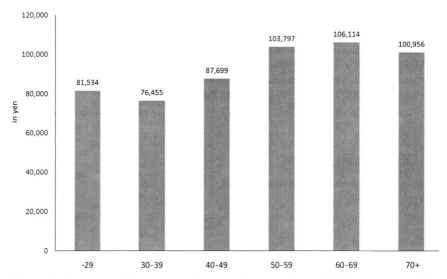

Figure 2. Average monthly consumption expenditures per household by age group of the household head, 2008 (average spending for one person in two-or-more-person households) (Source: MIC 2009, Table 3.2)

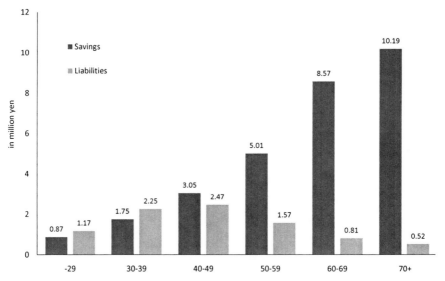

Figure 3. Average savings and liabilities held per household by age group of household head, 2008 (average for one person in two-or-more-person households) (Source: MIC 2009, Table 8.5)

Seniors' high purchasing power also stems from their financial wealth: On average, Japanese households with heads aged 60+ have savings of about 20 million yen (approximately 160,000 euro). Seniors are therefore the top age group in terms of savings. Per person, the generation of people over 70 has savings of more than 10 million yen (approximately 80,000 euro), closely followed by the 60 to 69-year-olds, with 8.6 million yen (cf. Figure 3). As a matter of fact, according to the latest estimates (2009), older people hold a disproportionately large amount of personal financial assets, with those in their 50s and 60s owning 21% and 31% respectively of the total, and those aged 70+ holding 28%. This means that people aged 50+ hold about 80% of the total personal financial assets in Japan (The Nikkei Weekly 2010). Furthermore, the older Japanese generally have no debts and own the property where they live (cf. also Conrad 2007). However, this does not apply to all of Japan's elderly, and the number of poorer seniors is expected to rise in future (Fukawa 2008; Kohlbacher and Weihrauch 2009).

2.2.2 Supply side

On the supply side, new industries and business opportunities are developing in response to the ageing population and their emerging needs. Various Japanese companies have already successfully started adjusting existing products and developing new products and technologies for this target group. As shown by user-friendly mobile phones, robots that take care of the elderly, and premium offerings for enjoying life after retirement – innovative products designed for the ageing population –, Japanese companies are increasingly adapting to this growing market. However, this is true of only a few pioneering firms, and even they have only addressed the tip of the iceberg of this market's huge potential (Kohlbacher forthcoming).

According to Clark et al., *"a careful assessment of the impact of population decline and rapid ageing in Japan can provide insights and important lessons for the future of Europe and other developed countries"* (2010, p. 208), as it is at the forefront of the demographic transition. Indeed, it has often been argued that Japan is playing a pioneering role in the silver market (Conrad and Gerling 2005; Coulmas 2007; Gassmann and Keupp 2005), and can thus be regarded as the silver industry's lead market (Kohlbacher and Herstatt 2008a; Kohlbacher et al. 2010b). As mentioned, attractive lead markets can be found in countries in which an innovation is first widely adopted and accepted and eventually also diffuses from there to other countries; i.e. most other countries follow the first country in adopting an innovation widely (Beise 2001, 2004). However, a *lead market* is not necessarily the country or market in which the innovation was first developed or even first used.

Bartlett and Ghoshal (1990) use the term lead markets in the context of these markets' ability to stimulate global innovations. According to them, lead markets are *"the markets that provide the stimuli for most global products and processes of a multinational company"* because *"local innovation in such markets become useful elsewhere as the environmental characteristics that stimulated such innovations diffuse to other locations"* (p. 243). In this case, the stimulating environmental characteristics are the demographic change and the resulting shifts in demand and market structure. Beise (2001, 2004) has derived a system of five groups of a country's *lead advantages*: (1) price advantage, (2) demand advantage, (3) transfer advantage, (4) export advantage, and (5) market structure advantage.

Demand advantage is the most straightforward when applying this theory to the silver market. Indeed, demographic changes cause new demands or shifts in existing demands and can therefore influence the lead market potential of the affected countries.

3   German companies in Japan

3.1 Empirical study

Japan is the world's second largest economy as well as one of the most important export markets for Western companies in Asia. As the most advanced in terms of demographic change, it can be assumed that Japan should also attract foreign companies to enter its silver market. A study of German companies doing business in Japan, jointly conducted by the German Chamber of Commerce and Industry in Japan (GCCIJ), the German Institute for Japanese Studies (DIJ) Tokyo, and the Institute for Technology and Innovation Management at Hamburg University of Technology (TUHH), sheds light on the question whether foreign companies really regard Japan as an attractive business opportunity in the silver industry.[2]

The results of the quantitative survey show how German companies in Japan deal with the implications of demographic change. The study also helps evaluate how active (or passive) German companies are in the Japanese silver market in terms of product development and marketing. These results will be complemented by two case studies of two pioneering German companies that decided to seize the demographic opportunity presented by Japan.

3.2 Product development and marketing in times of demographic change

The vast majority of German companies are convinced that the silver market offers business opportunities. More than 90% of all companies surveyed believe that the senior segment will develop into an interesting market within the next five to ten years. However, only 45% of companies see potential business opportunities for their own company in this market, and believe that ageing will dramatically influence their business model in the coming years. Most of the surveyed business-to-business suppliers feel that, on the market side, they will hardly be affected by demographic change (see below).

According to the survey, one in five German companies in Japan offers products and services for older consumers. These are not only items related to medical devices and health care, but also include food supplements, clothing, transport, and walking aids, household appliances, and services such as financial and insurance products (cf. Figure 4).

---

[2] Please refer to the Appendix for further information on the study.

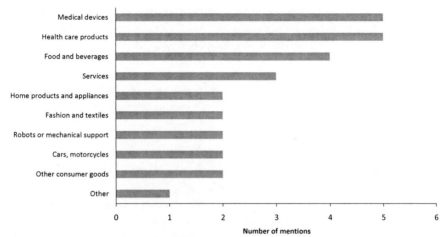

(n=28 responses, the rest of the companies does not develop special offers)

Figure 4. Responses to "What kind of products or services have you been developing specifically for senior customers?" (Source: Kohlbacher et al. 2010a, p. 16)

Although there is potential, the marketing and the development of new customer groups in the silver market is still new territory for many German companies in Japan. One in four companies have noticed that demographic change has directly affected their businesses. A quarter of the companies that felt these demographic effects (i.e. 6% of the total sample) reported declines in sales or changes in the customer base and the target market (cf. Figure 5).

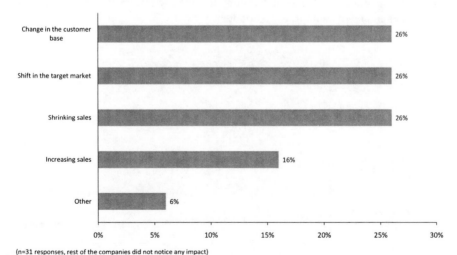

(n=31 responses, rest of the companies did not notice any impact)

Figure 5. Responses to "In which way did demographic change affect your sales/market(s)?" (Source: Kohlbacher et al. 2010a, p. 14)

A total of 16% of the companies concerned reported that they were able to profit from demographic change through increased sales. Several examples illustrate how companies are taking advantage of demographic change and, as a result, improving their business opportunities.

However, most of the 135 companies surveyed are reluctant to conduct business in the silver market. This is true across different sectors and applies to market research, marketing efforts, and product development for seniors. Only 10 of the 135 companies reported carrying out market research among the elderly. At the same time, only 10% of the companies believed that surveying the elderly was more difficult than surveying other age groups. This percentage indicates that the survey and focus group age is not perceived as an obstacle. Overall, marketing activities are rarely specifically directed at older consumers.

The vast majority of the surveyed companies, namely 92.2%, said they did not advertise any products specifically for older target groups. Only 5.4% of the companies undertake marketing in respect to a limited portion of their products directed at seniors . These companies are pioneers trying to appeal more strongly to seniors by either adjusting or expanding their product range as well as by strategically reorienting their communication.

The number of companies that develop products for seniors (cf. Figure 6) is very limited: 79.9% of German companies in Japan do not develop products or services specifically for the elderly. Only 6.5% mentioned that they develop products designed to meet older customers' needs. Other companies offer products featuring a 'universal design' or have modified existing products. However, the finding that almost no product development takes place in Japan reflects the fact that research and development is, in many cases, done by the parent company in Germany (even though some larger companies have set up technology offices in Japan to observe the market and learn about the latest trends).

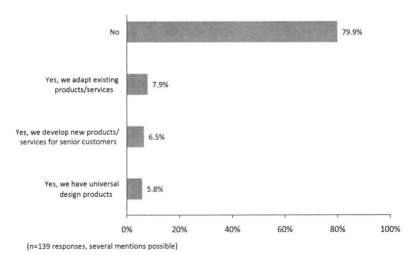

(n=139 responses, several mentions possible)

Figure 6. Responses to "Do you develop products or services specifically for senior customers?" (Source: Kohlbacher et al. 2010a, p. 23)

Finally, in the survey and during the follow-up interviews, the manufacturing companies held that business-to-business companies that do not manufacture products for final customers do not need to deal with the silver market. However, it should be kept in mind that machines and other equipment for the workplace would need to be adjusted to suit the needs of older employees (cf. also Mertens et al. 2008). As a starting point, it is useful to provide ergonomically designed, easy-to-use, and intuitive items as well as easily legible characters and signs on machines. Such products, designed specifically for the physical as well as mental needs of older employees, are often innovative and beneficial for younger staff as well.

3.3 Strategies for entering Japan's silver market

While foreign companies' activities in Japan's silver market remain limited, pioneering efforts by some German companies have been quite successful (as shown in Figure 5). These are not limited to obvious business sectors such as medical devices and health care, but also include transportation devices (e.g., home elevators), consumer goods (e.g., apparel), and the service sector (e.g., insurance).

Through interviews with managers of German companies and the analysis of several case studies, two generic strategies were identified that foreign companies pursue when entering Japan's silver market. In the cases (described in detail below), Japan's position as the world's most advanced ageing society has been a crucial factor in the company's decision to enter Japan's silver market. However, their strategies have differed significantly from the start. Although the two case studies do not represent all possible strategies, they do show two generic and very different approaches that companies can take when entering a new market with products and services for the silver generation.

3.3.1 Case 1: Introducing successful products from overseas markets to Japan

The first and most obvious approach is to apply successful products or services from the home market or other markets to Japan. This has been ThyssenKrupp Access's (a ThyssenKrupp subsidiary) approach to marketing its stair lift, called Flow. Developed in the Netherlands, this product was successfully introduced in the EU and the US prior to its launch in Japan in 2008. For ThyssenKrupp Access, demographic change was only the starting point in penetrating the Japanese market. Its decision to enter the Japanese market was based on the great potential for barrier-free solutions that would facilitate an easier life in senior-unfriendly residences in Japan's metropolitan areas.

With this product, ThyssenKrupp Access provides seniors with mobility. The stair lift, which runs on a single steel rail on the stairs, is easy to install in Japanese homes. The fact that this compact product provides sufficient space for other people to use the stairs at the same time seemed an important competitive advantage, especially in small Japanese condominiums. However, two years after its launch, the stair lift's sales, although increasing, are still below expectations. The company's greatest challenges are to overcome the lack of awareness of the stair lift, to find the right sales channels, and to overcome existing market barriers.

A decisive factor for companies pursuing this approach is to adapt existing products and services to local market needs, for example, the Japanese customer's specific service and quality requirements. In many cases, ergonomic adaptations are needed to accommodate different physical features or specific comfort preferences. Furthermore, Japanese customers often ask for additional options. ThyssenKrupp has used insights and requests from the Japanese market to further improve the quality of existing products and these have also been channelled into the development process of future products.

3.3.2 Case 2: Developing new products and business concepts in Japan as a test market

The size and growth potential of Japan's silver market has lead a few foreign companies to develop wholly new products and services in Japan. In these cases, Japan serves as a test and learning market and helps companies explore senior customer preferences. Successful products and business concepts can later be transferred to other markets or adapted to fit the needs of customers in other countries.

A good example of this strategy is Otto Japan, a leading German fashion catalogue company. Since its market entry in the 1980s, Otto's main customer group has consisted of Japanese women between 35 and 55. Over time, as these customers aged, Otto began adapting and expanding its product line to the tastes of mature customers. In 2006, it introduced a new catalogue called *Otto Madame*, in addition to its main catalogue (*Otto Women*), specifically targeting women between 50 and 65. In this catalogue, Otto also tests silver market products for women over 65.

In its product line, Otto Japan addresses the changing preferences and fashion styles of senior female customers. The product line for mature Japanese women is of particularly high quality as well as unique in terms of elegant materials, cuts, and colours. Customers can also expect a concierge service that assists senior customers in making purchasing decisions. The company has introduced a special VIP hotline for this customer group. Call centre staff are trained to advise customers in a very polite and professional manner about their orders as well as of possible selections for specific occasions.

A key success factor for Otto Japan has been its multi-channel strategy combining the traditional mail order operations (catalogue) with new e-commerce concepts (Internet) and points of sale (over-the-counter). Since its inception in 2006, the circulation of the *Otto Madame* catalogue has increased continuously, and now reaches almost half a million Japanese households. Besides the catalogue, online sales have risen in recent years, with online growth rates among senior customers being particularly high. Furthermore, in 2009, Otto opened its first point of sales at Keio Department store in Tokyo, targeting senior consumers with premium fashion products. This *touch-point* literally allows customers to touch products prior to purchasing. For Otto, the test store also serves as a basis to gain even more insights into the preferences of the ageing clientele. Market insights and experiences are later shared within the Otto Group.

4 Lessons learned from the survey and case studies

Against the backdrop of Japan's dramatic demographic shifts, there were two assumptions: (1) Foreign companies (in this case, German companies) react to the challenges and opportunities caused by demographic change, and (2) Japan is an attractive lead market as a result of these developments.

As seen from the quantitative survey and the two case studies, the high number of wealthy aged customers has already attracted considerable interest from German companies in very different industries. One can thus speak of demand-induced interest and a demand-induced market attractiveness. While not all German companies have profited from these opportunities, some already do. Many German companies seem to have difficulties in approaching the ageing clientele (including market segmentation, doing market research, and developing distinctive concepts). Other companies (a small fraction of the present sample) are developing solutions for their ageing customers. As is the case with all innovation-related activities and new businesses, such activities bear the risk of failure; the fact that Japan seems an attractive (lead) market for silver products is no guarantee of success.

Overall, this means that there are some interesting tendencies, but the vast majority of German companies doing business in Japan have not reached their potential (even though they are well aware of the challenges and opportunities); the reasons for this failure vary and cannot all be discussed here. Besides, the sales of silver products have not necessarily lived up to the expectations of the pioneering companies, even though there are exceptions such as Otto. Furthermore, companies can take very different strategic approaches to entering Japan's silver market from abroad. In one case, the strategy was to introduce successful products from the home market and adapt them to the specific market needs, while in the second, new products and business concepts were developed in Japan as a test market. No doubt, several other options are available, and the final assessment of which approach is the most successful or the most appropriate remains an open question.

Japan is not the only country with a rapidly ageing society. Sooner or later, other nations will experience similar developments. The activities of foreign companies doing business in Japan –the most advanced ageing society – might one day become extremely useful in their home markets. Some companies explicitly call Japan a test or a learning market for their products. It has been reported that insights from the Japanese market have been applied to product development at foreign companies' headquarters. Whether Japan will serve as a successful testing ground prior to the introduction of products developed and marketed in Japan into other markets remains to be seen.

According to the survey of German companies, very few companies have done market research among older consumers and/or developed products for the silver market. What does this really tell us? Are the companies front runners or pioneers? Are companies reluctant to invest in developing silver products because they lack confidence in the assumed market potential, or do they lack strategies to segment and properly serve this assumed market? Further research is needed if the answers to these questions are to be anything but speculative.

5   Conclusion

With almost 23% of its population at 65+, Japan is the most advanced ageing society in the world today. Japan became an aged society in 1994 – sooner than other industrial nations –, when its share of senior citizens exceeded 14%. Japan's share of people over 64 reached 21% in 2007, making it the first country to be labelled a *super-aged* or *hyper-aged* society (cf. also Coulmas 2007). As Japan was the first society to experience such dramatic demographic change, its companies were the first to be affected by its consequences and had to adapt their strategies and product lines to these new challenges early on.

At first, only the health care sector was expected to profit due to the rising demand for medical treatment and health care services, but the high number of aged wealthy people, especially in the baby-boomer generation, and their favourable spending behaviour soon focused attention on the opportunities in other sectors. The advent of a new, affluent senior customer segment was considered to contribute to the creation of a new and lucrative silver market beyond the medical industry. Various Japanese companies have successfully created demand among this target group, thus turning a potential threat into an opportunity. However, these are only pioneering efforts (Kohlbacher forthcoming; Kohlbacher et al. 2010a). Many companies are caught up in old patterns and risk shrinking sales unless they also target older customers. Even though most of the evidence is anecdotal, the number of Japanese companies developing products for the silver market seems to remain low.

However, the speed and intensity of Japan's demographic changes and the resulting shift in market segments and demand structure are among the reasons why Japan is often considered the forerunner in the area of the silver market, as mentioned. Besides the country's demographic development, researchers have also pointed to the peculiar Japanese consumer behaviour and the innovative capacity of Japanese companies (Kohlbacher forthcoming; Kohlbacher et al. 2010b). Japanese customers have generally been considered as very quality oriented and therefore demanding. This characteristic is considered especially true for mature customers, given their life experience and financial resources. High quality and excellent service are therefore indispensible for reaching wealthy Japanese customers. There is also a greater openness to technical novelties compared to other countries. However, the assumption that senior customers are generally also ready to pay a premium price must be questioned. On the contrary, Japanese consumers have recently reduced their expenditure and are now questioning their well-known inclination to pay for convenience (Salsberg 2010, p. 82). Even affluent older consumers in the baby-boom cohort are saving their money or are using it to support their children or grand-children in this time of economic downturn, instead of spending it on themselves (Nihon Keizai Shimbun 2010). This means that, despite the high potential demand, companies face consumers with a very tight grip on their purses, which further exacerbates the demographic challenge.

This chapter's leading question was whether Japan can offer an attractive business opportunity in the silver product industry with regard to new solutions (technologies, products, and services) corresponding to demand shifts rooted in its demographic changes. There are reasons to believe that the answer is yes, it generally can. This argument is supported by the obvious demographic developments and the many unique solutions from different industries in Japan, which have already been developed and can be clearly aligned to age-specific needs. Some of these solutions have already been exported to other countries and have proven successful in different cultural contexts. One prominent example is the care robot Paro (Kohlbacher et al. 2010a).

There are three main – preliminary – conclusions: Firstly, as powerful as they may be, demographic shifts and the resulting changes in demand structures are clearly not a sufficient condition to induce companies to enter the domestic and foreign silver market and to innovate in this area. Secondly, Japan is not yet a lead market for the silver industry, or at least not in all areas (robotics is one possible exception), even though it already offers attractive business opportunities in the silver industry. Thirdly, Japan is a pioneer in terms of demographic change, but not yet a leader in leveraging this trend as a business opportunity. We therefore make an urgent call for further research, especially on a more fine-grained company and industry level.

Appendix: Survey details

Between 23 May and 14 July 2008, this survey was sent to 411 German companies in Japan, questioning them about the implications of demographic change on their business. The analysis was carried out on the basis of 135 completed questionnaires, which corresponds to a representative response rate of 32.8%. The responses stem from eight industry sectors, primarily from machinery and engineering, automotive, consumer goods, services, and health care. The key points of the questionnaire were, on the one hand, the challenges and threats posed by demographic change such as labour shortage, loss of knowledge, and a shrinking customer base, and, on the other hand, new business opportunities in the silver market.

In addition to the survey, interviews were carried out with selected German companies in Japan to add qualitative aspects to the quantitative data, case studies, and best business practices. The interviews took place from 20 March to 3 April 2009, and consisted of face-to-face meetings with 20 company representatives from various industry sectors. The detailed results of the study are documented in Kohlbacher, Gudorf and Herstatt (2010a), and include examples of management strategies and successful products from Japanese companies.

References

Bartlett, C. A., & Ghoshal, S. (1990). Managing innovation in the transnational corporation. In C. A. Bartlett, Y. Doz & G. Hedlund (Eds.), *Managing the global firm* (Vol. 215-255, pp. 69-94). London: Routledge.

Beise, M. (2001). *Lead markets: Country-specific success factors of the global diffusion of innovations*. Heidelberg: Physica.

Beise, M. (2004). Lead markets: Country-specific drivers of the global diffusion of innovations. *Resarch Policy, 33*(6-7), 997-1018.

Cabinet Office. (2009). *Heisei 21-nenban shshika shakai hakusho [2009 white book on the society with fewer children]*. Tokyo: Cabinet Office, Government of Japan.

Clark, R. L., Ogawa, N., Kondo, M., & Matsukura, R. (2010). Population decline, labor force stability, and the future of the Japanese economy. *European Journal of Population, 26*(2), 207-227.

Conrad, H. (2007). Japanische Senioren als Konsumenten und der 'Silbermarkt': Ein Lehrstück für Deutschland? In M. Behrens & J. Legewie (Eds.), *Japan nach Koizumi: Wandel in Politik, Wirtschaft und Gesellschaft* (pp. 177-187). Baden-Baden: Nomos.

Conrad, H., & Gerling, V. (2005). Der japanische 'Silbermarkt' – Marktchancen und Best Practices für deutsche Unternehmen. In K. Bellmann & R. Haak (Eds.), *Management in Japan: Herausforderungen und Erfolgsfaktoren für deutsche Unternehmen in einer dynamischen Umwelt* (pp. 267-278). Wiesbaden: Deutscher Universitäts-Verlag.

Conrad, H., Heindorf, V., & Waldenberger, F. (Eds.). (2008). *Human resource management in ageing societies: Perspectives from Japan and Germany*. Basingstoke: Palgrave Macmillan.

Coulmas, F. (2007). *Population decline and ageing in Japan – The social consequences.* London: Routledge.

Coulmas, F., Conrad, H., Schad-Seifert, A., & Vogt, G. (Eds.). (2008). *The demographic challenge: A handbook about Japan*. Leiden, Boston: Brill.

Fukawa, H. (2008). Poverty among the elderly. In F. Coulmas, H. Conrad, A. Schad-Seifert & G. Vogt (Eds.), *The demographic challenge: A handbook about Japan* (pp. 921-931). Leiden, Boston: Brill.

Gassmann, O., & Keupp, M. M. (2005). Wachstumsmarkt der jungen Alten: Lernen von Japan. *io new management, 7-8*, 15-19.

Herstatt, C., Stockstrom, C., Tschirky, H., & Nagahira, A. (Eds.). (2006). *Management of technology and innovation in Japan*. Heidelberg: Springer.

Kohlbacher, F. (2007). Baby Boomer Retirement, Arbeitskräftemangel und Silbermarkt: Herausforderungen und Chancen des demographischen Wandels für Unternehmen in Japan. *Wirtschaftspolitische Blätter, 54*(4), 745-758.

Kohlbacher, F. (forthcoming). Business implications of demographic change in Japan: Chances and challenges for human resource and marketing management. In F. Coulmas & R. Lützeler (Eds.), *Imploding populations – Japan at the forefront of developments in the industrialized world*. Leiden: Brill.

Kohlbacher, F., Gudorf, P., & Herstatt, C. (2010a). Silver business in Japan: Implications of demographic change for human resource management and marketing. *German Chamber of Commerce and Industry in Japan*.

Kohlbacher, F., & Herstatt, C. (2008a). Preface and Introduction. In F. Kohlbacher & C. Herstatt (Eds.), *The Silver Market Phenomenon: Business Opportunities in an Era of Demographic Change* (pp. xi-xxv). Heidelberg: Springer.

Kohlbacher, F., & Herstatt, C. (Eds.). (2008b). *The Silver Market Phenomenon: Business Opportunities in an Era of Demographic Change*. Heidelberg: Springer.

Kohlbacher, F., Herstatt, C., & Schweisfurth, T. (2010b). Produktentwicklung in Zeiten des demografischen Wandels: Herausforderungen und Ansätze der Marktbearbeitung. *Wissenschaftsmanagement – Zeitschrift für Innovation, 16*(1), 30-36.

Kohlbacher, F., & Weihrauch, A. (2009). Japan's silver market phenomenon: Golden opportunity or rusty reality? *Japan Close-Up, May 2009*, 18-23.

McCreery, J. (2000). *Japanese consumer behavior: From worker bees to wary shoppers*. Honolulu: University of Hawai'i Press.

Mertens, P., Russell, S., & Steinke, I. (2008). Silver markets and business customers: Opportunities for industrial markets? In F. Kohlbacher & C. Herstatt (Eds.), *The silver market phenomenon: Business opportunities in an era of demographic change* (pp. 353-370). Heidelberg: Springer.

MIC (Ministry of Internal Affairs and Communications). (2009). *Family income and expenditure survey.* Retrieved 2010/02/19. from http://www.e-stat.go.jp/SG1/estat/Xlsdl.do?sinfid=000002209380 (Table 3.2, consumption), http://www.e-stat.go.jp/SG1/estat/XlsdlE.do?sinfid=000002932542 (Table 8.5, savings and liabilities).

MIC (Ministry of Internal Affairs and Communications). (2010). *Population estimates, Monthly Report, May 2010.* Retrieved 2010/06/10. from http://www.stat.go.jp/english/data/jinsui/tsuki/index.htm and http://www.e-stat.go.jp/SG1/estat/ListE.do?lid=0000010 63847.

Nihon Keizai Shimbun. (2010). Dankai sedai, zeitaku oazuke (Baby boomers postpone consumption of luxury goods). *5 February 2010,* p. 27.

Salsberg, B. (2010). The new Japanese consumer. *McKinsey Quarterly, 2010*(2), 80-87.

The Nikkei Weekly. (2010, 2010/01/11). Boomers wield financial clout,

UN Population Division DESA (2009). *World population prospects – The 2008 Revision Population Database.* New York: UN Population Division DESA (= Department of Economic and Social Affairs).

List of Authors

Sabrina Adamczyk is a doctoral candidate and Research Associate at the chair for Information Systems I – Innovation & Value Creation at the University of Erlangen-Nuremberg. She graduated from the Technische Universität München as a Diplom-Kauffrau (equivalent to a Master's in business) with majors in technology and innovation management as well as information and organisation management. Her current research interests are open innovation and innovation contests.

Miriam K. Baumgaertner is a Research Associate and doctoral candidate at the Center for Disability and Integration (CDI-HSG) at the University of St. Gallen (Switzerland). She studied psychology at the Universities of Constance and Mannheim (Germany) and at the University of North Carolina and at Western Carolina University (USA). She worked as a Research Assistant at gesis (The Leibniz Institute for the Social Sciences, formerly ZUMA) for several years. At Kenexa, she gained practical experience as a Consultant in the areas of employee surveys and HR management solutions.

Dr. Eva Bilhuber Galli, the Managing Director of human facts ag, is a Management Consultant and Executive Coach. Her interdisciplinary approach combines insights from business administration and psychology in order to balance humanity and efficiency in organisations. She is particularly interested in the creation of trust in companies, transformation processes and leadership development. Prior to this, she worked in executive functions for ten years in the area of employee, management and organisational development in a multinational company. She received a doctorate in business administration from the University of St. Gallen (topic of dissertation: "Strategic alignment of leadership development") and a Master's from the University of D-Freiburg i. Brsg. in education sciences and psychology.

Dr. Stephan A. Boehm is a Senior Lecturer and Director of the Center for Disability and Integration (CDI-HSG) at the University of St. Gallen (Switzerland). He studied business administration at the University of St. Gallen, the HEC Lausanne (Switzerland), and the University of Stellenbosch Business School (South Africa). He received a Master's (2003) and a Ph.D. (2008) from the University of St. Gallen. In 2008 and in the spring of 2009, he served as a Visiting Research Fellow at the Oxford Institute of Ageing at the University of Oxford, Great Britain. His research interests include diversity management, with a focus on the integration of disabled employees and the management of demographic change as well as group-level and organisational-level processes of categorisation, stereotyping, and discrimination. Stephan works as a Consultant and Trainer for several European companies and has gained additional practical experience while working at Siemens, Deutsche Telekom and Mercer Management Consulting.

S. Kunisch et al. (eds.), *From Grey to Silver*,
DOI 10.1007/978-3-642-15594-9, © Springer-Verlag Berlin Heidelberg 2011

Michael Boppel is a Research Associate and a doctoral candidate at the Institute of Management of the University of St. Gallen (Switzerland). His research interests are in the field of strategy processes, focusing on the set-up and evolution of corporate initiatives in multi-business firms. He is a board member of the doctoral network at the University of St. Gallen. Previously, he was a Consultant for KPMG Germany, advising companies on financial distress and turnaround situations. He holds a Master's in business computing from the University of Paderborn (Germany).

Prof. Dr. Heike Bruch has been the Director of the Institute for Leadership and Human Resources Management of the University of St. Gallen (Switzerland) since 2001. Professor Bruch is also the Academic Director of the International Study Program (ISP) at the University of St. Gallen, a member of the McKinsey Academic Sounding Board, and a member of the Executive Board of DGFP (the German Association for Leadership). Between 1999 and 2001, Heike served at the London Business School (UK) as a Visiting Scholar and later as a Senior Research Fellow. She received her habilitation from University of St. Gallen (2001), her doctorate from the University of Hanover (1996) and her Master's (1991) in business administration from the Free University of Berlin. Heike's research interests include managers' emotion, volition and action as well as leadership in change processes and organisational energy.

Dr. Angelika C. Bullinger is an Assistant Professor at the chair for Information Systems I – Innovation & Value Creation at the University of Erlangen-Nuremberg. She graduated from the University of St. Gallen with majors in information, technology, media, and communication management. At the same time she also earned a Master's in business from the HEC Paris. Angelika Bullinger received her Ph.D. from the Technische Universität München, where she served as a Research Associate at the Institute for Information, Organisation and Management. Her research interests lie at the boundaries between information systems and innovation management, particularly the interplay of open innovation and the collaboration of research and development teams in academia and practice.

David J. G. Dwertmann is a Research Associate and doctoral candidate at the Center for Disability and Integration (CDI-HSG) at the University of St. Gallen (Switzerland). He studied psychology with business administration as minor at the universities of Mannheim (Germany) and Bern (Switzerland). Before joining the Center for Disability and Integration, he conducted research at the University of Mannheim and San Diego State University. His research interests focus on diversity management, organisational culture, and job attitudes.

Dr. Matt Flynn is a Senior Lecturer in HRM at Middlesex University (UK). His research interests include age management, age discrimination, employment relations and trade union management. He has written for the UK and EU governments on age diversity, knowledge management, retirement and flexibility. Matt was the co-investigator in the project 'Age Diversity at the Workplace' and lead the project 'Older Workers in the UK and Japan'. He was a Research Fellow at the Centre for Research into the Older Workforce at Surrey University (UK). He received his M.Sc. in public policy and public administration from the London School of Economics (UK) and his Ph.D. in trade union management from Cranfield University (UK).

Dr. Peder Greve obtained his Ph.D. in international management in 2009 from the University of St. Gallen (Switzerland). His research focuses on the international market for executives and the role of top management teams in the firm internationalisation process. He is currently employed as a Research Fellow at the Research Institute for International Management at the University of St. Gallen.

Pascal Gudorf is Communications Manager at the German Chamber of Commerce and Industry in Tokyo (Japan). He is also Editor-in-Chief of Japan Markt, a German monthly that covers business trends in Japan. His primary research topics include changes in Japan's outward and inward foreign direct investment, marketing strategies of foreign companies in Japan as well as the impacts of globalisation on Japanese corporate strategies.

Golo Henseke is a doctoral student and Research Assistant at the Institute of Economics of the Rostock University. He is associated with the Rostock Center for the Study of Demographic Change. His research interests include the consequences of demographic change on labour force dynamics, innovation patterns, and economic growth. He has attended Ph.D. courses at the Max Planck Institute of Demographic Research, Rostock (Germany), has participated in the DFG Summer School 'Labor Economics – Theory, Empirical Methods, Current Research', Mannheim (Germany), and has presented his work at several international conferences.

Prof. Dr. Cornelius Herstatt is Director of the Institute for Technology and Innovation Management at Hamburg University of Technology (TUHH). He is the author of numerous books and more than 160 scientific contributions in the area of technology and innovation management. He regularly consults to companies in different industry sectors. His research focuses on customer-centred innovations, designing innovation processes, open source innovation and innovation in global added-value networks.

Kurt Hoerhager has been the CEO of Consenec AG since 2006. Consenec is an internationally active consulting company founded by ABB (Switzerland), ALSTOM (Switzerland) and Bombardier (Switzerland). The Consenec model was developed by ABB Switzerland in 1993 in order to rejuvenate its management as well as to continue to profit from the experience and knowledge of its former top-level managers. The managers of the three companies leave their original posts at the age of 60 and transfer to Consenec, where they continue their careers as Senior Consultants. Prior to joining Consenec, Kurt held various management positions, most recently managing ABB's Semiconductor Unit. In addition to his duties as CEO, he also works as a Consultant in the fields of strategy development/implementation and production relocation.

Dr. Martin Karlsson is an Assistant Professor in applied econometrics at the Technische Universität Darmstadt and a Research Fellow at the University of Oslo. He wrote his Ph.D. thesis on incentive regulation in health care. As a Researcher, he participated in several projects in applied health economics at Cass Business School in London and at the University of Oxford. His primary research interests lie in the domain of health economics and span a range of topics, including the effect of economic inequalities on individual health, information asymmetries in health insurance, and the effect of sickness pay on labour supply. At the Technische Universität Darmstadt his teaching activities are predominantly in applied micro-econometrics.

Florian Klohn (Dipl. oec.) is a Research and Teaching Assistant at the Chair for Applied Econometrics at the Technische Universität Darmstadt. He studied economics at the Ruhr-Universität Bochum, with an emphasis on econometrics and economic policy. In his diploma thesis, he empirically evaluated the relationship between unemployment and crime in Germany. His main research interests lie in the fields of applied econometrics, health economics, labour markets and competition policy.

Dr. Florian Kohlbacher is a Senior Research Fellow and Head of Business & Economics Section at the German Institute for Japanese Studies (DIJ) (Tokyo). He currently manages a research project on the implications of demographic change for businesses. Florian is a Fellow of the World Demographic & Ageing Forum as well as an Advisor to the International Mature Marketing Network (IMMN). He is the author of *International Marketing in the Network Economy: A Knowledge-Based Approach* (Palgrave 2007) and, with Cornelius Herstatt, the co-editor of *The Silver Market Phenomenon: Business Opportunities in an Era of Demographic Change* (Springer, 2008) as well as *The Silver Market Phenomenon: Marketing and Innovation in the Aging Society* (2nd edition, Springer, 2011).

Sven Kunisch is a doctoral candidate at the Institute of Management of the University of St. Gallen (Switzerland). His research interest focuses on strategic management, specifically corporate strategy. He holds a diploma in business informatics from the University of Rostock (Germany). Since the autumn of 2007, he has been Chief Editor of *M&A REVIEW,* a German monthly dedicated to mergers and acquisitions. Prior to this, he served as a Management Consultant at Accenture and gained additional work experience with Dr. Ing. h.c. F. Porsche AG. He is a board member of the doctoral network at the University of St. Gallen. He has published several conference papers and practitioner-oriented articles on management topics and co-edited two books.

Dr. Florian Kunze is a Senior Research Fellow at Institute for Leadership and Human Resources Management of the University of St. Gallen (Switzerland). In 2010, he completed his Ph.D. dissertation on demographic change in companies. His research focuses on the management of demographic change, processes triggered by diversity in teams and companies, and adjusted leadership behaviour for age-diverse teams and differently aged individuals. Florian studied politics and management at the universities of Konstanz (Germany) and Pavia (Italy) and gained practical experience while working for PricewaterhouseCoopers and Daimler-Chrysler, among others.

Frank Leyhausen holds a degree in insurance business, marketing and direct marketing. He joined MedCom International in 2001 after working in the marketing of financial industries for more than 10 years. At MedCom, he set up a demographic consulting business unit; here, he and his team focus on communication and product development in all age-related issues as well as in workforce management. He became General Manager in 2005 and Partner in 2006. MedCom International has joined forces with NGOs and other enterprises to inform and educate seniors in their decision-making processes.

Dr. Stéphanie Moerikofer-Zwez has been the President of the Swiss Home Care Association (Spitex) since 2002. Prior to this, she was first Minister (Regierungsrätin) of Public Health and then Minister of Finance in the canton of Aargau (Switzerland) for eight years. She studied biochemistry at the ETH in Zurich. After receiving her Ph.D. from the University of Berne, she worked at the University of Basel as a Scientific Collaborator and Lecturer (Habilitation 1985) from 1977 to 1993, specialising in the regulation of carbohydrate metabolism. She has also been politically active since the 1970s.

Prof. Dr. Michael Muller-Camen is a Professor in International Human Resource Management at Middlesex University (UK). Michael's main research interests are the comparative study of HRM, age diversity, and sustainable HRM. He has published widely in journals such as *Human Relations, Journal of International HRM*, and *Organisation Studies* on comparative and international HRM. He led the research project 'Age Diversity at the Workplace'. Michael received his M.Sc. in industrial relations from the London School of Economics (UK) and his Ph.D. in occupational behaviour from London University (UK). He has taught at the University of Innsbruck (Austria), DeMontfort University (UK), and the International University (Germany).

Dr. Guenter Pfeiffer has been the Chief Personnel Officer and a member of the Swisscom Group's Executive Board since 2004. In this role, he shapes and supports the company's continuous transformation towards customer centricity. Before he switched to the HR side of the business, he was in charge of Swisscom's participation management and served as a member of several Supervisory Boards (e.g., debitel and Cesky Telecom). Prior functions include responsibility for corporate development, marketing and international projects at E.On, T-Mobile, and Detecon. Guenter studied economics at Bonn University, followed by a P.hD. at the University of Cologne (Germany). He lives with his family in Berne.

Matthias Rass is a doctoral candidate and Research Associate at the chair of Information Systems I – Innovation & Value Creation at the University of Erlangen-Nuremberg. He graduated from this university as a Diplom-Kaufmann (equivalent to a Master's in business), with majors in information systems, strategic management and health care management. His current research focuses on open innovation, innovation contests and innovation communities.

Prof. Winfried Ruigrok, Ph.D. is a Professor in international management and the Academic Director of the MBA programme at the University of St. Gallen, Switzerland. His research focuses on corporate governance, the internationalisation of top management teams and boards as well as internationalisation and restructuring strategy. Prior to his professorship at the University of St. Gallen, he held positions at Warwick Business School (UK), Erasmus University/Rotterdam School of Management (NL), the University of Amsterdam (NL), and the European Commission (B), among others.

Heike Schroder is a doctoral candidate in HRM at Middlesex University (UK). Her research interests lie in HRM and the employment of older workers in Britain and Germany as well as in life course transitions and trajectories in later life. As a Researcher, Heike was involved in the ESRC-funded research project 'Age Diversity at the Workplace' and served as a Visiting Research Fellow in the British-Council-funded project 'Older Workers in the UK and Japan' at Keio University (Japan). She received an MBA from the International University (Germany) and an M.Sc. in research methods from Middlesex University (UK).

Alexander Vossen is a Research Associate at the Technology and Innovation Management Group at RWTH Aachen University (Germany), where he previously received a Master's in business administration (Diplom-Kaufmann) in 2008. His main research interests lie in the field of external idea generation and the integration of consumers into new product or service development. While working on his PhD thesis on ideation with consumers, he also coordinates university classes and a research project in this field.

Prof. Dr. Norbert Walter was Chief Economist of Deutsche Bank Group and Head of Deutsche Bank Research until the end of 2009. He subsequently founded Walter & Daughters Consult in January 2010. Before his position at the Deutsche Bank Group, he was Professor and Director at the renowned Kiel Institute for World Economics as well as a John J. McCloy Distinguished Research Fellow at the American Institute for Contemporary Studies at the Johns Hopkins University in Washington, DC (1986-1987). He holds a doctorate in economics from the Johann-Wolfgang-Goethe University, Frankfurt/Main (Germany). Professor Walter was also a member of the Committee of Wise Men on the Regulation of European Securities Markets (Lamfalussy Group), a member of the Economic and Monetary Affairs Committee of the European Banking Federation, and Chairman of the International Conference of Commercial Bank Economists.

Prof. Markku Wilenius, Ph.D., is a Professor in futures studies at the University of Turku (Finland) and Senior Advisor to Allianz (the world's largest property and casualty insurance company, based in Munich). He has worked in the field of trends and risks for the past 20 years, owns three companies, and chairs three foundations in Finland. He is particularly interested in the long-term developments of the global system and is also a member of the Club of Rome.

Carola Wolf, Dipl.-Kff., Maîtrise d'Economie d'Entreprise, is a business study graduate from the universities of Augsburg (Germany) and Rennes (France). During her studies she specialised in human resource management and organisation studies. Since 2007, she has been a Research Associate at the Institute of Management at the University of St. Gallen (Switzerland), where she is engaged in her doctoral studies on strategy processes.

Company and Organization Index

Country and Region Index

Index

The World Demographic and Ageing Forum

The World Demographic and Ageing Forum (WDA Forum) is a foundation established in 2002 in St. Gallen, Switzerland. Its key topic is the upcoming demographic change: What will the world's population structure look like in future? What consequences and challenges will the ageing population bring? How can the latest research findings be translated into practice? What can individuals, companies, NGO and governments do to prepare for these changes?

These questions, which concern age and generations, are key themes of our time and the future. The WDA Forum recognises that demographic change offers a formidable challenge but also a unique opportunity to find sustainable solutions through an integrated approach. Therefore, the WDA Forum offers an international, inter-generational, and permanent platform to coordinate the worldwide efforts and activities related to demographic change.

The WDA Forum addresses a global audience of economists, politicians, non-government organisations, researchers, and the general public. One of the main activities is the *World Ageing & Generations Congress*, an international congress held annually at the University of St. Gallen. Together with well known partners, the WDA Forum also organises several specialised conferences each year.

Moreover, the WDA Forum has a positive reputation and has had evident influence in the science arena. Together with the University of St. Gallen (HSG), the WDA Forum has established a global network of over 100 Fellows. The Fellowship system arranges visiting professorships at the University of St. Gallen, and organises conferences, publications (e.g., the high-quality *WDA-HSG Discussion Paper Series on Demographic Issues*) and advocacy (preparation of recommendations, statements, position papers, etc.).

For more information about the WDA Forum, please visit www.wdaforum.org.

Kohlbacher, Florian; Herstatt, Cornelius (Eds.):

The Silver Market Phenomenon
Marketing and Innovation in the Aging Society

2nd Edition, 2011, 450 p., Hardcover
ISBN: 978-3-642-14337-3

The current shift in demographics – aging and shrinking populations – in many countries around the world presents a major
challenge to companies and societies alike. One particularly
essential implication is the emergence and constant growth of the
so-called "graying market" or "silver market", the market segment
more or less broadly defined as those people aged 50 and older.
Increasing in number and share of the total population while at
the same time being relatively well-off, this market segment can
be seen as very attractive and promising, although still very
underdeveloped in terms of product and service offerings.

This book offers a thorough and up-to-date analysis of the
challenges and opportunities in leveraging innovation, technology,
product development and marketing for older consumers and
employees. Key lessons are drawn from a variety of industries
and countries, including the lead market Japan.

LaVergne, TN USA
29 October 2010

202690LV00002B/9/P